New Inside Out

Sue Kay & Vaughan Jones

with Peter Maggs & Catherine Smith

D0784150

Upper intermediate

Student's Book

MACMILLAN

WB = **Workbook**. Each unit of the Workbook contains a one-page section which develops practical writing skills.

1 Impressions

Grammar Verb structures. Auxiliaries. Indirect questions
Vocabulary Collocation. Word formation. Clothing
Useful phrases Talking about appearance

Speaking

1 Work with a partner. Look at the photos (*a–d*) and match them with the events in the box.

> Beijing Olympics   Death of Princess Diana   First Moon landing
> Millennium celebrations

Put the events in the order in which they happened.

2 Work with your partner. Write down as much additional information as you can about the events in the photos.
Discuss your information with other people in the class. Did any of these events make an impression on you?

Listening & Reading

1 　🌐 1.01–1.04 Listen and match the speakers, Alec, Belinda, Chris and Dana, with the photos (*a–d*) on page 4.

2 　Read and complete what each person said with an appropriate verb structure.

▲ Alec

It made a huge impression on me because, when I was a kid, I always (1 think) *used to think* I hope I (2 live) _____ long enough to see a man on the Moon. So when it (3 happen) _____ – I don't know how old my son was, but I said to him, 'Sit down and watch all of this. This is one of the most momentous things that (4 ever happen) _____ in your life.'

▲ Belinda

What (1 annoy) _____ me is people who think the royal family had something to do with Diana's death. It was a tragic accident. That's what I (2 believe) _____ anyway. I was never a big fan of Diana, but she raised a lot of money for charity, and I (3 think) _____ she was a good mother to those boys. I just hope the press can leave them alone and not hound them as they hounded their mother.

▲ Chris

We (1 stand) _____ really close to the Harbour Bridge. We'd decided to get there early to get a good place, so we (2 wait) _____ since six o'clock in the evening. Then, at midnight, the fireworks (3 explode) _____ across the sky. I (4 never see) _____ anything so spectacular. I (5 feel) _____ proud to be an Australian.

▲ Dana

It was the first time I (1 visit) _____ an Asian country. It was so different. I was amazed at how many people there were. After the Games (2 finish) _____ , we (3 do) _____ some sightseeing. The Great Wall was definitely my favourite. It's the most incredible thing I (4 ever see) _____ .

Listen again and check.

3 　Write down three memorable events that have been important …
- in your own life.
- in the history of your country.

Tell a partner about the events you have chosen. Find out as much as you can about the events your partner has chosen.

Grammar

Verb structures

Present/Past simple
I **work** / I **worked**

Present/Past continuous
I'**m working** / I **was working**

Present/Past perfect simple
I'**ve worked** / I'**d worked**

Present/Past perfect continuous
I'**ve been working** / I'**d been working**

used to / would
I **used to work** / I'**d work**

1 　Underline the most appropriate verb structure.
a) **I've been knowing** / <u>**I've known**</u> / **I know** Alice since I was a child.
b) **I had** / **I've had** / **I used to have** breakfast with Ben this morning.
c) **I'm talking** / **I've been talking** / **I was talking** to Cathy just before the lesson started.
d) **I like** / **I'm liking** / **I'd like** Dan a lot – he's one of my best friends.
e) **I've learnt** / **I've been learning** / **I'm learning** English for about the same number of years as Erica.
f) **I've gone** / **I've been** / **I've been going** out to dinner with Frank lots of times.
g) **I've already met** / **I already met** / **I'd already met** Gina before I joined this class.
h) **I was having** / **I used to have** / **I'd have** a friend called Harry, but we've lost touch with each other.

2 　Choose five sentences from Exercise 1 and change the names to make the sentences true for you. Read your partner's sentences and find out as much as you can about the people they mention.

3 　Grammar *Extra* 1, Part 1 page 132. Read the explanations and do Exercise 1.

Vocabulary

1 What do you notice most about a person when you meet them for the first time? Look at the ideas in the box below and discuss with a partner.

> clothes   eyes   face   hair   handshake
> manner   smile   voice

2 'Collocation' refers to the way that words form predictable relationships with other words. Look at the alternative adjectives (a–h) and cross out the adjective which does NOT form a strong collocation with the noun. Use your dictionary if necessary.

a) **designer / ~~brand~~** clothes
b) **shiny / bright** eyes
c) **round / circular** face
d) **spiky / pointy** hair
e) **strong / firm** handshake
f) **charming / fair** manner
g) **heated / warm** smile
h) **profound / deep** voice

'You never get a second chance to make a first impression.'

3 Match the nouns from Exercise 1 to the adjectives below to make additional strong collocations.

a) hearty / limp *handshake*
b) expressive / impassive _____
c) fake / forced _____
d) close-set / staring _____
e) sleek / tousled _____
f) husky / shrill _____
g) old-fashioned / scruffy _____
h) abrasive / mild _____

Which of the characteristics described above or in Exercise 2 would you find appealing / unappealing? Tell your partner.

Listening

1 🌐 1.05 Listen to a man and a woman who meet in a New York coffee shop. Answer the questions.

a) Where are they from?
b) What are they doing in New York?
c) Why does the conversation stop?

2 Complete the table with a ✔ or a ✗. Then listen again and check your answers.

	The man	The woman	
a)	✔	✔	is English.
b)	✗	✗	is on holiday.
c)			is working in New York.
d)			works for a bank.
e)			likes New York.
f)			has been in New York a long time.
g)			is an artist.
h)			is from London.
i)			was a good student.
j)			left school in 1989.

3 Have you ever 'put your foot in it' – accidentally said something that was embarrassing or that annoyed someone? Or have you been with someone when they 'put their foot in it'? Tell your partner.

Grammar

Auxiliaries (1):
so / neither (nor)

'I went out last night.'
✔ 'So did I.'
✗ 'I didn't.'

'I haven't done my homework.'
✔ 'Neither have I.'
✗ 'I have.'

1 Work with a partner. Make ten sentences based on the information in the table on page 6. Use *and so ...* , or *and neither ...* , or *but ...* as appropriate.

   a)   *The man is English and so is the woman.*

2 Use the sentence beginnings to write some sentences which are true for you and which you *believe* are also true for your partner. (Do *not* check with your partner yet.)

   a) I was born ...   d) I used to ...   g) I've never been to ...
   b) I'm not used to ...   e) I've got ...   h) I'd like to ...
   c) I'm interested in ...   f) I can't ...   i) I hardly ever go ...

   I was born in the 1980s. / I was born in a hospital. / I was born in this city. / I was born ... etc.

3 Work with your partner. Go to the Additional material on page 128.

Grammar & Pronunciation

Auxiliaries (2): Question tags

We've finished, **haven't we**?

You're not listening, **are you**?

1 Work with your partner. Look at the examples from the conversation on page 6 and match the information in columns A and B to explain the form and use of question tags.

   1   *Sorry, but you're English, aren't you?*   2   *It isn't very busy here today, is it?*

A	B
positive statement	asking a real question
negative statement	negative question tag
rising intonation	asking for agreement
falling intonation	positive question tag

2 Choose the correct question tag for each statement. Is each question tag more likely to be said with a rising or falling intonation?

   a) It's a bit chilly today, **isn't it? / is it?**
   b) I'm late again, **isn't it? / aren't I?**
   c) The traffic was dreadful, **isn't it? / wasn't it?**
   d) You haven't been waiting long, **isn't it? / have you?**
   e) Nobody's away today, **isn't it? / are they?**
   f) You don't have Mike Smith's phone number, **isn't it / do you?**

   🌐 **1.06** Listen, check and repeat.

3 ▌ Grammar *Extra* 1, Part 2 page 132. Read the explanations and do Exercises 2 and 3.

Speaking: anecdote

You are going to tell your partner about a person who made a big impression on you.
- Ask yourself the questions below.
- Think about *what* to say and *how* to say it.
- Tell your partner about the person.

   a) Who was this person? A teacher? A boss? A member of your family? ...
   b) What was his/her name?
   c) When and how did you meet him/her?
   d) How old were you? How old was he/she?
   e) What were you doing at this time? What was he/she doing?
   f) How did you get to know him/her?
   g) Why did he/she make such a big impression?
   h) What did you learn from him/her?
   i) What is he/she doing now?
   j) When was the last time you saw him/her?

Reading

1 Work with a partner. What do you know about Madonna? Which of her songs do you know/like/have? What did she look like the last time you saw a photo or a video of her?

2 Read the article on page 9. Choose the best summary of the writer's opinion of Madonna.
   a) Madonna is an exceptionally talented singer, actor and writer.
   b) Madonna is a talented business woman who's brilliant at selling her image.
   c) Madonna is too old to wear a leotard, and should retire to the country.

3 Read the article again and label the paragraphs with the words in the box.

> Controversy   Early life   Pop icon   No plans to retire
> Motherhood   Reinventing the brand

4 Complete the comprehension questions with the words in the box.

> controversy   criticism   date   gracefully   on   raised   trademark   with

   a) What did she register as a _____ ?
   b) What does she pride herself _____ ?
   c) Where was she born and _____ ?
   d) At school, who did she find it difficult to fit in _____ ?
   e) What has she produced over her career to _____ ?
   f) Why did adopting a child attract strong _____ ?
   g) Why is she described as being no stranger to _____ ?
   h) Is it likely that she'll soon retire _____ ?

   Answer the questions.

5 Who is your favourite female singer / male singer / band? Tell your partner.

Vocabulary

Word formation

re prefix meaning *again*: used with many verbs, nouns and adjectives: *rearrange, rebuild, reconsider, reconstruct, rediscover, redo, redraft, re-examine, reinvent, relocate, remake, reorganise, repackage, reschedule, rethink, reunite, reword, rewrite*

1 The article on Madonna talks about her *reinventing* and *repackaging* herself. Cross out the word on each line which does *not* form a new verb with re, according to the Word formation panel.
   a) change / do / invent / package
   b) arrange / organise / prepare / schedule
   c) build / construct / erect / make
   d) consider / contemplate / examine / think
   e) copy / draft / word / write
   f) discover / find / locate / unite

2 Look up words with the prefix re (meaning *again*) in your dictionary. Tick the words you know or can understand easily. Choose three more to learn. Write your own example sentences.

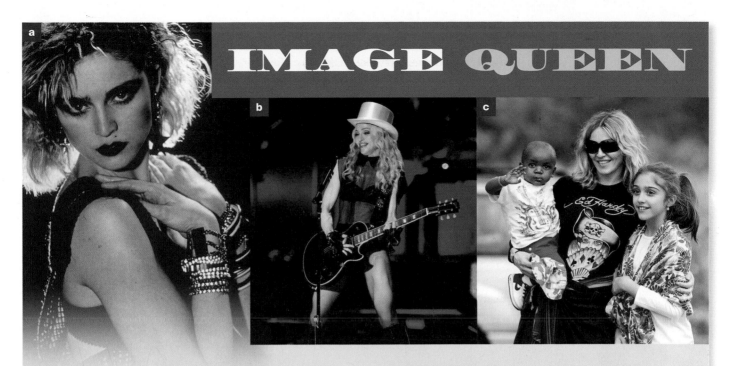

IMAGE QUEEN

a) *Pop icon*

Her career is older than most of her fans, and some may say that, now in her fifties, it's time she slowed down and left the stage to younger performers. But the truth is that Madonna
5 still puts on an amazing show, and her tours continue to sell out.

She's had more top ten hits than Elvis Presley and is the most successful female recording artist in history. To say that Madonna is a celebrity is an understatement: she's a
10 veritable pop icon.

b) _____

So how did she reach iconic status? The genius of Madonna is in the way she manages her image and markets the global super-brand that is Madonna. It was her genius to realise that
15 marketing was the key to her success as long ago as 1979, which was when she registered 'Madonna' as a trademark.

Madonna has always been a brilliant consolidator of trends, picking up on an existing look and making it her own. Think back on her career. It may not be the songs
20 you remember first, nor the films, nor the videos. It's much more likely that you'll recall her career as a series of images: Madonna in lacy gloves, bare midriff and bangles; Madonna as Marilyn in satin; Madonna as Evita; Madonna as geisha, dominatrix, cowgirl and mystic earth mother. It's no wonder
25 that she's known as the queen of reinvention. In fact, she prides herself on an ever-evolving look, style and sound. She even called one of her world tours the 'Re-invention tour'.

c) _____

But behind all the masks, who is the real Madonna?
30 Madonna Louise Veronica Ciccone was born in 1958 in Michigan and raised in the suburbs of Detroit, the third of six children. Her mother died when she was six. At school, she was bullied because she was different. In an interview for *Vanity Fair*, she explains: 'I didn't fit in with the popular
35 group. I wasn't a hippie or a stoner, so I ended up being the weirdo. I was interested in classical ballet and music,

and the kids were quite mean if you were different. I was one of those people that people were mean to.'

Madonna later hitchhiked to New York with $35 in her pocket, where a short struggle was followed by a swift
40 ascent to stardom. She began to bleach her dark hair, and the 'material girl' was born – she had her first mainstream pop success with *Holiday* in 1984 and has never looked back. Over her career to date, she has produced an impressive catalogue of albums, world tours, videos, feature
45 films, documentaries and books.

d) _____

Meanwhile, her personal life has not stood still. She had her first child, Lourdes, with fitness trainer Carlos Leon in 1996. Four years later she had met and married British film director
50 Guy Ritchie and had a son, Rocco. The couple adopted a third child, David Banda, from Malawi, attracting criticism from some people who felt that Madonna had used her wealth and fame to fast-track the adoption. Madonna and Guy divorced in 2008.

55 **e)** _____

Both on and off-stage, Madonna is no stranger to controversy: over the years, she has shocked people with her choice of clothes, song titles, religious imagery and, at the MTV music awards in 2003, a lingering kiss with Britney
60 Spears. The Queen of Pop is well aware of the importance of keeping her name in the headlines and, ever the marketing genius, she knows exactly how to do it.

f) _____

But she isn't ready to relinquish her share of the limelight
65 yet. At an age when many wealthy pop stars would opt to retire gracefully to their country residence, put on a few kilos and give the young ones a chance, Madonna comes back again and again, repackaged, new and improved. In her own words: 'I want more, more, more. I'm not stepping down,
70 I'm stepping up career-wise. There's no exit plan.'

Glossary

trend noun [C]: direction in fashion
mask noun [C]: cover to disguise your face
bullied adj: frightened by older or stronger children
weirdo noun [C]: strange person
mean adj: cruel or unkind

swift adj: quick
fast-track verb [T]: make sth happen quickly
relinquish verb [T]: give sth up
limelight noun [U]: public attention

Listening

1 **Look at the photos and answer the questions.**

a) How would you describe the image each man is trying to achieve: cool, professional, trendy, casual, sporty, etc?

b) What kind of image do you find most/least appealing?

c) Do you think men are more image-conscious these days than in the past?

▲ Charles   ▲ Rick   ▲ Adam   ▲ Matt

2 🌐 **1.07–1.10 Listen to the way each man describes his personal style to a journalist. In what order does the journalist speak to the men?**

Charles ☐
Rick ☐
Adam ☐
Matt ☐

Tick the words in the box that best describe the journalist's attitude towards the four men.

| angry | apprehensive | friendly | frustrated | nervous | polite | respectful | rude |

3 **Work with a partner. Answer the questions about the four men in Exercise 2.**

a) Who never dresses up to go out?

b) Who couldn't live without his trainers?

c) Who wants people to notice his clothes?

d) Who bought something pink recently?

e) Who just wears clothes he feels comfortable in?

f) Who hasn't changed his style for years?

g) Who thinks it's important to make a good impression?

h) Who likes his jeans and T-shirts to be clean and neat?

Listen again and check your answers.

Try to answer the same questions with the names of men you know. Tell your partner about the men you have noted down.

Grammar & Speaking

1 The journalist on page 10 used indirect questions to interview the four men. Complete the table by writing some of the questions she asked. Check the Recordings on page 144 if necessary.

Direct questions	Indirect questions
a) What image are you trying to achieve? →	Could you tell me what *image you're trying to achieve*?
b) Are you aware of fashion? →	Do you think that _____ ?
c) What do you wear to go out in the evening? →	Do you mind telling me what _____ ?
d) What do your clothes say about you? →	I'd like to know what _____ .
e) Do you care about your image? →	Would you say that _____ ?
f) Does your appearance affect your life? →	I'd like to know whether _____ .
g) What was the last thing you bought? →	Do you know what _____ ?

🔘 **1.11** **Listen, check and repeat the indirect questions.**

2 Work with a partner. What are the main differences between direct and indirect questions? Discuss the following.

    a) word order   b) *do / does / did*   c) *if / whether*   d) formality

3 Complete these indirect questions. Then ask your partner.

    a) Where is the cheapest clothes shop in town? *Do you know …?*
    b) Are cheap clothes good value for money? *Do you think …?*
    c) Where is the best place to buy jeans? *Where do you think …?*
    d) Have you ever sewn a button on a shirt? *I'd like to know …*
    e) How much money would you spend on a leather jacket? *Do you mind telling me …?*
    f) How many pairs of trainers have you got? *Could you tell me …?*
    g) Do clothes and fashion matter to you? *Would you say …?*

Use the indirect question beginnings to write three more questions to ask your partner.

Vocabulary

1 Work with your partner. Note down items of clothing that have the following parts or accessories. Use your dictionary if necessary.

    a) a belt: *trousers, a skirt, a dress, a coat …*   e) cuffs
    b) a buckle   f) a hem
    c) buttons   g) sleeves
    d) a collar   h) a zip

2 Choose the correct alternative to complete these common idiomatic expressions. Discuss with your partner and use a dictionary if necessary. Which expressions are similar to ones in your language?

    a) Tom is very funny. He's always coming out with amusing **off-the-cuff / off-the-sleeve** remarks.
    b) Richard is very lazy. He needs to **belt down / buckle down** soon if he wants to do anything with his life.
    c) Julie is very clever. She's **as bright as a button / as bright as a zip** and always comes top in exams.
    d) Ann is very boring. She always **belts / collars** me at parties so I have to listen to all her problems.
    e) Harry is very careful. He knows how to **tighten his belt / tighten his buttons** when he hasn't got much money.
    f) Zoë is very open. She wears her heart **on her hem / on her sleeve** so you always know what she's feeling.

Which descriptions could you use to describe people you know? Tell your partner.

Useful phrases

1 🌐 **1.12 Listen to the conversation and answer the questions.**

a) Where are Rose, Ian and Mike?
b) What are the relationships between them?
c) Who does Mike meet at the bar?

2 Match the useful phrases (*a–f*) used in the conversation with their function (*1–6*).

a) Calm down.
b) You're so annoying.
c) You're so easy to wind up.
d) It can't be her.
e) You'll never guess …
f) You were saying.

1 I'm going to tell you something surprising.
2 I think you're angry.
3 You make me angry.
4 I'd like you to continue speaking.
5 I'm sure it isn't her.
6 I think you believe things too easily.

Who said the useful phrases (*a–f*)? Write *Rose*, *Ian* or *Mike* next to each expression. Listen again and check.

3 Work with a partner. Complete more useful phrases (*a–j*) from the conversation to talk about people's appearance. Use the phrases in the box.

> a very   changed so   in the   look anything   looking woman   no resemblance
> spitting image   that smile   ~~that woman~~   the same

a) Look at *that woman* over there.
b) The one _____ white jacket?
c) She's the _____ of Gwyneth Paltrow.
d) She doesn't _____ like Gwyneth Paltrow.
e) She's got _____ hair.
f) I'd recognise _____ anywhere.
g) She's got _____ distinctive smile.
h) That woman bears absolutely _____ to Gwyneth Paltrow.
i) I saw this amazing-_____ walking towards me.
j) I didn't recognise her. She's _____ much.

4 Complete the second sentence so that it has a similar meaning to the first sentence, using the word in brackets.

a) I look exactly like my father. ➔ I'm *the spitting image of him*. (image)
b) Our eyes are identical. ➔ We've _____ . (same)
c) His way of walking is unusual. ➔ He has _____ . (distinctive)
d) I look very different from my mother. ➔ I don't look _____ . (like)
e) She looks completely different from the rest of the family. ➔ She bears _____ . (resemblance)
f) She was an extremely attractive woman when she was younger. ➔ She _____ . (amazing-)

Change the sentences to make them true for you and your family.

Writing *Extra*

Informal letter

1 **Work with a partner and discuss these questions.**

a) Have you (or anybody you know) ever had a pen friend?

b) How long did you/he/she have one for?

c) Did you/he/she ever meet this pen friend?

2 **Read this letter from Ling Chun to her pen friend, Hanna West. Do you think the language is appropriate? If not, why not?**

3 **The underlined words and expressions (1–16) make the letter very formal. Replace these words and expressions with these more informal alternatives (a–p).**

1 – j, 2 – …

a) I've been up to my eyes in work.

b) By the way,

c) anything else you think I should know about you.

d) PS Hope you like the photo!

e) Love,

f) I can't wait to hear from you again

g) I'd love to hear

h) I'm afraid

i) here's

j) Thank you for your letter which I received on

k) I'm really sorry I haven't written back sooner,

l) There are three of us

m) Anyway,

n) I'd love to be

o) I'm really pleased

p) on the back

Are there any other things in the letter that you would change in order to make it more informal?

4 **Write a letter introducing yourself to a pen friend. Include information about the following.**

• Your family
• Your work/studies
• The place where you live
• What you would like to know about your pen friend

5 **Exchange letters with another student in the class and write a reply, answering his or her questions.**

---

14 Jalan Hajijah
Changi
Singapore

21st April 2009

123 Clifton Crescent
Bristol BS8 3HT
England

Dear Hanna,

(1) <u>With reference to your letter of</u> 12th April, (2) <u>I would be pleased to accept your offer of becoming</u> your new pen friend.

First of all (3) <u>I should apologise for the delay in replying to your letter,</u> but (4) <u>I have been extremely busy with work.</u> I'm a trainee lawyer and have been revising for my final exams.

(5) <u>I would be grateful if you could tell me</u> more about you, your family, what kind of music you enjoy, what you do in your free time and (6) <u>any other relevant information.</u>

I'm from quite a big family. (7) <u>It consists of three <u>children</u></u> – two girls and a boy. I'm number three in the family and only I live at home now with my parents. My elder sister has just had a baby, and my brother got married last year.

(8) <u>I regret to inform you that</u> I haven't got an up-to-date photograph of us all together, but (9) <u>I enclose</u> a photo of me and my sister taken at my brother's graduation. I've put the names (10) <u>on the reverse side</u> so you know who's who.

(11) <u>Incidentally,</u> I agree with what you say about email. It's very convenient, but perhaps it's not the best way for me to improve my English, because nobody bothers about punctuation or spelling!

(12) <u>In conclusion,</u> (13) <u>I am delighted</u> to be in touch with you and (14) <u>I look forward to hearing from you again</u> as soon as possible.

(15) <u>Yours sincerely,</u>

Ling

Ling Chun

(16) <u>Enc: 1 family photograph</u>

2 Generations

Grammar Verb patterns (1). Adjective structures
Vocabulary Sayings. Social register
Useful phrases At home: showing someone around your house

Reading & Vocabulary

1 **Work with a partner. Decide what ages you think correspond to each stage in life.**

Ages	Stages
0 – ☐	infancy
☐ – ☐	childhood
☐ – ☐	adolescence
☐ – ☐	adulthood
☐ – ☐	middle age
☐ – ☐	old age

Do the following tasks.

a) Match each of these important life events with a stage in the chart.

> buying a car   changing a baby's nappy   first words   a free bus pass
> learning to swim   leaving home   retiring   school trips or exchanges

b) Think of other important life events associated with each stage.
c) Decide which is the best age or stage to learn a foreign language.

▲ Viv Groskop

2 **Read the article on page 15 about Viv Groskop's experiences of school exchanges. Answer the questions.**

a) How many exchange students did she stay with and where were they from?
b) What are the reasons she gives for the success of the exchanges?
c) What happened to each of her exchange relationships over time? Why?

3 **Look at the highlighted words and phrases in the article. Categorise them under the headings in the table. There are five words or phrases in each column. Use your dictionary if necessary.**

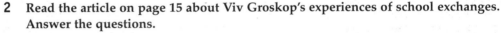

Language learning	Relationships	Describing people
pen friend		

4 **Use a word or phrase from Exercise 3 to complete the comprehension questions.**

a) What will Viv Groskop do if her children show any _____ for languages? Why?
b) Which of the languages she learnt are now a bit _____ ?
c) Which exchange student's parents were older and _____ their two children?
d) Why were the _____ and _____ Spanish girls disappointed in the English nightlife?
e) Why were Viv and Axelle _____ at Axelle's wedding?
f) Who is Viv's mother still _____ with?

Answer the questions.

5 **Work in small groups. Discuss the following questions.**

a) What are the advantages and disadvantages of school exchanges or study trips abroad?
b) Do you agree that 'immersion is the only way to learn'? Why? / Why not?
c) What are your own school-age experiences of learning languages?

Vive la différence!

By Viv Groskop

In many ways, I am the ultimate poster-girl for the school exchange. From the age of twelve and for the next six years I exchanged visits at
5 least twice a year with my French pen friend Axelle Perron from Angers; at fifteen, I went to stay with my German exchange, Frauke Schoon, near Bremen; and at sixteen I started
10 a Spanish exchange with Amalia Muñoz Ruano in Salamanca. By the age of eighteen, I had a degree of fluency in all three languages.

Which just goes to show that
15 when a school exchange works, it really works. If my children show any aptitude for languages whatsoever, I would not hesitate to send them to live with host families in their teens,
20 because immersion is the only way to learn. Although my Spanish and German is now a bit rusty, in the case of French the experience gave me fluency for life.

25 But beyond the learning opportunities, the real reason these exchanges worked for me is because I relished my escape from rural life in Somerset. And I loved the exoticism
30 of my new friends. Axelle was slim, beautiful and, at the age of twelve, had fabulously blow-dried hair. Frauke was tall, sporty and earnest. Amalia was quiet, sweet and had a secret
35 wild side.

It helped that all three families were extremely amusing. The Germans were jolly, smothering older parents who doted on their two children and
40 never stopped trying to make you eat cake. The Spanish were a large, loud extended family, all of whom were comically short – except for Amalia's brother, who was, inexplicably,
45 about seven feet tall. The father in the French family, Alain, had a very wiggly moustache which he used to excellent effect.

As I grew older, faultlines developed
50 in my exchange relationships. Frauke always got on better with my mother than she did with me, and with Amalia I had the opposite problem: I was not really cool enough for her. It
55 didn't help that the Spanish exchange girls were all hip and urban, used to eating tapas at 10.00 p.m. and then

going out dancing until 4.00 a.m. The prospect of trying to get into
60 the Studio Nightclub in Yeovil with our fake ID, to dance on the sticky carpets and get home for an 11.00 p.m. curfew was somehow not so exciting.
65 Eventually, even my wonderful friendship with Axelle soured. We grew apart during our university years, and I never forgave her for holding me to the rash promise (made at the
70 age of thirteen) of being a witness at her wedding in 1999, at a time when we were barely speaking. We haven't spoken since.

My mother, however, is still in
75 touch with both Axelle and Frauke, though she pretends not to be as she knows it irritates me. I don't know what happened to Amalia. I like to think that she is still out partying.

Glossary

go to show phrase: help to illustrate
relish verb [T]: enjoy a lot
smothering adj: loving to excess

curfew noun [C]: a time by which you must be home
rash adj: describes sth done too quickly without thought

Reading

1 Work with a partner. Look at the three photos and discuss the questions.

a) What do you think the parents' jobs or hobbies are?

b) How do you think these teenagers feel about their parents?

Read the article and decide which of these parents you would *least* like to have.

Problem **Parents**

ALEX COURTLEY finds it difficult to see the funny side of his father's job. His father, Paul, is better known to his fans as Corky
5 **the Clown.**

Alex says: 'My dad couldn't have become Corky at a worse time. I was at the age where I knew what it was like to feel really, really embarrassed.
10   At first I <u>dreaded my friends finding out</u> what he did, but eventually everyone at school <u>got to hear</u> about it, and they nicknamed me Corky Junior. But the worst times were when he took me to
15 children's parties and <u>made me join in</u> the act. He used to pay me a bit of money, but nothing could compensate for the humiliation.
   My dad is always clowning around.
20 He sings out loud when we go shopping and he's always whistling.
   I used to wish he wasn't Corky, but I never <u>wanted him to have</u> a boring, ordinary job in an office.'

25 **KAYLEIGH ROLLS is thirteen years old, a difficult age to have an embarrassing parent. Her mum is the club mascot for Cardiff City Football Club.**

30 **Kayleigh says:** 'Even though she wears a bird costume, everyone knows it's our mum underneath. She has to wear a really silly Bluebird costume and fool around to entertain the crowd.
35   Once, she went over to my Maths teacher who was in the crowd and shook his hand. Then she took her bird head off and said, 'I'm Kayleigh's mum!' I just <u>wanted the ground to open up</u> and
40 swallow me. I'm one of the ball girls for the club, and our mum <u>loves to chase</u> me around the ground. I <u>try to run away</u> as fast as I can, but sometimes she catches me and <u>makes me cuddle</u> her
45 in front of the whole crowd.
   She does cause us a lot of embarrassment, but life is never dull, and she's our mum, and I think we're lucky to have her.'

50 **GINA CLARK cannot believe that her mother, a singing and piano tutor by day, performs as singer and film star Cher in her spare time.**

55 **Gina says:** Everyone round here knows my mum as Cher, but it's a nightmare if she's performing at a club when I'm there, because a lot of people look at me while she's doing her act, and we're
60 so different. She <u>loves being</u> in the limelight, whereas I <u>can't stand being</u> the centre of attention. Cher is known for her outrageous clothes, and so Mum's got some incredible little see-through,
65 all-in-one black body stockings in lace that cost a fortune. I find it embarrassing to see her in her Cher costumes, but at least when she's not Cher, she looks more normal in jeans and casual stuff.
70 I have to admit, my mum is gorgeous, and she <u>manages to stay</u> in shape without spending a fortune on cosmetic surgery.

2 Answer the questions about the article.

a) Who <u>enjoys being</u> in the limelight?

b) Who <u>forced his son to join in</u> his act?

c) Who <u>hates being</u> the centre of attention?

d) Who <u>makes her daughter cuddle</u> her in public?

e) Who <u>attempts to run away</u> from her mum as fast as she can?

f) Who really didn't <u>want his friends to find out</u> what his father did?

Do you know anybody who has an unusual job or hobby? Tell your partner.

Grammar & Vocabulary

Verb patterns (1)

verb + *to*-infinitive
I didn't **want to dance**.

verb + object +
to-infinitive
She **asked me to dance**.

verb + gerund
I **hate dancing**.

verb + object + gerund
I **watched her dancing**.

verb + object + infinitive
without *to*
She **made me dance**.

1 Look at the underlined verb patterns in the article and in Exercise 2 on page 16. Record the different verb patterns in the appropriate boxes below.

> a) verb + *to*-infinitive
>   *get to do sth*

> b) verb + object + *to*-infinitive

> c) verb + gerund

> d) verb + object + gerund

> e) verb + object + infinitive without *to*

"I said, would you mind turning down your fan?"

2 Work with a partner. Look at twenty more common verbs and verb phrases in the box. Categorise them according to the five patterns outlined in Exercise 1. Some verbs can belong to more than one category. Use a dictionary if necessary.

> aim   allow   arrange   ask   avoid   can't afford   decide   expect   finish
> encourage   help   hope   let   (not) mind   offer   spend time   teach   tell
> urge   warn (not)

3 Complete the sentences with the correct form of the verb in brackets.

a) My family always avoids (talk) _____ about politics or religion.
b) My parents always encouraged me (save) _____ money for a rainy day.
c) I don't mind (lend) _____ money to my brothers and sisters.
d) My father taught me (drive) _____ .
e) My parents always let me (stay out) _____ till after midnight.
f) When I've finished (study) _____ I want to go travelling.
g) I'd rather do something active than spend my time (sit) _____ at home
    (watch) _____ TV.
h) I hope (start) _____ a family of my own one day.

Which sentences are true for you? Compare with your partner.

4 Work with your partner. Match the sentence halves to make *sensible* pieces of advice for parents with teenagers.

a) You should help them   keep their rooms tidy.
b) You shouldn't let them   to take drugs.
c) You should make them   smoke.
d) You should tell them not   to respect their elders.
e) You should warn them not   to keep fit.
f) You should encourage them   to play their music too loud.
g) You should ask them not   to do well at school.
h) You should expect them   to believe everything they hear.

What advice did your parents give you as a teenager? Tell your partner.

5 Grammar *Extra* 2 page 132. Read the explanations and do Exercises 1 and 2.

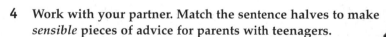

Pronunciation & Vocabulary

Single vowel sounds

/ɪ/ big gym
/iː/ green beans
/ʊ/ should look
/uː/ blue moon
/e/ well said
/ə/ about mother
/ɜː/ learn words
/ɔː/ short talk
/æ/ fat cat
/ʌ/ must come
/ɑː/ calm start
/ɒ/ what shop

See *Phonetic Symbols & Spelling* on page 158.

1 🌐 1.13 **Listen and repeat the twelve single vowel sounds in English and the example words.**

2 🌐 1.14 **Listen and repeat these sayings about family and friendship. Write the correct phonetic symbol for the vowel sound in each underlined syllable.**

a) Charity begins at home. /æ/ /ɪ/
b) Blood is thicker than water.
c) Home is where the heart is.
d) Birds of a feather flock together.
e) Two's company. Three's a crowd.
f) One good turn deserves another.

3 Match the sayings (*a–f*) in Exercise 2 with their meanings (*1–6*).

1 If someone does you a favour, you should do them a favour in return.
2 People of a similar type often spend time with each other.
3 Look after your family and friends first.
4 Two people can be happy together. A third can get in the way.
5 Wherever your loved-ones are, that's where your home is.
6 Family relationships are the most important.

4 Which of the sayings in Exercise 2 do you like best? Are there any similar sayings in your language? Discuss with a partner.

Speaking & Listening

1 Work in groups. Which of these points do you think parents would consider important / not important in their son or daughter's future partner?

He or she should …

- have good table manners.
- be clean and smartly dressed.
- be from a good family background.
- be kind.
- be good-looking.
- be about the same age as their son/daughter.
- have good academic qualifications.
- like children.
- have a good job / good job prospects.
- have the same religion as their son/daughter.
- be wealthy / have wealthy parents.
- be the same nationality as their son/daughter.

Do you think any of the points are more (or less) important for a son than a daughter?

▲ Sarah and Andy

2 🌐 1.15 Listen to Sarah's parents talking about how they feel about meeting their daughter's boyfriend, Andy, for the first time. Are the statements true or false? Correct the false statements.

a) Sarah's parents don't know anything about Andy.
b) Sarah has had a lot of boyfriends.
c) Her parents have met all of them.
d) They don't think many of Sarah's boyfriends have been good enough for her.
e) Sarah ended her relationship with Jeremy because her parents didn't like him.
f) Sarah's parents think that Andy is a serious boyfriend.

▲ Sarah's parents

3 Choose the correct verb form to complete these sentences from the conversation in Exercise 2.

a) We're looking forward to **meet / meeting** Andy at last.
b) It's difficult **to know / knowing** with Sarah really – she changes boyfriends like other people change their socks.
c) I think it's essential for him **to come / coming** from the same kind of background.
d) It's very important for him **to have / having** some kind of qualifications.
e) He needs **to be / being** a strong character to stand up to Sarah.
f) The poor chap is unlikely **to last / lasting** very long.

Listen again and check your answers.

Listening

1 🌐 1.16 **Listen to Andy talking about how he feels about meeting Sarah's parents. What reason does he give for meeting them?**

2 **Underline the items in the box that Andy says might make a bad impression on Sarah's parents.**

> his shyness   his conversation skills   his background
> his age   his job   his education   his red hair   his religion

Listen again and check. How does he intend to make a *good* impression?

Grammar & Vocabulary

Adjective structures

Adjective + *to*-infinitive
It's **difficult to understand.**
I find it **hard to imagine.**

Adjective + *for* + object + *to*-infinitive
It's **easy for you to talk.**

Adjective + prepositions
I'm **fed up with** TV.
I'm **useless at** sport.
What are you **interested in**?

1 **Look at these extracts from the conversations with Sarah's parents and with her boyfriend. Underline the correct preposition in each extract.**

a) I'm always amazed **at / for / in** how awful they are.
b) … Jeremy. Lovely chap. We were impressed **of / to / with** him.
c) I'm worried **about / of / on** making a bad impression …

Who makes each of these statements?

2 **Complete these sentences with prepositions from the box. You can use each preposition only once.**

> about   at   for   in   of   on   to   with

a) Were there any school subjects you were particularly hopeless _____ ?
b) If you could be famous, what would you like to be famous _____ ?
c) What sort of music are you keen _____ ?
d) Which insects or animals (or people!) are you afraid _____ ?
e) Is there anything you're allergic _____ ?
f) What kind of sports are you interested _____ ?
g) Who was the last person you got angry _____ ?
h) Is there anything you are particularly optimistic or pessimistic _____ ?

Work with a partner. Ask and answer the questions.

3 **Think about three different situations. On a piece of paper write down how you feel about each one. Use sentence structures from the table or your own ideas.**

It's embarrassing to see my parents dancing. OR
I find it embarrassing to see my parents dancing.

| It's
It isn't | difficult
embarrassing
easy | for me | to look at photos of myself as a child.
to talk about relationships with my parents.
to discuss politics with my parents. |
| I find it
I don't find it | boring
irritating
amusing | — | to see my parents dancing.
to annoy my brothers and sisters.
to visit relatives. |

4 **Fold your piece of paper and give it to your teacher. Then follow the instructions.**

• Take one of the pieces of paper with the sentences written by another student.
• Ask questions to find out which student it belongs to. Use the following question structure.

Is it / Do you find it   **adjective**   ***to*-infinitive clause**
Is it / Do you find it   *embarrassing*   *to see your parents dancing?*

Reading & Listening

1 Read the two conversations: the first between Sarah and Andy; the second between Sarah's parents and Sarah and Andy. Choose the most appropriate options (*a*, *b* or *c*) to complete each conversation.

1 a) The door's open   b) Do come in   c) Enter
2 a) thank you – that's very kind of you   b) greetings   c) cheers – that's great
3 a) what's the matter   b) how's it going   c) how are you
4 a) totally shattered   b) absolutely exhausted   c) completely full
5 a) What've you been up to   b) What do you do   c) What's the matter
6 a) hurry up   b) relax   c) chill out
7 a) Do you want   b) Would you prefer   c) Are you looking forward
8 a) Anyone   b) Whatever   c) I don't mind
9 a) I can't help it   b) I'm afraid I don't know   c) No idea
10 a) rather old   b) on its last legs   c) elderly

Conversation 1

Sarah arrives at Andy's flat and knocks at the door.

Sarah: Hello!
Andy: Hiya. (1) *The door's open*!
Sarah: Here, I remembered to bring you that CD.
Andy: Oh, (2) _____ .
Sarah: So, (3) _____ ?
Andy: All right, but I'm (4) _____ .
Sarah: Why? (5) _____ ?
Andy: Nothing – it's just that I didn't finish work until five o'clock this morning.
Sarah: Oh right. Well, you'd better just (6) _____ this evening. (7) _____ to watch TV, or shall I go and get a DVD?
Andy: (8) _____ .
Sarah: Do you know what's on TV tonight?
Andy: (9) _____ . Rubbish as usual, I should think.
Sarah: Oh dear, you are in a bad mood. You're not nervous about meeting my parents, are you?
Andy: No – why should I be? But I am a bit worried about the long drive – my car's (10) _____ .
Sarah: Oh well, let's worry about that tomorrow. Come on – make me a nice cup of tea.

Conversation 2

Sarah and Andy arrive at Sarah's parents' house.

Mum: Hello. Welcome. (1) *Do come in.*
Sarah: Mum, Dad, this is Andy.
Parents: Nice to meet you.
Andy: Nice to meet you. These are for you – Sarah says they're your favourites.
Mum: Oh (2) _____ . And (3) _____ , darling?
Sarah: I'm (4) _____ , actually.
Mum: Oh dear. (5) _____ ? Have you been working too hard?
Sarah: Oh no, nothing like that – it's just a long drive, isn't it?
Mum: Yes, of course. You must sit down and (6) _____ , both of you. (7) _____ coffee or tea, Andy?
Andy: (8) _____ . Whatever's easiest.
Dad: How many miles is it exactly?
Andy: Oh, (9) _____ . The journey's taken us five and a half hours, but my car is (10) _____ .
Dad: Oh yes, I always take the M4, followed by the A34, except during the summer when I tend to avoid motorways and go through Winchester on the backroads.
Mum: Well, we're not going to talk about roads all day, are we? Now Andy, what exactly do you do? Sarah tells us you're in the music industry …

🔊 1.17–1.18 **Listen to each conversation and check your answers.**

2 Work in groups. Imagine someone you know is going to meet their girlfriend's or boyfriend's parents for the first time. Discuss what advice you would give.

Listening & Speaking

1 Work with a partner. List the things you would expect to experience on a visit to the UK to learn English. Think about: the people, the food, the climate, the language, etc.

2 1.19 Listen to Nora talking about the time she spent with an English family. Are the statements true or false? Correct the false sentences.
  a) Nora felt positive about her trip to England.
  b) She was worried about English food.
  c) She was hoping for hot weather.
  d) Her host family didn't like talking about personal matters.
  e) They made Nora feel at home.

3 Put Nora's account of her stay in the correct order. Then listen again and check.

  1 I knew there were lots of things I would have to get used

  8 on talking about the weather all the time. So I was surprised when I met my English family for the first time and they gave me a big hug and then asked me

  4 about trying new things, especially fish and chips! Also, I hate hot summers, so I was dreaming

  2 to when I decided to go to England and stay with a family. But I was looking forward

  5 of the typical English grey days. I was a bit worried

  11 with the language at first – I couldn't understand anything! But the family made me feel

  6 about the reserved British character. I'd heard that British people objected

  12 at home, and it was definitely the best way to improve my English. In a family situation, you have to sink or swim. It's as simple as that.

  10 in turning England into a hot country! I had problems

  3 to experiencing a new culture. I'm not difficult when it comes to food, so I was excited

  7 to talking about anything personal but insisted

  9 about my family, my work and even my boyfriend. The other surprise was the weather – I think global warming has succeeded

4 Use the verb + preposition structures from Nora's account to make true statements about yourself.
  a) I've always dreamt of …
      I've always dreamt of learning to fly.
  b) I'm looking forward to …
  c) I worry about …
  d) I don't object to …
  e) I always insist on …
  f) I've never succeeded in …

Discuss your sentences with your partner.

Speaking: anecdote

You're going to tell your partner about somebody's home you have stayed in.
* Ask yourself the questions below.
* Think about *what* to say and *how* to say it.
* Tell your partner about somebody's home you have stayed in.

a) Whose home did you stay in? A relative's? A friend's? A homestay family's? …
b) When did you stay there and how long did you stay for?
c) What was the purpose of your stay?
d) How did you get there?
e) Who lived in the house and what were they like?
f) How did their lifestyle differ from yours?
g) What was the house / your room like?
h) What were the best / worst moments of your stay?
i) Would you like to stay there again? Why? / Why not?

Useful phrases

1 🌐 1.20 **Listen to Jill Brown showing her new au pair, Marie, round her house. Answer the questions.**

   a) How many children does Jill Brown have?

   b) Which is Jill's favourite room?

   c) What colour are the bathroom walls?

2 **Listen again and number the rooms in the order Jill shows them. Which three rooms does she not show?**

> Marie's bedroom   the bathroom   Ben's bedroom   Jill's bedroom   Katy's bedroom
> the dining room   the kitchen   the living room   the study

3 **British people often apologise, even when there doesn't seem to be any reason to. What was Jill referring to in each case below?**

   a) It's not very big …   d) Excuse the mess.

   b) I hope you don't mind …   e) Sorry about the pink walls.

   c) I'm afraid … is broken.

4 **Match the two halves of the useful phrases that Jill uses to welcome Marie.**

a)	Did you have	1	give me a shout.
b)	Welcome to	2	you around.
c)	Let me introduce you	3	our home.
d)	Then I'll show	4	a pleasant journey?
e)	You must call	5	tea and coffee.
f)	Help yourself to	6	at home.
g)	Make yourself	7	to the rest of the family.
h)	If there's anything you need, just	8	me Jill.

🌐 1.21 **Listen, check and repeat.**

5 **The useful phrase beginnings can be used in a variety of ways to welcome somebody into your home. Cross out the option which is inappropriate in each case.**

   a) Let me **introduce you** / **help you** / **entertain you** / **take your bags**.

   b) Did you have a pleasant **journey** / **trip** / **flight** / **surprise**?

   c) Make yourself **at home** / **comfortable** / **scarce** / **a hot drink anytime**.

   d) Help yourself to **tea and coffee** / **the computer** / **my money** / **an extra pillow**.

   e) You must **call me Jill** / **tell me if the dog annoys you** / **get up at 6.30 a.m.** / **ask me if you need anything**.

6 **Draw a plan of your home on a piece of paper and then 'show' your partner round your house, introducing any other people or pets that live there.**

Vocabulary *Extra*

Learning about words

1 Work with a partner. Discuss the following questions.

a) What does it mean to 'know' a word?

b) How many words do you think you 'know' in your language?

c) How many words do you think you 'know' in English?

2 Read the text about word frequency and answer the questions.

Word frequency

It is a remarkable fact about all languages (not just English) that they consist of a small number of very frequent words, and a large number of very rare ones. As the graph shows, the hundred most frequent words in English make up about 45% of most texts. More importantly, the 7,500 most frequent words make up well over 90% of everything we read. This is important for language learning because a good working knowledge of these 7,500 common words provides a valuable basis for understanding what we read and hear.

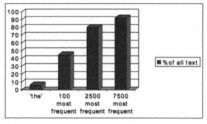

a) What is the most frequent word in the English language?

b) What percentage of text is made up of the most common 100 words?

c) If you know the 2,500 most common words, what percentage of most texts can you understand?

d) If you want to understand over 90% of all texts, how many of the most common words do you need to know?

3 Most common words have more than one meaning. Look at the dictionary entry for *word* and answer the questions.

a) How many main meanings of *word* as a noun are listed?

b) What is the third most common meaning of *word*?

c) What is the meaning of *word* when it is uncountable?

d) How many different phrases with *word* are listed?

e) How many phrases are you familiar with?

4 Work with your partner. When might someone say the following?

a) 'Tell us in your own words how it happened.'

b) 'I don't know the words to this.'

c) 'I'd just like to say a few words.'

d) 'Can I have a quick word?'

e) 'Keep it to yourself. You know how word spreads.'

5 Underline the correct verb to complete some common phrases.

a) Just **say** / **tell** the word.

b) I always **hold** / **keep** my word.

c) I won't **hear** / **see** a word against him.

d) Don't **put** / **throw** words into my mouth.

e) **Have** / **Take** my word for it.

f) Words **fail** / **lose** me.

Check your answers and the meaning of the phrases in the extract.

6 Check your own dictionary. How does it show information about word frequency? How does the entry for *word* differ from this extract?

Choose five useful phrases with *word* to learn.

---

word¹ /wɜː(r)d/ *noun* ★★★

1 unit of language	**4** news/information
2 things sb says/sings	**5** of advice/praise etc
3 short conversation/talk	**+** PHRASES

1 [C] a single unit of written or spoken language: *The first word that many babies speak is 'Mama'.* ♦ *Can you read the words on this page?* ♦ *The Latin word for a table is 'mensa'.*

2 words [plural] someone's words are things that they say: *I was remembering the words of my old friend.* ♦ **in your own words** *Tell us in your own words how the accident happened.* **2a.** used about the words of a song, rather than the music: *I can hum the tune, but I don't know the words.* → EAT, MARK²

3 [singular] a short conversation or discussion, usually without other people listening: **want a word (with sb)** *David wants a quiet word with you.* ♦ **have a word (with sb)** *Can I have a quick word with you?* **3a.** [C] a short speech on a particular subject: **+about/on** *Let me say a word on the subject of security.* ♦ **say a few words** (=give a short speech) *I would just like to say a few words about our guest.*

4 [singular/U] news or information about someone or something: *We've had no word from Brian yet.* ♦ **send word** (=send a message) *He sent word that they had arrived safely.* ♦ **word spreads** *Word of the incident spread quickly.*

5 [C] [usually singular] if someone gives you a word of something such as advice, praise, or warning, they advise, praise, or warn you: *A word of advice – don't take anything Gina says too seriously.*

PHRASES **from the word go** from the time when something starts: *We expected business would start slowly, but from the word go we were really busy.*

give/say the word to give someone an order to do something: *All you have to do is say the word, and I'll leave.* ♦ *When I give the word, start the machine.*

give (sb) your word to promise to do something: *You gave me your word that you would look after him.*

have/exchange words (with sb) to have an argument with someone: *Tom and I have already had words about that today.*

keep your word to do what you promised to do: *She always keeps her word.*

in a word used for giving the shortest answer possible, without explaining anything: *'Did you like Vince?' 'In a word, no.'*

in other words used for introducing another way of saying or explaining something, especially a more simple way: *These were people who fought for money – mercenaries, in other words.*

a man/woman of his/her word a man or woman who does what he or she promises to do

my word or **upon my word** *old-fashioned* used for showing surprise or anger

not have a good word for to think that someone or something is not very good: *He never seems to have a good word for me.*

not hear a word (said) against or **not hear a bad word about** used for emphasizing that you think someone or something is extremely good: *Jan won't hear a word against him.*

not hear/understand etc a (single) word used for emphasizing that someone does not hear/understand etc anything that you say to them: *Jane could hardly understand a word Mervyn said.* ♦ *I don't believe a single word he told me.*

not in so many words used for saying that someone says something in a very indirect way: *'Did he say he was unhappy?' 'Not in so many words.'*

put in a (good) word for sb to tell someone about the good qualities that a particular person has, usually in order to get an advantage for that person: *He promised to put in a word for me with the boss.*

put words into sb's mouth to claim that someone has said a particular thing, although they have not said it, or they did not mean what you say they meant: *He accused the interviewer of putting words into his mouth.*

take sb at their word to do something as a result of what someone has said, even though they may not have meant exactly what they said: *He said he didn't mind what we did, and we took him at his word.*

take my word for it used for emphasizing that what you are saying is completely true: *Take my word for it, she still loves you!*

too...for words used for emphasizing a particular quality that someone or something has: *If her father came to pick her up, that would be too embarrassing for words!*

word for word if you repeat something word for word, you repeat it exactly as someone else said it or wrote it: *I swear that's what he said, word for word.*

(the) word is that used for telling someone what other people have said about something: *Word is that her latest book is the best yet.*

word of mouth communication that consists of comments that people make to each other in an informal way, not formal communication such as news reports and advertisements: *The book became a worldwide best-seller, largely by word of mouth.* ♦ *Most of our customers hear about us by word of mouth.*

words fail me *spoken* used for emphasizing that you are very pleased, surprised, or angry

words to that effect used for reporting the general meaning of what someone has said, rather than their exact words: *He told me, 'Go away,' or words to that effect.*

your word (of honour) a sincere promise that you make: *I give you my word of honour this will never happen again.*

→ DIRTY¹, GOOD¹, LAST WORD

---

3 Gold

Grammar Reported speech. Unreal conditionals
Vocabulary *have, make, take* collocations. Metaphor. Money expressions
Useful phrases Shopping: money expressions; explaining what you want

Reading

1 Read the article and explain the links between the following.
   a) John Sutter – a private empire – disillusion
   b) James Marshall – a sawmill – half the size and shape of a pea
   c) President James Polk – the gold rush – the 'Forty-Niners'

GOLD FEVER

IN 1848, when gold was discovered in California, John Sutter was already one of the wealthiest people in the state. By 1850 he was a ruined man.

A PRIVATE EMPIRE
Sutter was a Swiss immigrant who came to California in 1839, intent on building his own private empire. At that time, the state was a distant outpost that only a handful of Americans had seen. San Francisco had just a few hundred residents. Sutter built a fort, and soon he had 12,000 head of cattle and hundreds of workers.

By the mid-1840s, more and more Americans were trickling into California by wagon and ship. Sutter welcomed the newcomers: he saw them as subjects for his new kingdom. But he had no idea that the trickle would become a flood, a deluge of humanity that would destroy his dream.

DISCOVERY
At the beginning of 1848, Sutter sent James Marshall and about twenty men to the American River to build a sawmill. It was nearly complete when a glint of something caught Marshall's eye. Later he wrote, *'I reached my hand down and picked it up; it made my heart thump, for I was certain it was gold. The piece was about half the size and shape of a pea. Then I saw another.'*

THE FORTY-NINERS
By the end of the year, whispers of a gold strike had drifted eastward across the country – but few easterners believed it until President James Polk made a statement to Congress on December 5th 1848. The discovery, he declared, was a fact. Within days 'gold fever' descended on the country.

The news was telegraphed to every village, to every town. Hundreds of thousands of people, almost all of them men, began to prepare for the epic journey west. They sold possessions, mortgaged farms, borrowed money, banded together with others from their towns to form joint stock companies. They said their goodbyes and streamed west – thousands of young adventurers willing to take a chance on gold: a year of pain in return for a lifetime of riches. They were called 'Forty-Niners' because they left home in 1849. When they would return was another matter entirely.

By early 1849, gold fever was an epidemic. By the end of 1850, Sutter's grand empire had completely collapsed. Sutter did not have gold fever. He wanted an agricultural empire and refused to alter his vision. In the new California, he was simply in the way. The Forty-Niners trampled his crops and tore down his fort for the building materials. Disillusioned, he eventually left the state. The man who had the best opportunity to capitalise on the discovery of gold never even tried.

2 Which words would you use to describe: a) John Sutter; b) one of the Forty-Niners?

> businessman   conservative   dreamer   entrepreneur   farmer
> opportunist   risk-taker   visionary

Can you use any of these words to describe people you know? Tell a partner about them.

▲ Sam Brannan

Listening

1 🌐 **1.22 Listen to the story of Sam Brannan – the first gold rush millionaire. What is the connection between the items in the photo of the Forty-Niner and Sam Brannan's fortune?**

◀ A Forty-Niner with a bottle of liquor, a pick, a prospecting pan and a shovel

2 **Work with a partner. Match the sentence beginnings (a–j) with the sentence endings (1–10) to retell the story of Sam Brannan.**

a) Sam Brannan became …
b) He was running …
c) He quickly recognised …
d) He bought up …
e) He ran …
f) He cornered …
g) He keenly understood …
h) He made …
i) In the end he lost …
j) He died …

1 all the picks, shovels and pans.
2 the laws of supply and demand.
3 a successful businessman in California.
4 the market for picks, shovels and pans.
5 his fortune and his health.
6 the only store near the gold fields.
7 an unnoticed death.
8 a gap in the market.
9 $36,000 in just nine weeks.
10 up and down the streets shouting 'Gold, gold, …'

Listen again and check your ideas.

Vocabulary

1 **Look back through the article on page 24 to complete these verb-noun collocations with *have*, *make* and *take*.**

a) 'But he had no _____'
b) 'James Polk made a _____'
c) 'thousands of young adventurers willing to take a _____'

2 **Complete some more verb-noun collocations by adding *have*, *make* or *take* to these lists.**

a) _____	b) _____	c) _____
a fortune	action	a chat
a fuss	advice	difficulty
a living	a deep breath	a duty
a loss	an exam	a go
a mess	notes	a guess
money	office	a laugh
a profit	place	a look
sense	responsibility	a right
a start	a risk	a think
way	sugar	a word

Work with your partner. Tick all the collocations you already know.

3 **Complete the sentences with an appropriate noun from Exercise 2. Which sentences are true for you?**

a) I always make a _____ when I cook.
b) I don't understand my dreams. They never make _____ .
c) The president of my country took _____ two years ago.
d) I always have _____ finding somewhere to park near here.
e) I don't take _____ in coffee or tea.
f) In my job I have a _____ to twenty-five days' holiday per year.

Choose five other collocations from Exercise 2 that you think would be useful for you. Write example sentences for them. Use a dictionary if necessary.

Metaphor:
MOVEMENT = WATER

deluge noun [singular]: a very heavy fall of rain → a huge number of people moving together

drift verb [I]: be pushed along slowly by air or water → to move somewhere slowly and randomly

flood noun [C]: a large amount of water that temporarily covers a dry area → a large number of people moving together

stream verb [I]: flow continuously / to move in large numbers

trickle noun [singular]: a small amount of liquid that flows slowly → a few people moving slowly

Vocabulary

1 Look at the words in the dictionary definitions. What do they all have in common?

2 Work with a partner. Try to complete the extracts from the article on page 24 with appropriate words from the dictionary definitions.

a) 'He [Sutter] had no idea that the _____ would become a _____ , a _____ of humanity that would destroy his dream.'

b) 'By the end of the year, whispers of a gold strike had _____ eastward across the country.'

c) 'They said their goodbyes and _____ west – thousands of young adventurers willing to take a chance on gold.'

Look back at the article to check your answers.

3 Read the conversation between Martha and her dad. Use the words in the box to complete some expressions which illustrate two more metaphors: TIME = MONEY and IDEAS = FOOD.

chewing digest food half-baked precious profitably running out ~~spare~~ spend wasting worth

Martha:	Morning!
Dad:	You're in a good mood today. Any particular reason?
Martha:	Yes, there is actually. I've decided to become a millionaire.
Dad:	You've decided to become a millionaire. I see. And how exactly do you propose to do that?
Martha:	Well, if you can (1) *spare* **a couple of minutes**, I'll tell you.
Dad:	Martha, you know how (2) _____ **my time is** ...
Martha:	Dad, I promise you it will be (3) _____ **your while**.
Dad:	Oh, OK – but just five minutes or else I'll be late for work.
Martha:	Right. I've got this idea for a website ...
Dad:	Oh come on, you're (4) _____ **your time** if you think you can make money out of the internet. All the best ideas have been used up. You should be **using your time more** (5) _____ , getting a proper job ...
Martha:	I promise you it's not some (6) _____ **idea**. It's something I've been (7) _____ **over** for the last few weeks. Please just have a look at these plans, then tell me what you think.
Dad:	Hm, yes, interesting. There's certainly (8) _____ **for thought** here. How are you going to find the money to do it?
Martha:	Ah, well, I was rather hoping you might help me. Will you?
Dad:	Well, I can't tell you until I've had time to (9) _____ **all this information**. But you've certainly got a good idea. Very original.
Martha:	But **we're** (10) _____ **of time**. If we don't do it very soon, somebody else will.
Dad:	Yes, you could be right. Look, I've got to go now, but as soon as I get back from work I'll (11) _____ **the rest of the evening** looking at it. Have you told anybody else your idea?
Martha:	No, not yet.
Dad:	Well, don't ... I think you've really got something here.

🔊 **1.23** Listen and check your answers.

4 Complete the table with the expressions from the conversation. Do you have similar expressions based on the same metaphors in your language?

TIME = MONEY	IDEAS = FOOD
to spare a couple of minutes	

5 Look at the opinions. Complete the expressions with an appropriate word.

a) Don't rush decision-making. Always take time to _____ things over.

b) The difficult thing about exams is that you always _____ out of time.

c) Going to the gym is a huge _____ of time.

d) It's best to read serious books. They give you _____ for thought.

e) Everyone should _____ at least one year living in a foreign country.

Do you agree or disagree with the opinions? Tell your partner.

Reading & Grammar

1 **Work with a partner. Discuss the following questions.**

a) When was the last time you splashed out (spent a lot of money) on clothes, on a meal, on a present, etc.?

b) When did you last feel guilty about spending money?

c) What is the most extravagant thing you've ever done?

2 **Read a newspaper report about a nineteen year old called Christopher Townsend. Why did he have to pay his mother £68.70?**

Where's my car?

Son steals mum's car!

UNEMPLOYED teenager, Christopher Townsend, had a strange way of showing concern when his mother went
5 into hospital. He sold her car without her knowledge and used the money to splash out on an extravagant champagne holiday for himself and his girlfriend at a
10 five-star hotel in Paris.

Townsend, 19, received £6,000 for the car when he took it to a garage near his home in Little Dibden, Wiltshire. Although the
15 car was registered in his mother's name, he told people in the garage that she had gone abroad and had asked him to sell the car.

With the £6,000 in his pocket,
20 he then phoned his girlfriend and told her that he had arranged a surprise for her birthday. When he said that they were going to Paris the following weekend and that
25 he'd booked a luxury suite in a five-star hotel, she asked him how he could afford it. He told her that he had inherited a sum of money from his grandfather who had
30 died a few months previously.

The teenager appeared in court yesterday, charged with theft. His mother, Mrs Hawkin, told reporters that prosecuting him
35 had been the hardest thing she'd ever done. She said that her son had apologised, but that she still had no idea why he had done it.

The young con-man is now
40 serving six months' community service and has been ordered to pay his mother £68.70, the total amount she has spent on public transport since she has been
45 without her car.

Reported speech

I told her we **were having** a party **the following Saturday**.
I said she **could come**.
She asked me who else
I **had invited**.

---

3 **Look through the newspaper report again and underline examples of reported speech. Then answer the questions (a–e) by writing what each person probably said in direct speech.**

a) What did Christopher Townsend say to the people in the garage? 'My mother's *gone abroad*. She _____ .'

b) What did he say to his girlfriend? 'I _____ a surprise for _____ . We _____ Paris _____ weekend. I _____ .'

c) What did she ask him? 'How _____ ?'

d) What did he say to her? 'I _____ a sum of money from my grandfather. He _____ .'

e) What did his mother say? 'He _____ , but I _____ .'

4 **Work with your partner. Find examples from Exercise 3 and the newspaper report of the changes (a–d) that usually occur when speech is reported.**

a) Tense changes: *has gone abroad* ➔ *had gone abroad*

b) Word order changes (questions): _____

c) Pronoun changes: _____

d) Time reference changes: _____

5 Grammar *Extra* 3, Part 1 page 134. Read the explanations and do Exercise 1.

Pronunciation

1 Underline the correct word to complete this explanation about the schwa /ə/ sound.

The schwa /ə/ is the most common (1) **vowel / consonant** sound in English. It is particularly common in (2) **stressed / unstressed** short words like *a, the, as, for* and *your*. Stressed syllables within single words are (3) **never / always** pronounced with a schwa.

2 Read the sayings about money and underline the vowel sounds that are pronounced using a schwa.

a) Money makes the world go round.
b) There's no such thing as a free lunch.
c) Put your money where your mouth is.
d) In for a penny, in for a pound.
e) Watch the pennies, and the pounds take care of themselves.
f) The love of money is the root of all evil.

🌐 **1.24 Listen, check and repeat.**

3 Which of the sayings in Exercise 2 do you like best? Are there any similar sayings in your language? Discuss with a partner.

Listening & Vocabulary

1 Work in small groups. Think about the questions (*a–f*). Then discuss your answers.

a) It's impossible to have too much money – do you agree?
b) Would you prefer fame or fortune?
c) Were you given or did you earn pocket money as a child?
d) What was the first thing you saved up for and bought yourself?
e) If you could buy yourself a skill or a talent, what would it be?
f) What can't money buy?

🌐 **1.25 Listen to Patti, Eric and Lee. Are any of their answers similar to yours?**

2 Who talks about the following things? Put *P* for Patti, *E* for Eric or *L* for Lee.

1 being broke
2 football
3 happiness
4 being practical
5 two shillings a week
6 toy soldiers

3 Patti, Eric and Lee then answered two more questions. Underline the correct alternative for each highlighted money expression in their answers. Who do you think gave each answer?

Question 1: Does it matter if a wife earns more than her husband? How would you handle it?

a) 'I would feel like a failure if my wife earned more than I did. It's a man's job to earn a **life / living**, and a woman's place is in the home.'

b) 'It wouldn't worry me. I know lots of couples where the woman is the main **breadwinner / breadbasket**. In fact, it would be really good to have a wife who **was loaded / full up!**'

c) 'It wouldn't matter to me, but it might matter to my husband. It shouldn't matter, but human nature being what it is, it probably would.'

Question 2: If you were given £1,000 to save, spend or invest, what would you do?

a) 'Um, the sensible thing to do would be to **save it for a rainy / windy** day or pay off my **overdraft / overflow**, but I think I'd rather **splash out / across** on a family holiday.'

b) 'Well, I certainly wouldn't save or invest it – I'd probably **throw / blow** it on a new music system and some massive speakers.'

c) 'I think I'd be tempted to get a new computer. Mine's getting a bit slow. You can **get them for peanuts / doughnuts** these days you know…'

🌐 **1.26 Listen and check your ideas. What are your answers to these questions? Tell your partner.**

▲ Patti, Eric, Lee

Grammar

Unreal conditionals

If I'd bought it on my credit card, **I'd still be paying** for it now.

1 Look at these conditional sentences. Match the *if*-clauses with the main clauses.

if-clauses	Main clauses
a) If you have dreams, …	1 I didn't get any pocket money.
b) If I were single with no kids and no responsibilities, …	2 it would have to be football.
c) If I didn't behave well, …	3 I'd want fame instead of fortune.
d) If I'd known that they would become valuable antiques, …	4 I'd have kept them.
e) If I had to choose one sport I couldn't live without, …	5 money makes them possible.

Discuss these questions with a partner.

a) How many clauses do conditional sentences have? Can you put them in any order?
b) Which two sentences talk about real situations (*real conditionals*)?
c) Which three sentences talk about hypothetical situations (*unreal conditionals*)?
d) Which auxiliary verb appears in the main clause of all the unreal conditionals?

2 Look at the table below and explain what happens to the verb form when you move from a real situation to a hypothetical one.

Real situation	Hypothetical situation (Unreal condition)
I'm not single.	If **I were** single, I'd want fame instead of fortune.
It's not raining.	If **it were raining**, I'd have come here by car.
I've been saving.	If **I hadn't been saving**, I wouldn't be able to go on holiday.
I left home late.	If **I hadn't left** home late, I'd have arrived here on time.

In modern English all the following *if*-clauses are grammatically acceptable – except for one. Which one?

a) If I was single, …   c) If I was a child, …   e) If I was you, …
b) If I was rich, …   d) If I was English, …

▲ *If I were single, …*

3 Work in groups. Discuss the following situations.

If you governed your country …

a) where would you build your palace?
b) what laws would you change?
c) what new laws would you bring in?
d) what would you spend most money on?
e) what would you tax?
f) what would you ban?
g) who would you appoint as your ministers?
h) what would you have named after you?

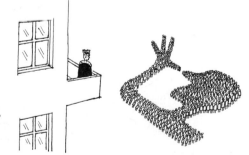

4 Complete the sentences to make them true for you. Discuss your sentences with your partner.

a) If I'd been born in a different country, …
b) If I'd been born a member of the opposite sex, …
c) If I'd had famous parents, …
d) If I'd started learning English earlier in my life, …
e) If I'd listened to my parents' advice when I was younger, …
f) If I hadn't come to this English class today, …

5 Grammar *Extra* 3, Part 2 page 134. Read the explanations and do Exercise 2.

Reading & Vocabulary

1 **Work with a partner. You are going to read about a man who sold his life on eBay. Before you read, discuss the following questions.**

   a) For what reasons might somebody want to sell their life and then start a new one?
   b) If you were selling your whole life, what sort of items would you include?
   c) How much money would you expect to get?

Read and compare your own answers with the answers given in the article.

What price a life?

FRANCES BOOTH

IAN USHER has sold his whole life on eBay, including the car, the hammock and the barbecue.

On days when the Earth seems to be turning in an opposite direction to me, I have thought of packing it
5 all in. Home, job, the city I live in. But actually going through with it? That takes guts.

Step forward Mr Ian Usher, who has sold his life on eBay. The British-born 44-year-old sold his house in Australia (three-bedroom), car (1989 Mazda 929), kite
10 surfing gear, hammock, spa, motorbike, jet ski, BBQ, DVDs, job (as a rug store shop assistant in Perth), PlayStation and friends.

Yes, Melanie, Em, Paula, Marty, Baxter, Andy, Karen, Dazz and the others were included in the deal.
15 The point was to leave everything behind, and Mr Usher walked off with only his passport and wallet in his pocket, to 'get on the train, with no idea where I am going or what the future holds for me'.

So why on earth did he do it?
20 'I have had enough of my life! I don't want it any more! You can have it if you like!' was how he explained things on his website, www.alife4sale.com.

'I am still not sure whether this is inspired madness, complete foolishness, or just some sort of mid-life
25 crisis,' he said.

Of course, at the root of it all was a girl.
He 'met and married the best girl in the world' (she's

called Laura). But after twelve years together he was 'hit with a bolt from the blue' – the details of which he won't
30 discuss. They separated two years ago and this – the sale of a life – is his attempt to start afresh.

Cynics could argue that he is after the book deal, the movie money or just a short spell in the spotlight of fame.
35 Certainly others who have undertaken similar schemes in the past have profited. John D Freyer sold his life in 2001 (item by item, rather than as a job lot). Then he sold the book of the sale of his life – *All My Life For Sale*.
40 The starting price for Usher's life was $1. Within two minutes the first genuine bid was made, at $200. The bidding hotted up by midweek, and on Wednesday jumped from $315,000 to $390,200. Usher's life was sold after sixty-six bids for $399,300.00 AUS (about
45 £190,000 or €250,000).

But as he walks away from his previous life will Ian Usher be any happier? Will it have been life-affirming to see that so many people from around the world are interested in his existence?
50 Or did he expect it to be worth more?

Glossary
pack sth in verb (*informal*) [T]: stop sth
guts noun [U]: courage
bolt from the blue phrase: something completely unexpected

spell noun [C]: time
bid noun [C]: offer

2 Decide whether the sentences are true or false. Correct the false sentences.

a) Not many people would consider selling their whole life on eBay, but Ian Usher <u>did it</u>.
b) His friends weren't included in <u>the price</u>.
c) He <u>left</u> with only his passport and wallet in his pocket.
d) He knows exactly what <u>is going to happen next</u> for him.
e) <u>The main cause</u> of his decision to sell his life was his separation.
f) The sale is his attempt to <u>begin a new life</u>.
g) Some people say that he is <u>hoping to get</u> a book or film deal.
h) He decided to sell things item by item rather than <u>everything together</u>.

Find words or phrases in the article that mean the same as the underlined words above. You may need to change the form of the words or phrases.

a) Not many people would consider selling their whole life on eBay, but Ian Usher went through with it.

3 If you had to sell your whole life, what would be the one possession you'd try to keep? Tell a partner.

Listening

1 🔊 1.27–1.29 Listen to three people talking about their most treasured possessions. Match the possessions (*a–c*) with the notes about the stories (*1–3*).

a) Chris' camera   b) Katie's mobile phone   c) Heather's neckwarmer

1   expensive – GPS – addresses and numbers – three hundred people
2   vintage – South Africa – bargain – tax – family photos – 70th birthday
3   saved life – avalanche – over face – mouth and nose – breathe

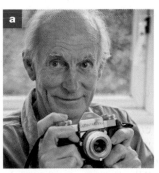
▲ Chris

▲ Katie

▲ Heather

2 Work with your partner and try to reconstruct the stories using the notes in Exercise 1. Listen again and check.

Speaking: anecdote

You are going to tell your partner about your most treasured possession.

• Ask yourself the questions below.
• Think about *what* to say and *how* to say it.
• Tell your partner about your most treasured possession.

a) What is your most treasured possession?
b) What's it made of?
c) How old is it?
d) How long have you had it?
e) Did somebody give it to you or did you acquire it yourself?
f) What special significance does it have?
g) Did it belong to somebody else before?
h) Does it remind you of a particular person? Who?
i) Does it remind you of a time, a place or an event in the past? What?
j) Where do you keep your treasured possession?
k) Who will you leave it to when you die?

Useful phrases

1 🎧 1.30 **Listen to a conversation between John and Cara. Answer the questions.**

a) Who's Julia?
b) What's John's original budget?
c) How much does he spend in the end?

2 Match each pair of useful phrases from the conversation to a suitable meaning (*1–4*).

a) It wasn't worth much.
b) I just got something cheap and cheerful.

c) I was really hard up at the time.
d) I'm not made of money.

e) You have to be prepared to splash out.
f) This is a time when you have to push the boat out.

g) My budget is two or three hundred pounds.
h) I could stretch to £1,000.

1 poor

2 spend a lot of money

3 the most I can pay is

4 inexpensive

Listen again and number the useful phrases (*a–h*) in the order in which you hear them.

3 What does John mean when he says, 'They're a little out of my price range'? Choose the correct option.

a) They're much too expensive.
b) They're a little too expensive.
c) They're not expensive enough.

Put John's words in the correct order.

1 I want a (much) bigger diamond. = 'I was hoping for *slightly / something / sparkly / more.*'
2 I want something (much) cheaper. = 'I suppose, I was thinking of *little / pricey / something / less / a.*'

🎧 1.31 **Listen and check.**

4 Use the prompts to rewrite the following requests in less direct language.

a) I want something less tight. (I was looking for / a little)
b) I want more comfortable trousers. (I'd prefer / slightly)
c) I want something more fashionable. (I'm looking for / slightly)
d) I want something more formal. (I'd like / a little)
e) I want a smarter pair of shoes. (I was looking for / slightly)
f) I want a less colourful jacket. (I was wondering if you might have / slightly)

🎧 1.32 **Listen, check and repeat.**

5 Work with a partner. Tell your partner about the following.

a) shops in your city that are out of the average person's price range
b) the kind of things you'd splash out on if you could afford to
c) the last time you pushed the boat out and bought an expensive gift for someone

Writing *Extra*

Description

1 Read this description of an imaginary day in the life of a very wealthy person. Complete the description using appropriate linking words and expressions from the box. Use each word and expression only once.

> after   as   as soon as   by the time   during   just as   then   until   when   while

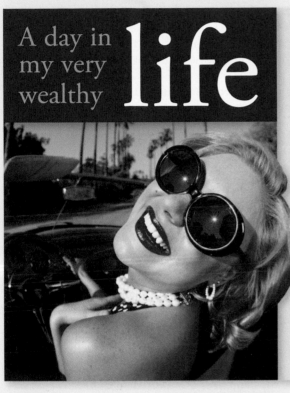

A day in my very wealthy **life**

The first thing I did (1) _____ I woke up in my favourite house this morning was to admire the *breathtaking* view from my bedroom window. **A** (2) _____ I did an hour's exercise with my personal fitness trainer (3) _____ my housekeeper prepared my breakfast. **B** (4) _____ a bath, I spent some time with my secretary and told her to send cheques to all the charities I support. **C** (5) _____ I was leaving the house, a special delivery arrived. It was a parcel from Paris. **D**

I didn't get to the airport (6) _____ midday, so I instructed the pilot to use our fastest plane and take me to my favourite city. **E** (7) _____ the flight, I had lunch and looked at photographs of my last holiday. **F** (8) _____ we'd landed, I contacted a friend who has just finished making her film and arranged to meet her for dinner later. **G** I spent the rest of the afternoon doing what I love doing most. **H**

(9) _____ I met my friend at the restaurant I was starving, so I ordered all my favourite things on the menu. **I** (10) _____ we were leaving the restaurant, I spotted somebody I'd always wanted to meet. **J** It was the perfect end to a perfect day.

2 Insert the adjectives and adverbs from the box into the description in appropriate places. Use the words in the order in which they appear in the box. Compare your ideas with a partner.

> ~~breathtaking~~   vigorous   luxurious   extremely efficient   huge   a light   close   latest   absolutely

3 Imagine that this is a description of how a day might be in your life if you were very wealthy. Add the following details using your own ideas. Exchange descriptions with other students in the class.

A Describe the view.
Steps lead down from the garden to the white sands of my private beach and in the distance I can see dolphins playing in the deep blue sea.
B What did you have for breakfast?
C Which charities?
D What was in the parcel?

E Which city?
F Describe your last holiday.
G Describe your friend.
H How did you spend the afternoon?
I What did you order?
J Who was it and what happened?

4 Choose one of the titles below and write a description. Use all the linking words from the box in Exercise 1 and add adverbs and adjectives to make your description more interesting.

A day in my life as a secret agent
A day in my life on a desert island

A day in my life as a famous sports personality
A day in my life as the leader of my country

5 Exchange your description with other students and choose the most interesting description in the class.

Review A

► Grammar *Extra* pages 132–135

Grammar

1 **Underline the correct alternative.**

I (1) **'ve had** / **had** some great experiences in my life, especially since I (2) **'ve been working** / **worked** as a doctor here in Africa for the last ten years. I (3) **'ve met** / **am meeting** some wonderful people, and (4) **have travelled** / **was travelling** to some amazing places.

One date I will never forget is 1 January 2000. It (5) **was** / **has been** one of the most important days of my life! My wife, Cassie, and I (6) **were living** / **lived** in South Africa. Cassie (7) **expected** / **was expecting** our first baby, but the baby was late. We (8) **has been** / **had been** in hospital for two days, and we (9) **are** / **were** feeling very tired and fed-up. All our friends and family (10) **were** / **have been** out celebrating the new millennium, but Cassie and I (11) **were having to** / **had to** stay inside, just waiting. Our son, Tom, was born just after midnight. I could hear the fireworks outside, but I didn't care! I (12) **had never seen** / **never saw** anything as beautiful as my new baby son.

2 **Match the sentences (*a–f*) to the responses (*1–6*).**

a) I'm not interested in politics.
b) I can speak Arabic.
c) I really enjoyed the new James Bond film.
d) I've never seen a Shakespeare play.
e) I've been to New York.
f) I'd love to visit China one day.

1 So have I. 2 Neither am I. 3 So would I.
4 Neither have I. 5 So did I. 6 So can I.

Give true responses to sentences *a–f*. Compare with a partner.

a) Neither am I. / I am.

3 **Complete the question tags with the words in the box.**

aren't do don't have isn't shall

a) It's a lovely day, _____ it?
b) You like sushi, _____ you?
c) You're coming to dinner tonight, _____ you?
d) You don't live in Paris, _____ you?
e) You haven't been to this class before, _____ you?
f) Let's go and have a coffee, _____ we?

Give true responses to the questions.

4 **Write the questions in the correct order.**

a) what / you / tell / is / me / Could / time / it ?
b) is / Do / station / know / where / the / you ?
c) you / today / think / it's / to / Do / rain / going ?
d) a sandwich / you / I / whether / can / buy / Do / here / know ?
e) coffee / you / think / is / the / Where / do / place / to / have / a / best ?

5 **Complete the conversation with a gerund or a *to*-infinitive.**

Len: Would you mind (1 help) _____ me, Kay?
Kay: Sure. What's the matter?
Len: Sara's asked me (2 go) _____ with her to Spain.
Kay: That's great, isn't it?
Len: Yeah, but I can't afford (3 have) _____ a holiday this year. I was hoping (4 spend) _____ some time (5 work) _____ this summer to pay off my loan.
Kay: Oh, I see.
Len: Mum's offered (6 lend) _____ me the money, but I can't borrow money from her again! She helped me (7 buy) _____ my car.
Kay: Well, I don't mind (8 lend) _____ you the money.
Len: Really? Wow. Thanks, Kay. You're a really great sister.
Kay: Yes. But I'll expect you (9 pay) _____ it back soon.
Len: No problem, sis!

6 **Write the sentences in reported speech.**

a) 'I've got an idea to make some money,' said Jerry.
   Jerry said that _____ .
b) 'I've been thinking about it for a long time,' he added.
   He added that _____ .
c) 'I want to open a shop,' he said.
   He told me that _____ .
d) 'Can I borrow some money?' he asked.
   He asked me if _____ .
e) 'I promise I'll pay you back within five years.'
   He promised that _____ .

7 **Complete the conditional sentences with the correct form of the verbs in brackets.**

a) If I (be) _____ rich, I (buy) _____ a bigger house.
b) If you (borrow) _____ my phone again without asking, I (be) _____ very angry with you!
c) If I (win) _____ a million pounds I (not keep) _____ all the money. I (give) _____ a lot of it away.
d) When I was a child, if you (not have) _____ the money for something, you (not buy) _____ it.
e) If Julie (know) _____ about Paul's past, she (not marry) him _____ . But it's too late now.
f) If I (be) _____ you, I (get) _____ rid of that old car.

Vocabulary

1 Match the adjectives (*a–f*) with nouns (*1–6*) to make collocations.

a) impassive   1 clothes
b) forced   2 smile
c) close-set   3 voice
d) husky   4 hair
e) tousled   5 eyes
f) scruffy   6 face

2 Label the pictures (*a–h*) with the words in the box.

> belt   buckle   button   collar   cuff   hem
> sleeve   zip

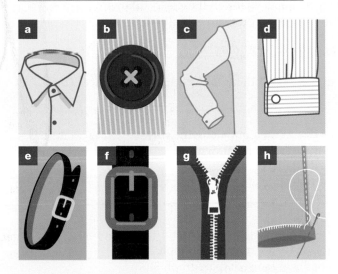

3 Replace the words in bold with the words in the box.

> rearrange   reconsider   reconstruct   relocate
> reword

a) I'm going to **change the date of** the meeting next week.
b) Joe asked me to **think again about** his big idea.
c) Your report is good, but please **change** the last sentence.
d) After the floods, they had to **build** the bridge **again**.
e) Pam's company is going to **move** to Scotland.

4 Complete the sentences with the words in the box.

> aptitude   barely speaking   dotes on
> in touch with   pen friend   rusty

a) I used to speak French very well, but now I'm a bit _____ .
b) I was good at art at school, but I showed no _____ for music.
c) Gina's been writing to her _____ in Japan for five years.
d) Blanca _____ her grandchildren. She just adores them!
e) Are you still _____ Alex from university?
f) I had a row with Phil, and now we're _____ .

5 Complete the text with the correct form of *have*, *make* and *take*.

Louise had been running a small business for two years, but had been (1) _____ difficulties for some time. Her bookshop should have been (2) _____ money, but it wasn't. In fact, the business was (3) _____ a loss. Louise was desperate, and she knew she had to (4) _____ action. She almost gave up and sold the business, but she decided she wanted to (5) _____ a go at saving the bookshop, so she asked a business advisor for help. The advisor visited Louise's shop and spent two days talking to local people and (6) _____ notes. He realised that people didn't know about the shop, and advised Louise to (7) _____ a look at ways of getting the shop noticed. Louise (8) _____ his advice. She painted the shop bright red and put advertising up all over town. Now the bookshop (9) _____ a fortune and Louise is delighted.

6 Complete the sentences with the words in the box.

> blown   breadwinner   loaded   peanuts   rainy

a) She was _____ after her lottery win.
b) I've got some money put aside for a _____ day.
c) His wife's the _____ and he stays at home and looks after the children.
d) His suit was a bargain. He paid _____ for it.
e) Mark's just _____ all his money on a new car.

Pronunciation

1 Look at some words from Units 1–3. Say the words and add them to the table.

> ~~advantages~~ appearance businessman
> decision designer embarrassing everything
> impression memorable relationship
> spectacular talented

A: □■□	B: ■□□	C: □■□□
		advantages

2 Underline the stressed syllable.

🔊 1.33 **Listen, check and repeat.**

▶ 🔊 1.34 **Song**

Challenge

Grammar Narrative tenses. Future continuous and future perfect
Vocabulary Word formation. Collocations. Phrasal verbs
Useful phrases Common ailments; showing sympathy; recommendations and advice

Reading & Vocabulary

▲ Ben Saunders

1 **Look at the photos of Ben Saunders on page 37 and discuss the questions with a partner.**

a) What sort of expeditions do you think he takes part in?
b) What are the potential dangers he may face on these expeditions?
c) What reasons might he have for going on these expeditions?

Read the article on page 37 and check your ideas.

2 **Sentences *a–e* are from the article. Match them to the appropriate places (*1–5*) in the article.**

a) I'm absolutely average.
b) So that's one of the lessons I've figured out along the way.
c) There are, as Ben says, 'no maps left to be drawn'.
d) Everything that could go wrong did go wrong.
e) Meet Ben Saunders: adventurer, athlete, motivational speaker.

3 **Are these sentences are true or false?**

a) Ben isn't planning an <u>immediate trip back</u> to the Arctic. (paragraph 1)
b) British explorers are all <u>excessively wealthy</u>. (paragraph 2)
c) Ben's first expedition was <u>badly organised</u>. (paragraph 3)
d) They didn't actually reach the North Pole, so there was no <u>press coverage</u>. (paragraph 3)
e) After his first expedition, he got a <u>contract to write a book</u>. (paragraph 3)
f) It's Ben's <u>absolute conviction</u> that the more you stretch yourself, the more you can achieve. (paragraph 5)
g) Ben is excited that his Antarctic expedition might be <u>achievable</u>. (paragraph 6)
h) Ben says that you have to be <u>especially talented</u> to do these types of expedition. (paragraph 7)

Find the words or phrases in the article that mean the same as the underlined words.

Word formation

self- prefix relating to yourself: used with many nouns and adjectives: *self-belief, self-conscious, self-discipline, self-employed, self-esteem*

able / ible suffix something that can be done: used with many verbs to make adjectives: *accessible, doable, edible, enjoyable, reasonable, unbearable*

4 **Ben talks about 'self-belief' and expeditions that are 'doable'. Look at more examples of words formed with the prefix *self-* and the suffix *able/ible*, in the Word formation panel. Complete the sentences.**

a) I feel very _____ when I speak English to a native speaker.
b) I don't like working for other people – I'd rather be _____ .
c) I have a friend who suffers from low _____ even though she's very successful.
d) I never go to expensive restaurants. I prefer places where the food is good but prices are _____ .
e) I recently spent a very _____ evening with my old school friends.
f) I can't stand the summer. I find the heat and humidity _____ .

Are any of the sentences true for you?

5 **Look up the list of nouns and adjectives with the prefix *self-* in your dictionary. Tick the ones you know or can understand easily. Choose three more to learn. Write your own example sentences.**

Ben Saunders: POLAR explorer

1 Ben, at the age of twenty-three, was the youngest man to ski solo to the North Pole. He dragged a 180 kilogramme sledge over 1,420 miles through Arctic conditions described by NASA at the time as some of 'the worst since records began'. This year, as well as planning an imminent return to the Arctic, Ben plans to ski solo from the Antarctic coast to the South Pole and back in the autumn, carrying all his supplies on his sledge – 1,800 miles, 200-odd kilogrammes, minus 40 degrees Centigrade.

This is a fundamentally pointless thing to do. 'Arctic explorer' isn't much of a job title when a tourist can pay $22,000 to do the same thing in a cruise ship. ' **2** But we do still have adventurers in Britain. They tend to be either obscenely rich – Richard Branson – or to have convinced us that, somehow, their endeavours and achievements have emotional significance for the rest of us – Ellen McArthur.

Well, Ben Saunders isn't rich. He was 'fired from the only sensible job I ever had' after persuading the firm to sponsor his shambolic first expedition.' **3** We were attacked by a bear. I got frostbite in my toe. We started running out of food. It was just desperate. And we didn't get to the Pole, we didn't get there, so we had no media interest. No one heard about it: no book deal, no speaking, no nothing. I was so miserable.'

('Sorry, attacked by a bear?' 'Menaced ... but you never really know if they're going to have a go or if they're just being inquisitive.')

'Environmental scientists in Canada said it was impossible for me to get to the Pole in 2004 ... I said 'No, it's still OK, and I can still get there,' and I did. Self-belief, I see it as being a bit like a muscle – and I'm slipping into motivational speaking mode now – but it's my genuine belief that the more you stretch yourself the stronger it gets. And the reverse is true: if you never do anything that's uncomfortable or risky then your self-belief gets weaker. **4** The thing that I've stretched and tested, more than any part of my physiology, is my self-belief.'

'My Antarctic expedition is just about doable, just feasible and that's what is exciting to me. If I knew it was possible, if I knew I could do it without too much bother, I wouldn't be interested.' Why? 'Personally I'm fascinated by the human performance element to it. Not that long ago, running a marathon was seen as the pinnacle of human endeavour, and now I wouldn't be that surprised if my mum said she was going to run one next year.'

People's horizons are changing. 'I'm not particularly gifted, I'm not genetically freakish in any sense, **5** I've just chosen this one goal to pursue and I've been dedicated to it. That's it. And that's the thing that intrigues me: with enough training and enough determination, enough focus and preparation, how far can we go? And I don't think I've found out yet.'

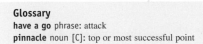

Glossary
have a go phrase: attack
pinnacle noun [C]: top or most successful point
freakish adj: not normal or natural
pursue verb [T]: try to achieve

Listening & Vocabulary

1 Work with a partner. Do you think these facts about polar bears are true or false?

a) Polar bears hibernate in winter.
b) They don't usually eat seals.
c) They are the largest land-based carnivores in the world.
d) If you meet a polar bear, you need to stay quiet and make yourself as small as possible.
e) They can move at nearly fifty kilometres per hour.

🌐 **1.35** **Ben Saunders and his colleague, Pen Hadow, met a polar bear on a North Pole expedition in 2001. Listen to the first part of their story and check your answers.**

2 Discuss the answers to these questions with your partner.

a) How many people went on this expedition, and who was navigating?
b) Why did Ben stop, turn round and look back along his tracks?
c) The year was 2001, but which month of the year was it?
d) Where had they practised what to do in case they met a polar bear?
e) How did they intend to deal with the polar bear?
f) What happened when Pen pulled the trigger on his shotgun?

Listen again and check your answers.

3 Discuss what you think happened next.

a) What did Pen do?   b) What did Ben do?   c) What did the polar bear do?

🌐 **1.36** **Listen and check your ideas.**

4 Read and listen again to extracts from the climax to the story. Which tenses are used for the verbs in bold?

The bear (**walk**) towards us. Pen (**reload**) the gun … so Pen (**be**) is now halfway through our supply of ammunition. He (**pull**) the first trigger … he (**walk**) around his sledge … I (**remember**) thinking, 'Wow, Pen's gone mad … He's going to get eaten. What (**do**)?'

Why do you think these tenses are used at this point in the story? Discuss your ideas.

5 Complete these collocations from the story.

a) I couldn't quite f_____ out what wasn't right.
b) I shouted at Pen … and our bear drill swang into a_____ .
c) There was no w_____ we could outrun the bear.
d) Pen was in ch_____ of the gun.
e) Pen l_____ the gun … closed the barrels, pulled the trigger …
f) He said, 'The gun's still j_____ .'
g) Everything went into s_____ motion.
h) I couldn't even u_____ the zip on the sledge.

Check your answers in the Recordings on page 147. Choose the three most useful expressions for you to learn. Write your own example sentences.

Grammar

Narrative tenses

Past simple
She **came** into the room.

Past continuous
He **was standing** there.

Past perfect simple
She**'d never met**
him before.

Past perfect continuous
He**'d been waiting**
for ages.

1 **Match the sentence endings (*a–d*) with the correct meaning (*1–4*).**

I got home yesterday and my father …

a) made dinner.

b) was making dinner.

c) had made dinner.

d) had been making dinner.

1 'Making dinner' happened **before** I got home. (a single completed action)

2 'Making dinner' happened **after** I got home.

3 'Making dinner' happened **before**, **while** and **after** I got home.

4 'Making dinner' started **before** I got home. (an action that was in progress but was not necessarily completed)

Name the tenses used in the sentence endings (*a–d*). Write the negative and question forms. Use each tense to make true statements about different situations when you got home yesterday. Tell a partner.

2 **Work with your partner. Look at the sentence beginnings (*a–e*) based on Ben Saunders' polar bear story. In each case, choose the ending that best describes the facts of the story.**

a) Ben Saunders was just 23 and …

(1) he hadn't been on a polar expedition.
(2) he didn't go on a polar expedition.

b) When Ben and Pen met the polar bear, …

(1) they had been travelling for a day.
(2) they travelled for a day.

c) When Ben looked back along his tracks, …

(1) the polar bear walked towards him.
(2) the polar bear was walking towards him.

d) They had a 'bear drill' which …

(1) they had practised in a car park in the UK.
(2) they had been practising in a car park in the UK.

e) When the gun went off, …

(1) the polar bear had walked away.
(2) the polar bear walked away.

3 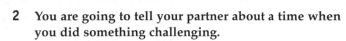 **Grammar *Extra* 4, Part 1** page 134. Read the explanations and do Exercise 1.

Speaking: anecdote

1 **Work with your partner. Discuss which of the following challenges you think is the most daunting. How many of these challenges have you had to face?**

- taking part in a race or a competition
- doing an audition for a part in a play
- performing on stage (acting, singing, etc.)
- giving a speech or a presentation
- taking an exam or a driving test
- attending a job interview

- travelling abroad on your own
- cooking a meal for lots of people
- asking somebody out on a date
- meeting your boyfriend or girlfriend's parents

2 **You are going to tell your partner about a time when you did something challenging.**

- Ask yourself the questions below.
- Think about *what* to say and *how* to say it.
- Tell your partner about your experience.

a) What did you do?
b) Why did you decide to do it?
c) Was it your first time?
d) How did you prepare for it?
e) What were you most afraid of?
f) How did you feel while you were doing it?
g) Did anything go wrong? What?
h) How did you feel afterwards?
i) Was it as challenging as you thought it would be?
j) Would you do it again?

Reading

1 Read the article and label the sections (*a–e*) with the headings in the box.

| Clothing | Fitness and training | The mind | ~~MoonWalk?~~ | Nutrition |

Personal challenges: MoonWalk

Claire Jones is aiming to raise money for a breast cancer charity by doing a 'MoonWalk'. She will be joining 15,000 women in bras in a 26.2-mile power-walk through the night around Hyde Park, London. She has two months to prepare. Here, she outlines her training plan.

a) *MoonWalk?*
The MoonWalk is a power-walking marathon set up by Walk the Walk, a charity that raises money for breast
5 cancer all over the world. Participants always wear decorated bras, and that includes the men!
b) _____
As you can see, I'm not a health freak,
10 but for the MoonWalk I need to be in good general health, so I'll be working on my stamina and general fitness levels. I'll be going to the gym four times a week, doing a combination of
15 cardio, aerobics and strength-training.
c) _____
I'm the type of person who likes chips with my chips, and so I'm a bit worried about the diet. Apparently,
20 carbohydrates are crucial for keeping

energy levels up when you're training for a marathon, but they have to be the right carbs. I'll probably be supplementing my diet with protein
25 drinks and vitamins.
    During the MoonWalk, it's important to maintain blood sugar levels, so I'll be eating energy bars, bananas and other fruit snacks at regular intervals.
30 Of course it's also vital to stay hydrated, so I'll be drinking plenty of water along the way.
d) _____
Power-walking gear is very similar to
35 running gear: light clothes that allow the air to circulate and your skin to breath. I'll definitely be investing in a good pair of trainers. Although power-walking doesn't put as much pressure
40 on the joints as running does, it's still

essential to have the right support for the soles of your feet and your ankles. Most of the heat from your body escapes from your head, so I'll
45 be wearing a hat. And like everybody else, I'll be wearing a decorated bra.
e) _____
Any exercise is a huge mental challenge for me. It's a constant battle for me to
50 stay motivated enough to keep up with the training. I need to visualise myself reaching the finishing line ... hopefully not on my hands and knees.
    Also, in the back of my mind I need
55 to remember the reason for doing this: when I've completed this MoonWalk, I'll have contributed a sum of money to a very good cause, and that's what will keep me going.

2 Choose the correct collocation in these comprehension questions. Look back at the article, if necessary.

a) Which good cause does the MoonWalk **earn** / **raise** money for?
b) What will Claire be doing to improve her general **fitness** / **health** levels?
c) How will she be supplementing her **diet** / **food**?
d) Why will she need to eat snacks at **constant** / **regular** intervals during the walk?
e) Why will she be investing in a good **pair** / **set** of trainers?
f) What will be at the back of her **brain** / **mind** when she is doing the MoonWalk?

Answer the questions.

Have you or has anyone you know ever done anything to raise money for a good cause? Tell a partner.

Grammar

Future continuous and future perfect

Future continuous
I'll be working on that report tomorrow.

Future perfect
I'll have finished it by 6.00 p.m.

1 Look back at the article about Claire Jones on page 40. Find examples of the future continuous and the future perfect to add to the table. Then answer the questions *a* and *b*.

Things *she'll be doing* to prepare for the MoonWalk	Things *she'll be doing* during the MoonWalk	Something *she'll have done* when she's completed the MoonWalk
She'll be working on her stamina and general fitness levels.		

a) Which tense describes an action that will be *in progress at* a certain time in the future?
b) Which tense describes an action that will be *completed by* a certain time in the future?

2 Write future continuous sentences. Use *will* or *won't* with *probably* or *definitely* to make them true for you.

a) In about an hour from now, I (have) _____ lunch.
In about an hour from now, I'll probably be having lunch.
b) In a few hours' time, I (drive) _____ home.
c) From eight o'clock this evening, I (work out) _____ at the gym.
d) At nine o'clock this evening, I (watch) _____ TV.
e) This time next year, I (work) _____ in an office.
f) Ten years from now, I (live) _____ at the same address.

3 Think about things you will have done by the end of today. Write future perfect sentences using these prompts.

By the end of today, …
a) spend / (money) *I'll have spent £100.*   d) go into / shops   g) eat / chocolate
b) send / text messages   e) do / exercise   h) spend online / (time)
c) speak to / people   f) drive / kilometres   i) say *sorry* / times

Make questions using *How many …?* or *How much …?* Then ask a partner.

By the end of today, how much money will you have spent?

4 | Grammar *Extra* 4, Part 2 page 134. Read the explanations and do Exercise 2.

Listening & Vocabulary

1 Work with your partner. Look at the 'Top ten' list and discuss the questions.

a) How much exercise do you do?   b) What stops you doing exercise?

▲ Steve

▲ Maria

▲ Sam

▲ Tim

Top ten excuses for **not** doing exercise

1 You hate it.
2 You can't afford a gym membership.
3 You're not motivated.
4 The weather's too bad.
5 You're too tired after work.
6 You don't know how to exercise.
7 It hurts.
8 You don't have time.
9 It doesn't make any difference.
10 You look terrible in Lycra.

2 🌐 1.37–1.40 Listen to four people (Steve, Maria, Sam and Tim) being asked the questions in Exercise 1. Which reasons do they give for not doing exercise?

3 Work with your partner. Go to the Additional material on page 128.

Reading

1 You're going to read an article about the challenge of giving up smoking. Think of …
  a) three good reasons for giving up smoking.
  b) three reasons why people smoke.
  c) three different methods people use to give up smoking.

2 Read the article and find out …
  a) the writer's reasons for wanting to give up smoking.
  b) the writer's reasons why he smokes.
  c) the method the writer has used to try to give up smoking.

Do you think the writer is likely to give up smoking in the near future? Why? / Why not?

I know it's bad for me, but I still can't STOP

Three packs of cigarettes were lying there on the pavement. I hopped down from Yefim Shubentsov's office doorstep, picked them up and pocketed them. Later, in a bar, when I opened the first pack, I
5 found – to my delight – the twenty cigarettes intact.

I'm still at the bar, telephone in one hand and the cigarettes in the other. I'm dialling Shubentsov, who told me to call the moment I felt the urge to smoke. I feel it, feel it even stronger than I felt Shubentsov's
10 healing energy. That's saying something, since Shubentsov is known around the world for curing smokers of their nasty habit, using a mystical method. He transmits his healing energy from his fingertips, he tells me – something he picked up
15 from another bloke in Russia. 'I help you for free,' he told me in his muddy accent. 'Just call me whenever.'

I went to see Shubentsov because I think it's time to stop. Time to stop because I'm getting old,
20 and I can't keep doing this to myself. But here's the real problem. I should quit, but like a lot of you struggling with the same habit, I really don't want to. At least, not yet.

Smoking has been very good to me. Cigarettes
25 have never let me down, never abandoned me on lonely, desperate nights. Smoking clears my head, helps me think. Smoking has started conversations, driven away annoying people. Smoking helps me celebrate victories, get over losses, comfort
30 the comfortless. It also chases away the mosquitoes.

I will quit. Soon. My body and my mind are demanding that I do, daily.

I claim to smoke for pleasure, but I realise that
35 slowly, steadily, I'm losing control of this close, special friend. I hate that. I realise it's not just a 'habit'. I'm hooked.

So here I am, attempting to give up again, at Shubentsov's place. I've tried all the other quitting
40 techniques available. Anytime the urge to smoke strikes, he said, just call him immediately and he'll help. The funny thing is, I realise that I'm not phoning him to stop me from lighting up. I'm phoning him so I can. If I call, I'll have done my
45 part. Then I can smoke this cigarette. Besides, I know that at 9.30 on a Friday night, I'll get the answering machine. I do. 'The office is open from ten to four. Call me back then. This machine does not take messages.'

50 I put the phone down and I can honestly say I'm relieved. You see, it's not Shubentsov's fault or anyone else's fault that I'm still smoking. It's mine.

Now if you'll excuse me, I'm going to smoke this cigarette. Whether I'll really enjoy it,
55 though, is another story.

It takes a lot of strength to do this.

Used with permission of Men's Health Copyright © 2008. All rights reserved.

Glossary

feel the urge phrase: feel a strong need or desire
cure sb of sth verb [T]: stop sb's bad habit

pick sth up phrasal vb [T]: learn
struggle verb [T]: try hard to do sth

Vocabulary

1   **Work with a partner. Discuss these questions about phrasal verbs. Use a dictionary if necessary.**

a)   What is the difference in meaning between *pick a book up* and *pick a language up*? Which meaning is idiomatic? Which meaning is literal?

b)   What is the difference in meaning between *I gave in* and *I gave my homework in*? Which verb is transitive? Which verb is intransitive?

c)   *Look sth up* is transitive and separable. Which of the following patterns is not possible: *I looked up the word / I looked the word up / I looked up it / I looked it up*?

d)   *Look into sth* is transitive and not separable. Which of these patterns are not possible: *I looked into the matter / I looked the matter into / I looked into it / I looked it into*?

Identify all the phrasal verbs in the article on page 42. For each one, decide …

• if the meaning is literal or idiomatic.
• if the verb is transitive or intransitive.
• if the transitive verb is separable or not separable.

2   **Use an appropriate phrasal verb from the article to rewrite the underlined phrases at the end of these sentences.**

a)   The writer found three packs of cigarettes on the ground – <u>he took them</u> – *he picked them up*.

b)   Shubentsov wasn't born with healing power in his fingertips – <u>he learnt it</u>.

c)   Cigarettes have been good to the writer – <u>they've never disappointed him</u>.

d)   Smoking is helpful with losses – <u>it helps you recover from them</u>.

e)   There's an answering machine in Shubentsov's office – <u>it says 'telephone me again later'</u>.

Phrasal verbs

come down with sth become ill

feel up to sth feel strong enough to do sth

put sb off make sb dislike sth

shake sth off get rid of sth, eg an illness

take after sb be like an older relative

wear sb out make sb feel very tired

3   **Complete the sentences by putting the object pronoun in brackets in the correct position.**

a)   I stopped smoking when I saw a film about it at school. It really put off. (me)

b)   Whenever there's flu going round I always seem to come down with. (it)

c)   If I catch a cold in winter it usually takes me ages to shake off. (it)

d)   My father has always been very fit. It's a pity I don't take after. (him)

e)   At the end of a day, the last thing I want to do is go running. I just don't feel up to. (it)

f)   I don't need to do any exercise – my kids wear out. (me)

Are any of these sentences true for you?

Speaking

1   **Identify the phrasal verbs in these statements about health. How many do you know? Look them up in a dictionary if necessary.**

a)   I can't keep up with all the new diets that come out every year.

b)   I know I need to lose weight but I keep putting it off.

c)   My problem is that I can't do without chocolate.

d)   I wish someone would come up with a non-fattening chocolate that tastes as good as the real thing.

e)   I'm also trying to cut down on caffeine.

f)   I need to take up a new sport, but not one that takes up too much time.

'James has given up smoking recently'

2   **Work in groups. Which of these statements do you relate to most? Tell your partner.**

Useful phrases & Pronunciation

1 Read the conversations and match an ailment to each one.

> difficulty sleeping   hay fever   a sore throat   a splitting headache
> sunburn   a twisted ankle

a

A: Oh dear – you look like death warmed up! Late night last night?
B: No, not really. But I couldn't sleep. I don't think I slept a wink, and now I feel exhausted.
A: Oh, it's horrible when that happens. You should try ...

b

C: Oh dear! What happened?
D: I've done something to my ankle. It's killing me!
C: Oh dear, you poor thing! It looks really swollen.
D: I know, and it's getting worse.
C: If you ask me, you need to ...

c

E: Ugh! I can't swallow anything.
F: Oh yes, I know what you mean. I was the same last week. I could only eat ice cream!
E: So, what did you do?
F: Well, you could try this. ...

d

G: Don't touch my back!
H: Why? What's up?
G: I wanted to get a tan quickly so I didn't bother to put any sunblock on.
H: Oh well, it serves you right then, doesn't it?
G: It really stings.
H: Have you tried ...

e

I: When did it start?
J: After I'd been playing computer games for a few hours. I feel as if my head's going to explode!
I: Oh well, you've only got yourself to blame, haven't you?
J: I know, I know. But I've taken aspirin, and it hasn't worked.
I: Well, you could try ...

f

K: Have you got a cold?
L: No, I'm all right – I always get a streaming nose and red eyes at this time of the year.
K: That must be awful. If I were you, I'd ...

2 Work with a partner. Look at the conversations in Exercise 1 and complete each one with your own advice.

  🔊 1.41 Listen and compare your ideas with the original conversations.

3 🔊 1.42 Read and listen to the highlighted useful phrases in the conversations. Are the listeners being sympathetic or unsympathetic?

  Practise the useful phrases with your partner. Try to use the same stress and intonation as the recording.

4 Work with your partner. Student A look at your problems on page 128. Student B look at your problems on page 131. Follow the instructions.

Vocabulary *Extra*

Phrasal verbs

1 Work with a partner. The diagrams show combinations of the two most common verbs with the six most common particles found in phrasal verbs.

- Choose six from the twelve possible phrasal verbs and think of a meaning for each one.
- Decide if the phrasal verbs you have chosen are transitive [T] eg I **took off** my coat, or intransitive [I] eg The plane **took off**.
- Write a 'vocabulary entry' showing the grammar, the definition and an example sentence. Use a dictionary if necessary.

    take sth up [T] = start doing something new – 'I've just taken up jogging.'

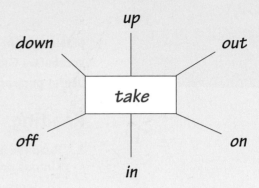

2 Complete the following questions with *take* or *get*.

a) What time do you _____ up during the week?
b) Do you always _____ out travel insurance when you go abroad?
c) How well do you and your brothers and sisters _____ on?
d) Do you find that grammar rules are easy to _____ in?
e) What time do you usually _____ off work?
f) What sort of things _____ you down?

Ask your partner the questions.

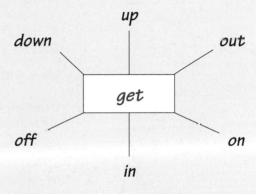

3 *Take, get, put, come, go* and *set* are the six most common verbs found in phrasal verbs. Decide which common phrasal verb is being defined by each of the 'meaning menus' *A–F*.

A) *come* up   C) _____ on   E) _____ off
B) _____ on   D) _____ up   F) _____ on

4 Replace the underlined words or phrases in sentences *a–f* with the correct form of an appropriate phrasal verb from Exercise 3.

a) I never miss the news. I like to know what's <u>happening</u> in the world.
b) I always try to <u>leave</u> early when I've got a long way to drive.
c) I buy a lottery ticket every week but my numbers never <u>win</u>.
d) You don't need a university education to <u>be successful</u>.
e) I'm so busy. I can't <u>accept</u> any more work at the moment.
f) My flat is quite small so when I <u>let people stay</u> they have to sleep on the sofa.

Are any of the sentences true for you? Compare with your partner.

5 Work with your partner. Some phrasal verbs are made up of a verb and two particles. Add *at, for, on*, or *with* to complete these sentences. Use your dictionary if necessary.

a) 'Is that the best you can come up _____ ?'
b) 'When does it come up _____ renewal?'
c) 'Just get on _____ it. We haven't got all day!'
d) 'Stop going on _____ me, will you?'
e) 'I can't put up _____ this any longer.'
f) 'I might take you up _____ that one of these days.'

Decide in what context somebody might say these sentences.

6 Check your own dictionary. Look up phrasal verbs under the entries for *come, get, go, put, set* and *take*. Choose five new phrasal verbs to learn.

A

1 go to speak to sb	7 to higher point/level
2 become available	8 appear in sky
3 need to be dealt with	9 win money with a ticket
4 travel further north	10 about plants
5 about information	11 be judged in court
6 when sb is sick	+ PHRASES

B

1 get into bus etc	6 be successful
2 continue doing sth	7 be friends with sb
3 be chosen for group etc	8 finally do sth
4 appear on a programme	+ PHRASES
5 asking how well sb did sth	

C

1 continue happening	7 time: pass
2 happen	8 base an opinion on sth
3 begin an activity/state	9 go to a place before sb
4 electricity etc: work	10 walk on stage etc
5 talk too much/again	+ PHRASES
6 do sth after	

D

1 build a wall etc	6 let sb stay in your house
2 fix sth to a wall/post	7 suggest sb for a position
3 increase the value of sth	8 suggest sth/sb
4 give money	9 try to achieve/prevent sth
5 raise sth	+ PHRASES

E

1 begin a journey	4 cause sth accidentally
2 make sth start working	5 make sb/sth look attractive
3 make sth explode	6 make sb laugh/cry/talk a lot

F

1 employ sb	4 fight or compete against sb
2 develop character etc	5 decide to do sth
3 accept work/responsibility	

5 Ritual

Grammar *will*, *would*, *used to* for present and past habits. Verb patterns (2)
Vocabulary Guessing from context. Expressions with *go*. Weddings
Useful phrases Annoying habits

Reading

1 Read the article on page 47. Link the famous people (*a–e*) with the objects (*1–5*).

a) Serena Williams   1   popcorn
b) Ana Ivanovic   2   furniture
c) Adrian Mutu   3   shoelaces
d) David Beckham   4   underwear
e) Prince   5   white lines

Work with a partner. Compare your answers and explain the links to each other.

2 Based on the article, underline the five possible endings to this sentence from the alternatives below.

Professional sports people perform rituals because they're …

a) experienced.   f) thirsty.
b) superstitious.   g) famous.
c) missing home.   h) obsessive compulsive.
d) rational.   i) worried about somebody's magical powers.
e) a bit crazy.

In your opinion, which of the famous people has the strangest rituals?

Vocabulary

1 Read the article on page 47 again and underline words or phrases that you don't know. Then answer the questions:

a) Is the unknown word or phrase a verb, a noun, an adjective, …?
b) Is it similar to another English word or a word in your language?
c) Can the context – the words in the surrounding text – help you guess the meaning of the unknown word?

2 Complete the glossary below with words or phrases from the article.

> **Glossary**
> 1 *stride* verb [I]: walk with confidence
> 2 _____ verb [T]: come from
> 3 _____ verb [T]: beat very easily
> 4 _____ noun [C]: set of regular fixed habits
> 5 _____ phrase: the advantage
> 6 _____ verb [T]: meet
> 7 _____ adj: crazy
> 8 _____ noun [C]: bad magical spell
> 9 _____ noun [C]: a force that brings bad luck
> 10 _____ adj: famous
> 11 _____ adj: not equal
> 12 _____ noun [C]: set of clothes
> 13 _____ adj: common
> 14 _____ adj: unaffected

How many of the words or phrases you underlined in Exercise 1 are included in the glossary? Write glossary definitions for any other words. Use your dictionary if necessary.

Mind games

AS SERENA WILLIAMS strides out onto the tennis court, most people will assume that her air of confidence derives from the knowledge that she is a super-talented and experienced player who's at the top of her game and can thrash most opponents with her eyes closed.

5 But for this tennis champion, it's much more complicated than that. Her winning formula includes tying her shoelaces in the same way, using the same shower cubicle before each match and bouncing the ball five times before the first serve and twice before the second.

▲ Serena Williams

10 Like many other professional sports people, Serena Williams is relentlessly superstitious both on and off the court. But what would happen if she came up against the equally ritual-bound Serbian star, Ana Ivanovic, who avoids stepping on the lines of the court and used to bounce the ball only once before serving, but lost that habit and now bounces the
15 ball exactly four times? Whose rituals would have the upper hand?

Ana Ivanovic believes that rituals are comforting, especially when she's travelling and away from the things she's used to. She says, 'I am on the road ninety percent of the year, so I miss the comforts that someone living at home enjoys. It's nice to have some rituals to fall back on.'

▲ Ana Ivanovic

20 But there may be another explanation, more to do with the type of person who gets to be very good at sport. There's nothing very rational about devoting every moment of your youth to perfecting the ability to hit a ball inside a white line. Only those with the ability to focus obsessively on a single, otherwise useless skill, will ever succeed. Most of us have come
25 across people like that once or twice and let's face it, they're always a bit loopy.

Romanian football player Adrian Mutu once declared, 'Curses cannot touch me because I wear my underwear inside out.' And during the 1998 World Cup, the entire Romanian team bleached their hair blond,
30 apparently to break a jinx put on them by the Romanian church.

▲ Adrian Mutu

But David Beckham, renowned for his perfectionism on the pitch, appears to take these rituals a stage further. He has to have everything just right at home as well. Beckham explains, 'I have got this obsessive compulsive disorder where I have to have everything in a straight line
35 or everything has to be in pairs. Beckham reportedly spends hours straightening the furniture at home, apparently buys exactly twenty packets of Super Noodles on each visit to the supermarket and wears a new pair of football boots for every match. His wife, Victoria, has had to get used to his ritualistic ways. She says, 'Everything has to match in the
40 house. If there are three cans of Diet Pepsi, he'll throw one away because it's uneven.'

▲ David Beckham

In the football world, fans are just as attached as players to their strange pre-match habits. Some will wear the same clothing to a match if that outfit brought victory in the previous game. Others will always try to sit in the
45 same seat at every game, believing this will bring the team good luck.

Superstition may be rife in professional sports, but other professions are not immune. Musicians and rock stars are renowned for their pre-gig rituals, of which here are a few: group hugging, saying prayers, chanting affirmations, stretching, doing mad dance routines to Michael Jackson
50 tracks, singing the national anthem, drinking large amounts of whisky … oh, and Prince always eats a bowl of his favourite popcorn before going on stage.

They're a superstitious lot, these sport and music stars, and they share a secret: their success is nothing to do with talent, practice or hard work. It's
55 all in the mind.

▲ Prince

Speaking

1 Work with a partner. What other examples of personal ritual can you think of? Think about the following situations.

a) Before taking an exam
b) Before a job interview
c) Before taking part in a sporting competition
d) Before leaving the house every morning
e) Before setting off on a long trip
f) Before going out on a Saturday night
g) Before sitting down to start working or studying

2 Tell your partner about your own rituals or the rituals of people you know.

Listening & Vocabulary

1 🔘 2.01 Listen to Laura talking about her dad and his car. Are these statements true or false?

a) Laura's dad is very fond of his car and treats it better than a pet.
b) When Laura was a child, her dad often took the family out in the car.
c) Laura's sisters vandalised the seats and damaged the car doors.
d) Her dad has always gone through exactly the same procedure before setting off.
e) He backs out of the drive very carefully and very slowly.
f) Laura thinks he probably used to go through a similar ritual before taking off in a plane.

2 Match words from column A with words from column B to make collocations from the recording.

A		B
a)	domestic	Air Force
b)	a cosy	speed
c)	a sudden	animals
d)	slam	blanket
e)	a box of	urge
f)	first	the door
g)	at breakneck	go
h)	Royal	matches

Listen again and check the collocations. With a partner, use the collocations to describe the relationship between Laura's dad and his car.

3 Do you know anybody who is very attached to their car (or motorbike, or computer or any other piece of equipment)? Tell your partner about them.

Vocabulary

Expressions with *go* (noun)

have a **go** at sth: attempt to do sth
have a **go** on sth: have a ride on sth
give sth a **go**: try sth for the first time
make a **go** of sth: succeed in doing sth
in one **go**: all at once
on the **go**: very busy or active

1 Laura's dad has *several goes* at lighting his pipe. Complete these sentences with more expressions containing *go* as a noun. Use each expression only once.

a) I've always wanted to _____ a big motorbike.
b) I was so hungry last night I ate a whole pizza _____ .
c) I've never been skiing so this winter I've decided to _____ .
d) I'd love to _____ writing a novel. I've got lots of ideas but I'm not sure if I can do it.
e) I've been _____ since 6.00 a.m. this morning. I'm absolutely exhausted.
f) I hate my part-time job but I need the money, so I'm determined to _____ .

2 Are any of the sentences in Exercise 1 true for you? Write your own example sentences for the expressions.

Grammar

Present and past habits

These days he**'ll clean** his car once a year.
When it was new, he**'d clean** it every Sunday.
He **used to love** that car.

1 Look at the verb structures in these extracts from the listening on page 48. Discuss the questions (*a–d*) with a partner.

*… he**'ll take out** his pipe … he**'ll get out** his box of matches … The pipe **won't light** first go – he**'ll have** several goes at it, and finally … he**'ll puff** and puff until the car is full of smoke.*

a) Which modal verb is used?
b) Are the extracts about present habits, future habits or past habits?
c) Does the main verb describe a repeated action or a state?
d) Are the actions characteristic of Laura's dad or unusual for him?

2 Read the description of a family's morning routines. If possible, and without changing the meaning, replace the verbs in bold with *'ll* (*will*) + verb.

My dad (1) **gets up** at around seven o'clock. He (2) **hates** wasting time in bed. He (3) **has** two cups of coffee and a slice of toast before driving off to work. Dad (4) **'s** never late. My mum (5) **doesn't usually get ready** for work till after breakfast. She (6) **likes** to take her time in the morning. Mum (7) **'s got** a part-time job and she (8) **always leaves** it till the last minute before running out of the house. As for me, my morning routine (9) **varies** from day to day. It (10) **usually depends** on what I've been up to the night before!

3 Prepare a similar text using *'ll* (*will*) + verb where possible to describe the morning routines of members of your own family. Read your text to your partner and compare your routines.

4 Now think about your life when you were twelve. Complete sentences *a–l* and then compare them with your partner.

My daily routine	My thoughts and feelings
a) Before setting out for school I'd _____ .	g) My favourite subject used to be _____ .
b) At break time I'd _____ .	h) I used to love _____ .
c) During English classes I'd _____ .	i) I didn't use to enjoy _____ .
d) At lunchtime I used to _____ .	j) I used to have _____ .
e) After school I'd _____ .	k) I used to believe _____ .
f) Before going to bed I used to _____ .	l) I didn't use to understand _____ .

5 Complete the statements with *used to, will* and *would*.

a) You can use _____ + verb to talk about present habits.
b) You can use _____ + verb to talk about past habits.
c) You can use _____ + verb to talk about past habits and past states.

6 Grammar *Extra* 5, Part 1 page 136. Read the explanations and do Exercise 1.

Speaking

1 Write five sentences – four true and one false – describing ways in which your life was different ten years ago compared to now.

1) I didn't use to have a car.   2) I'd wear trainers all the time.   3) I used to be blond.   4) I …

2 Read your five sentences. Your partner has to guess which sentence is false.

Reading & Vocabulary

1   Work with a partner. Look at the photo and decide if it represents your ideal setting for a wedding. What's the best location for a wedding that you've ever been to? Describe it.

2   Read a father's account of his son's wedding. Answer the questions.
   a)   Where and in what month did the wedding take place?
   b)   What roles did Hank, Mat, Rebecca and Ron DeCar have on the day?
   c)   Why did the groom and his father wear pink and black?

The King and I

Where better to get married than in the Wedding Capital of the world in a ceremony presided over by Elvis himself? Hank Wangford walks his son down the aisle to the tune of 'Fools Rush In'.

I flew in with Virgin on its first direct flight from London to Las Vegas, Wedding Capital of the world. My son was to be married by Elvis, and I was feeling emotional.

Forty million people came to Vegas last year, many, like
5   my son Mat, to get married. No wonder there are Wedding Chapels round every corner, in every hotel. No wonder you can get married in a helicopter over the Strip, down the Grand Canyon, in your car in a drive-through chapel, or sky-diving.

June is wedding month of the year. White-veiled
10   brides are ducking through the hotel casinos. Rebecca, my prospective daughter-in-law, insisted the only way she'd marry Mat was if Elvis conducted the service in Vegas.

So here we all were with the happy couple and little Duncan, nearly one year old, packed into the white
15   superstretch limo, duded out in serious pink and black polyesters and sky-blue Crimplenes. We were ready for the young people's moment of destiny with The King, the Elvis himself who had married Oasis' Noel Gallagher.

Our package included limo and video, three songs and
20   twenty-four poses by Elvis. We went for white Vegas flared rather than black leather Elvis. More matrimonial. More apt.

The Viva Las Vegas Wedding Chapel sits by the Thunderbird Motel. Outside was the pink Cadillac convertible with Elvis number plates.
25   Suddenly Elvis was there. He was a great, if skinny version of the real thing. He is Ron DeCar, 'the most sought after soloist in the Las Vegas wedding industry'.

After a run through we're ready. Let me tell you there was nothing more inspiring than walking my boy down the aisle,
30   both in contrasting pink and black – Elvis's favourite colours – with gold Elvis shades and Elvis up there singing: 'Wise men say / Only fools rush in ...'

After the vows, Elvis did his two-pronged stage point at each of them, passed the rings, and then uttered the magic
35   words: 'By the powers invested in me by The King, uh, I now pronounce you man and wife, man.'

Glossary
veiled adj: face covered by a thin piece of cloth
duck verb [I]: move quickly to avoid being seen
duded out adj (*US informal*): dressed up
crimplene® noun [U]: type of man-made cloth
apt adj: suitable
sought after adj: wanted by many people but not easy to get
aisle noun [C]: passage between rows of seats in a church
vows noun [C]: set of promises made during a wedding ceremony

3   Decide whether the sentences are true or false. Correct the false sentences.
   a)   A priest conducted the <u>ceremony</u> in the Viva Las Vegas Wedding Chapel.
   b)   The <u>bride and groom</u> and all the guests arrived together at the chapel in a long white limousine.
   c)   They <u>chose</u> a black leather 'Elvis' because they thought it would be more <u>suitable</u> for a wedding.
   d)   They had a <u>short practice</u> before the service began.
   e)   'Elvis' <u>accompanied</u> the groom down the aisle.
   f)   The father of the groom wore gold <u>sunglasses</u>.
   g)   After the vows, 'Elvis' <u>declared</u> the couple man and wife.

   Find words or phrases in the article that mean the same as the underlined words in the true/false sentences.
   a)   ceremony = service

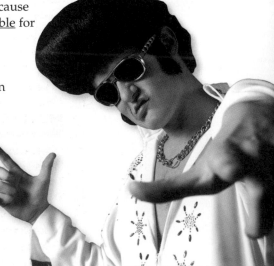

Listening & Vocabulary

1 Read these descriptions of wedding rituals. Are any of them common in your country?

a) The bride and groom cut the wedding cake together.
b) The bride and groom exchange gold coins during the church ceremony.
c) The bride has her hands and feet decorated in henna designs.
d) Guests pin money on the bridegroom's suit during the reception.
e) Guests throw rice over the bride and groom as they leave the church.
f) An older person holds a black umbrella over the bride's head as she leaves her home to go to the groom's house.
g) The bride throws her bouquet of flowers over her shoulder into the crowd of guests.
h) The father of the bride, the groom and the best man make speeches at the reception.

2 ⊕ 2.02–2.05 Listen to four people talking about wedding rituals. Match a ritual (*a–h*) from Exercise 1 with a person (*1–4*). What is the meaning of each ritual?

▲ Jorge

▲ Sandra ☀

▲ Ilhan ☾

▲ Laila ☆

3 Look at the words and phrases in the box, which you can use to describe weddings in the UK. Now complete the task.

| aisle   best man   bouquet of flowers   bridesmaid   church   confetti |
| honeymoon   photographer   priest   propose a toast   reception   rice   ring |
| speech   veil   vows   wedding cake   wedding presents |

a) Circle the words and phrases that you don't know and look them up.
b) Underline the stress in each word and practise saying all of the words and phrases.
c) Cross out the words that you *wouldn't* use to describe a wedding in your country.
d) Write a brief description of a typical wedding ritual in your country.
e) Read, compare and comment on your partner's description.

Speaking: anecdote

You are going to tell a partner about a wedding you have been to.

- Ask yourself the questions below.
- Think about *what* to say and *how* to say it.
- Tell your partner about your experience.

a) Who was getting married and how did you know them?
b) Where, when and what time of year did the ceremony take place?
c) What was the weather like?
d) What were you wearing?
e) What did the bride and groom wear?
f) How many people did you know at the wedding?
g) Where was the reception held?
h) What did you have to eat and drink?
i) Did anybody give any speeches? Who?
j) Did the guests give the bride and groom presents?
k) How did the day end?
l) Did you enjoy the wedding?

Reading & Vocabulary

1 Work with a partner. Read these funny quotes about marriage. Which one do you like best?

a) 'My wife and I were happy for twenty years. Then we met.' *Rodney Dangerfield*

b) 'A man in love is incomplete until he is married. Then he is finished.' *Zsa Zsa Gabor*

c) 'Some people ask the secret of our long marriage. We take time to go to a restaurant two times a week. A little candlelight, dinner, soft music and dancing. She goes Tuesdays. I go Fridays.' *Henry Youngman*

What do you think is the secret of a successful marriage? Discuss with your partner.

2 Work with your partner. You are going to 'read the minds' of husband Chris and wife Shirley as they celebrate their seventh wedding anniversary. Complete the task.

a) Student A read and complete Chris' thoughts. Use the *to*-infinitive or the gerund.

b) Student B read and complete Shirley's thoughts. Use the *to*-infinitive or the gerund.

c) Compare the two accounts and discuss your answers. Use a dictionary if necessary.

▲ **Chris and Shirley**

Chris is thinking ...

1 I remember (bring) *bringing* Shirley here for our third date – it must be nearly ten years ago ...

2 Yes, that was the evening I couldn't help (tell) _____ her that I loved her.

3 I'll never forget (look) _____ at Shirley that evening and thinking, 'This is the woman I want to marry.'

4 We both work so hard – we deserve (have) _____ a break.

5 Maybe we should try (spend) _____ a romantic weekend in Paris, just the two of us. My mother will have the children.

6 Yes – Paris. Good idea. I'll enjoy (practise) _____ my French.

7 I've tried (attract) _____ the waitress's attention but she won't look this way! I want to get a nice bottle of wine.

8 Mm, this wine's lovely. I regret (drive) _____ here now – we should have got a taxi.

9 I fancy (go) _____ to a club later – we haven't been dancing together for ages.

10 I can't stand (be) _____ at home all the time – we must do this more often.

Shirley is thinking ...

1 Oh dear, I hope I've remembered (bring) *to bring* the mobile phone. Oh good, here it is.

2 Oh no, I think I forgot (tell) _____ the babysitter what the number is. What if the kids wake up ...?

3 Calm down – she knows the name of the restaurant so she'll manage (find) _____ the number.

4 We both work so hard – I don't like (have) _____ so little time to play with the children.

5 From now on, I intend (spend) _____ more time with them. I'm going to stop working. Chris will understand.

6 We must stop (buy) _____ milk on the way home – I haven't got anything for breakfast.

7 He'd better stop (look) _____ at that waitress. Otherwise I'm going home!

8 I hope he doesn't expect me (drive) _____ the babysitter home.

9 I'm tired and I want (go) _____ home. I wish he'd finish his wine.

10 I'd just like (be) _____ at home relaxing in front of the television.

3 🌐 2.06 Listen and check. What are the main differences between Chris and Shirley's state of mind?

Vocabulary & Grammar

1 Look at the text about Chris and Shirley on page 52. Find four verbs that can be followed by either a *to*-infinitive or a gerund.

2 Complete the table with the verb patterns and example sentences you have identified in Exercise 1.

Verb pattern	Use	Examples
a) *remember doing sth* b) *remember to do sth* c) _____ d) _____ e) _____ f) _____ g) _____ h) _____	remember a definite past event remember sth you are/were supposed to do (never) forget a definite past event forget sth you are/were supposed to do say that an activity stops say why an activity stops try sth and see what happens try sth and not be able to do it	1 *I remember bringing Shirley here.* 2 *I hope I've remembered to bring the mobile.* 3 _____ 4 _____ 5 _____ 6 _____ 7 _____ 8 _____

Verb patterns (2)

verb + *to*-infinitive
or verb + gerund?
He **stopped to smoke.**
He **stopped smoking.**

3 Underline the correct verb structure in these sentences.

a) I remember **buying / to buy** my first English dictionary.
b) I've remembered **bringing / to bring** my English dictionary today.
c) I'll never forget **travelling / to travel** abroad for the first time.
d) I usually forget **packing / to pack** something important when I go abroad.
e) I had a really busy morning. I didn't even stop **having / to have** a coffee.
f) If I drink coffee in the evening, it stops me **sleeping / to sleep**.
g) I've tried **coming / to come** into town by bus but I prefer using my car.
h) I tried **taking / to take** the bus this morning but it was completely full so I drove.

Tick any sentences that are true for you. Rewrite the sentences so that they are true for you and compare with a partner.

4 Grammar *Extra* 5, Part 2 page 136. Read the explanations and do Exercise 2.

Listening

1 2.07 Listen to four people who were asked the question, 'Do you think you're romantic?' Put them in order: *1* = most romantic; *4* = least romantic.

> 'The best way to remember your wife's birthday is to forget it once.'
> *H.V. Prochnow*

2 Work with your partner. Complete the verb patterns and then put each comment in an appropriate column in the table.

a) Try (remember) _____ his/her birthday.
b) Stop (buy) _____ him/her flowers occasionally.
c) Remember (meet) _____ him/her for the first time.
d) Forget (say) _____ nice things to him/her.
e) Stop (look) _____ at other women/men.
f) Try (make) _____ him/her give up things he/she enjoys.

How to be romantic	
Do ...	**Don't ...**

What other do's and don'ts can you think of? Add them to the table.

Useful phrases & Pronunciation

1 🌐 2.08 **Read and listen to people talking about things that really annoy them. Match the picture to one of the people (1–6).**

Which of the habits mentioned would annoy you most?

1 Naomi 'I hate it when men wear too much aftershave. My brother-in-law, for example. He (insist on) _____ covering himself in this really strong aftershave – it makes me sneeze.'	**2 Kevin** 'Oh dear, there are so many things that annoy me! But I think the thing that annoys me most is when I watch a film with my girlfriend. She (always ask) _____ me questions about what's happening: 'Who's this? What happened there? Why did he do that?' Argh. That really gets on my nerves.'
3 Roz 'It really winds me up when people talk about how fat they are when they are stick thin! I've got this friend who's really slim – much slimmer than me. But she (go on about) _____ being fat. It's so annoying.'	**4 Dan** 'It really annoys me when my brother and his girlfriend are together. They (forever hug and kiss) _____ in front of me. Urgh – it makes me sick!'
5 Sally 'I can't stand it when people say they haven't done any work for an exam, and then they get the highest marks. One of my friends is like that. She (always tell) _____ us how worried she is because she hasn't done any work, but then she gets 90%.'	**6 Martin** 'I find it irritating when people keep losing things. For example, my mum (always lose) _____ her glasses. Why doesn't she put them on a chain? Or get a spare pair? She drives me mad.'

2 Listen again. Complete the highlighted description of the annoying habit with the correct verb structure.

3 🌐 2.09 Listen and repeat the highlighted useful phrases from Exercise 2. Mark the stressed words and note the intonation used. Practise them with a partner. Sound as annoyed as you can!

4 Complete the table with more useful phrases from the comments above.

Ways of beginning to explain what annoys you	Ways of saying how it makes you feel
a) I _____ it when … b) The thing that _____ me most is when … c) It really _____ me up when … d) It really _____ me when … e) I _____ stand it when … f) I _____ it irritating when …	g) That really _____ on my nerves. h) It's so _____ . i) It _____ me sick. j) She _____ me mad.

5 Think about all the people and things that annoy you. Make a list. Tell your partner about them.

Writing *Extra*

Article: expressing an opinion

1 Read the article and choose the best title.

   a) Weddings are a waste of money
   b) Weddings are for the family
   c) Weddings are a chance to escape

IN BRITAIN, the traditional white wedding in a village church, with in-laws wearing silly hats, is going out of fashion. One in six couples now prefer to get married abroad, and the more exotic or eccentric the location, the better. But are they making a terrible mistake? First
5 and foremost, a wedding, with all its traditions and rituals, is a rite of passage to be shared with family and close friends. Understandably, there are those who want to avoid the stress and expense of a big wedding and opt instead for a low-key affair. I have no problem with that – it's a matter of personal choice. But in my view, a couple
10 who opt for a holiday instead of a wedding, are running away from reality. Celebrities are renowned for their short-lived marriages, but not surprisingly, marriages that began in exotic locations appear to have even less chances of surviving. Britney Spears, for instance, married a childhood friend in the Little White Wedding Chapel in
15 Las Vegas and their marriage was annulled after 55 hours. Photos of Renée Zellweger and her country singer groom exchanging vows on a Caribbean beach looked idyllic, but they separated after four months. It is worth considering the list of top wedding destinations – Cyprus, Italy, Greek islands, Caribbean, Mauritius. What strikes me is that these
20 are honeymoon destinations and personally, I think that the honeymoon has a completely different function from the wedding. Honeymoons are for the couple, a welcome escape from everyday life, a once-in-a-lifetime holiday. A wedding, on the other hand, is all about family and friends. In my opinion, marriages for life need to be rooted in life, not
25 in fantasy. However lavish or modest the wedding, it has no meaning if the people who are there for you every day of your life cannot afford the airfare to the chosen exotic location. My advice to a couple who are tempted to tie the knot on a Caribbean beach is this: don't do it unless you can afford to pay for your nearest and dearest to go with you.

2 The article was originally written in five paragraphs as follows.

   paragraph 1   introduces the subject of the article
   paragraph 2   the writer states her opinion
   paragraph 3   she gives examples
   paragraph 4   she develops her ideas
   paragraph 5   she sums up her opinion and leaves the reader with food for thought

   Mark where you think each new paragraph begins.

3 Look at the highlighted expressions in the article and find the following.

   a) two expressions that mean 'I think'
   b) one way of giving an example
   c) one direct question
   d) three adverbs or adverbial phrases that show the writer's attitude
   e) three phrases that introduce a new point

4 Write an article giving your opinion on one of the following subjects.

   • Christmas has lost its meaning
   • Traditions should be kept alive
   • Marriage is an outdated institution

6 Eat

Grammar Present perfect simple and continuous. Passives review
Vocabulary Parts of the body. Food collocations. Linkers. Numbers
Useful phrases Complaints in a restaurant; food idioms

Reading & Speaking

1   🌐 2.10 **Read and listen to this description of a bad experience in a restaurant. How many potatoes did the customer eventually order?**

The worst waiter I've ever encountered was a chap in a suburban restaurant a few years ago. It may have been his first day, or he may have been dumped by his true love, but our conversation went like this.

Me: I'll have the soup and the lamb, please. And some spinach, and, er, potatoes.

Waiter: Soup, lamb, spinach. How many potatoes?

Me: Oh I don't know. A few.

Waiter: But how many?

Me: I don't know. A portion.

Waiter: Three? Four?

Me: I've never really been asked a number before.

Waiter: Six?

Me: Surely it depends how big they are.

Waiter: So are you saying you want three big ones or five really small ones?

Me: How about two spoonfuls? Would that be OK with you?

Waiter: How big a spoon?

Me: …

Imagine you were the customer in this situation. How would you have reacted?

2   **Read the questions about restaurant experiences and think about your answers.**

Have you ever …
a) had problems with a waiter?
b) sent the wine back?
c) told the waiter the food was lovely, but in fact it wasn't very good?
d) refused to pay for a meal?
e) flirted with the waiter or waitress?
f) asked the waiter to send your compliments to the chef?
g) decided not to tip the waiter?
h) felt annoyed by noisy children sitting near you?
i) pointed at the menu to indicate what you want because you couldn't pronounce it?
j) taken a seat in a restaurant, looked at the menu, realised it was too expensive and left?

Discuss the questions with a partner.

Reading & Vocabulary

1 **Read the first part of an article about communicating with waiters and answer the questions.**

a) What does WRIST stand for?
b) Is it a well-known abbreviation?
c) Can you make the gesture which is described in the article?

How to do
restaurant sign language

You are in a bustling Parisian brasserie, the approximate size of three football pitches. Your steak frites have arrived, piping hot. It would be nice to have some pepper with that steak, wouldn't it? However, there is none on your table.
5 Typical. Your waiter is miles away and you are not even sure what the French word for pepper is anyway. Peppe? Pipi? Peepe pourri? You should have studied harder at school.

Now is the perfect time to employ some WRIST action.
10 WRIST is the *World Restaurant International Sign Technique*, an ancient form of communication. To request pepper in a non-speaking situation, all you have to do is hold your hands high above your head. Loosely clench your fists and place them on 15 top of each other in an upright position, then rotate each fist 180 degrees in opposite directions simultaneously. This provides a convincing mime 20 of grinding pepper through a commercially produced pepper mill, and alerts the waiter to your seasoning needs. He will now be happy to 25 dash across the restaurant to provide you with a pepper mill and his profuse apologies.

Glossary

bustling adj: lively, noisy
piping hot adj: very hot

clench your fist verb phrase: close your hand
dash verb [I]: run quickly

profuse adj: a lot / a big amount

---

2 **Work with a partner. Read the next part of the article and try to make the gestures described. Guess the meaning of each gesture and complete the text.**

Other common forms of WRIST include the following.

1 Raise your right hand in front of your mouth, then squeeze your thumb and index finger together as if squashing a bee. Then make your whole hand tremble, as if the bee had just given you an electric shock. This means, 'Waiter, _____ , please'.

2 Using both hands, mimic the tying of a knot at the side of your neck, then raise one hand high, as if you're still holding one end of this imaginary tie or ligature. Now stick your tongue out and make your eyes bulge. This alerts everyone in the restaurant to the fact that you are finding your _____ a bit of a bore.

3 Lift the empty wine bottle out of your ice bucket. Hold it up, point to it with your free hand, then make a roll-over motion with this hand. This means, 'Can we have another _____ , please?'

4 Perhaps the most famous WRIST gesture is when customers take it upon themselves to sign an invisible cheque in the air. For centuries this has meant, 'Can I have the _____ ?' These days this action is so archaic it's almost amusing. In the UK, the correct WRIST for requesting _____ now means holding your hands apart, as if you are requesting a parrot-sized coffin. Now stab the palm of your hand four times with a finger, simulating the act of punching in your PIN.

🔘 2.11 **Listen and check your ideas.**

3 **In each of the following lists there is one noun that does not usually collocate with the verb. Cross it out. Use a dictionary if necessary.**

a) bend your **elbows / hair / legs / knees**
b) hold your **hand / head / thumb / ear** up
c) shake your **finger / fist / head / toes**
d) stick your **chest / eyes / leg / tongue** out
e) clench your **fist / hands / teeth / shoulders**
f) raise your **arm / eyebrows / hand / tongue**

Work with your partner. Test your understanding by asking each other to do some of the actions above.

Listening & Vocabulary

1 Work with a partner. You're going to listen to an interview with Jean Crowshaw, restaurant critic for *The Manchester Post*. Think about what her job involves and discuss whether you think the following statements are true or false.

a) She eats out every night of the week.
b) She never finishes everything on her plate.
c) She takes notes about the restaurant at the table.
d) She wears a wig to disguise herself.
e) She enjoys writing bad reviews most.
f) She always pays for her own meals.
g) She doesn't think waiters should ask you if everything's all right.
h) She likes waiters who tell you about their favourite items on the menu.
i) She enjoyed her best meal ever in a posh city centre restaurant.

🔘 **2.12 Listen and check your ideas.**

2 Correct the false statements in Exercise 1. Listen again and check.

3 Jean Crowshaw used the words in the box to talk about her job. Match each word to the appropriate adjective list (*a–f*) to make typical noun-adjective collocations.

> dish   flavour   food   meal   menu   plate

a) fast / fresh / organic / plain / rich / stodgy / vegetarian _____
b) gourmet / heavy / light / ready-made / square / three-course / vegetarian _____
c) cold / fish / local / main / regional / serving / vegetarian _____
d) clean / dessert / dinner / dirty / paper / plastic / side _____
e) bland / distinctive / mild / strong / subtle / unique / unmistakable _____
f) à la carte / extensive / lunch / set / varied / wine / vegetarian _____

Circle the collocations you don't know. Write example sentences for them using a dictionary if necessary.

stodgy food = In winter, I tend to eat more stodgy food, so I always go on a diet in spring.

4 Work with your partner. Decide which is the best and which is the worst restaurant in your area. Give reasons for your choices.

Speaking: anecdote

You are going to tell your partner about your favourite restaurant.

• Ask yourself the questions below.
• Think about *what* to say and *how* to say it.
• Tell your partner about your favourite restaurant.

a) What's the restaurant called and where is it?
b) What type of restaurant is it: a family business? A chain ...?
c) What's the interior like?
d) What's the atmosphere like?
e) What do the waiters and waitresses wear?
f) What kind of food do they serve?
g) What's the service like?
h) How often do you go there?
i) When was the last time you went?
j) Who did you go with and what did you have?

Grammar

Present perfect simple and continuous

Verbs describing actions or processes.
I've made dinner.
I've been making dinner.

Verbs describing <u>single</u> actions.
I've cut myself. (NOT ~~I've been cutting myself.~~)

Verbs describing states.
I've had that knife for years. (NOT ~~I've been having that knife for years.~~)

1 Look at this extract from the interview with Jean Crowshaw on page 58. Name the tenses of the verbs in bold and choose the best description (*a–c*) for each one.

Well I've been working for newspapers for more than twenty years. I started out as a journalist when I was twenty-three, and I've worked for several newspapers since then …

a) The action is **finished**. It happened at a **specified point** in the past. You **know** exactly **when**.

b) The action is **finished**. It happened at an **unspecified point** in the past. You **don't know** exactly **when**.

c) The action is **unfinished**. It started in the past and is **in progress** now. You usually know **how long**.

2 Use the same tense sequence as the extract in Exercise 1 to make three sentences about yourself: two true sentences and one false one. Write about your work, your studies, your hobbies, your habits, etc.

I … (something you've been doing).
I … (when or how you started).
I … (a thing or things you've done – or haven't done – in that time).

I've been driving for several years. I passed my test when I was eighteen. I've never driven abroad.

Work with a partner. Read your sentences out. Your partner guesses which is the false sentence.

3 Look at these sentence pairs. Choose the most appropriate form in each case. Discuss your answers with your partner.

1. a) I've **learnt / been learning** how to make paella. It comes out perfectly every time.
   b) I've **learnt / been learning** how to make paella. But I still overcook the rice.

2. a) I've **read / been reading** that new diet book. You can borrow it if you want.
   b) I've **read / been reading** that new diet book. I'm on the last chapter.

3. a) Have you **eaten / been eating** my birthday cake? There's only a tiny bit left!
   b) Have you **eaten / been eating** my birthday cake? There's none left!

4. a) I've **worked / been working** in a supermarket. I didn't like it very much.
   b) I've **worked / been working** in a supermarket. I need the extra cash.

4 The present perfect continuous can also describe an action which has *just* finished, especially when the results of the action are still evident. Look at the pictures (*a–d*) and describe what has been happening.

5 Verbs describing single actions or states are very rare in the continuous form. Discuss why the following sentences sound strange or wrong.

a) **I've always been hating** mushrooms. I just can't eat them.
b) **I've been stopping** watching programmes about food.
c) **I've been deciding** I should try and eat more healthily.
d) **I've been cutting myself** several times with the bread knife over the years.
e) **I've been having** the same dining table and chairs for years now.
f) **I've never been understanding** why people become vegetarian.

Rewrite the sentences using the simple form. Are any of the sentences true for you?

6 Grammar *Extra* 6, Part 1 page 136. Read the explanations and do Exercises 1 and 2.

Reading & Vocabulary

1 Write a list of what you ate yesterday. Work in small groups and find out the following.

   a) Who ate the most meat / the most fish / the most fruit / the most vegetables?
   b) Who could easily give up meat and fish?
   c) Who couldn't live without meat and fish?

2 What do you think are the advantages and disadvantages of more people becoming vegetarian? Think about health, animal welfare and the environment.

Read the article. How many of the points you thought of does it mention?

Is it time to give up meat?

I care about climate change, animal suffering and the condition of people in developing countries. So six months ago I became a vegetarian or, as a friend puts it, I stopped eating anything with a face or a fin.

5   It hasn't been easy, and I'm in danger of lapsing, but I'm glad I did it and I still believe in all the reasons that persuaded me to say 'no' to meat and fish.

   The first and most obvious reason why I gave up meat was because I'm against cruelty to animals. With the aim of 10 maximising profits and minimising cost, animals are crammed into confined spaces, and they rarely see the light of day before being slaughtered. These animals are deprived of exercise, fed drugs to fatten them up and genetically altered to grow faster. As a result, conditions are ideal for the spread 15 of diseases such as bird flu and foot-and-mouth.

   Secondly, I wanted to do my bit to fight global warming. The meat industry is one of the leading sources of the greenhouse gases that has lead to global warming. In fact, a United Nations report found that the meat industry produces 20 more greenhouse gases than all the cars, trains and planes in the world combined. In other words, there's no point in driving fuel-efficient cars and using energy-saving light bulbs if you eat meat every day of your life.

   Giving up meat also helps the global poor. 840 million 25 people are still going hungry today, and yet there is more than enough food in the world to feed the entire human population. The problem is that crops that could be used to feed the hungry are instead being used to fatten animals raised for food.

30   Finally, I became a vegetarian for health reasons. A diet high in meat and low in fresh fruit and vegetables leads to higher rates of heart disease, stroke, cancer and diabetes.

   And I must admit, I have felt better since I've shunned meat and fish. But my friends continue to treat me like an

35 eccentric animal-lover with a fussy attitude to food. They worry about inviting me for dinner, and I'm getting bored with soggy lasagne and goat's cheese salad. What is more, one of the reasons that I'm in danger of having to compromise my beliefs is that it's almost impossible to find a restaurant that 40 has a decent vegetarian menu.

   I still believe that being a vegetarian has many benefits. However, you don't need to give up meat altogether to make a difference. According to the Environmental Defense Fund, if every American skipped one meal of chicken per week 45 and substituted vegetarian foods instead, the carbon dioxide savings would be the same as taking more than half a million cars off the US roads.

   On balance, I think that it is possible to eat organic meat and fish from animals that have lived a wild and free life, and 50 retain the moral high-ground. Like so many things in life, it's all about moderation.

Glossary

a) *cram* verb: squeeze or pack tightly
b) _____ verb: stop doing sth (suggests failure)
c) _____ verb: avoid
d) _____ verb: miss / not eat
e) _____ verb: kill
f) _____ noun [C]: plant grown for food, eg corn

g) _____ noun [C]: flat, thin part of a fish
h) _____ noun [C]: medical condition in which blood is blocked from reaching the brain
i) _____ adj: difficult to please
j) _____ adj: unpleasantly soft and wet
k) _____ phrase: do what you can to help
l) _____ phrase: be morally correct

3 Look at the words and phrases highlighted in yellow in the article. Try to guess the meaning from the context and then complete the glossary.

4 Which do you think is the most convincing argument in the article for becoming a vegetarian? Does it convince *you*?

Vocabulary & Writing

1 Use all the linkers in the table below to complete the summary of the article on page 60. Some linkers can go in more than one place.

Organising ideas	Adding more information	Connecting contrasting ideas	Showing cause and effect	Concluding
	Furthermore	However even though Although	so Consequently	To sum up

The writer talks about becoming a vegetarian. He explains that the meat industry is focused on profits, and (1) _____ they don't care about animal welfare. Animals are kept in over-crowded conditions. (2) _____ , disease spreads quickly. He goes on to talk about the environment. He explains that vehicle emissions are among the biggest causes of greenhouse gases. (3) _____ , the meat industry is worse than all of them put together. He then explains that (4) _____ there is enough food in the world to feed the entire world population, people are still starving because crops are being used to feed animals, not people. The writer claims that if you eliminate meat from your diet you are less prone to heart disease. (5) _____ , vegetarians are less likely to develop other illnesses such as cancer and diabetics. (6) _____ the writer feels better since he gave up meat, he admits that it can be a problem when eating out. (7) _____ , he recommends becoming a vegetarian, but says that even cutting down on meat and fish will be beneficial for the environment.

2 There are ten more linkers highlighted in blue in the article on page 60. Add each of them to an appropriate column in the table in Exercise 1.

3 Read this article about bottled water and underline the correct linker (1–11).

'What's so bad about BOTTLED WATER?'

Production of bottled water has grown over the past thirty years from nothing into a
5 $16 billion-per-year business. (1) **However / Furthermore**, a backlash has begun, and environmentalists are urging people to go back to the tap.

(2) **In other words / The first reason why** you should seriously think about giving up bottled water, they say, is that it's bad for the environment. The manufacturing of plastic bottles requires vast quantities of petroleum. (3) **As a result, / Although** factories create toxic
10 waste and release it into the environment. (4) **What is more / So**, the overwhelming majority of plastic water bottles aren't recycled. In virtually every part of the world, discarded water bottles swell landfills and release hazardous toxins into air and water when they are burned in industrial incinerators. (5) **Even though / In other words**, bottled water is a major contributor to global warming.

15 (6) **Secondly / On balance**, the distribution of bottled water is fuel-intensive. In the USA alone, one billion bottles of water are moved around each week in trucks, emitting polluting gasses and wearing down the roads. (7) **In fact / However**, some high-priced waters are shipped from one side of the planet to the other.

(8) **Finally / To sum up**, bottled water isn't even better for your health. Tap water
20 regulations in many countries are far stricter than those for bottled water. (9) **Furthermore / So**, tap water contains fluoride, which promotes strong teeth and prevents tooth decay.
(10) **Consequently, / But** as bottled water consumption has increased, so has tooth decay.

(11) **As a result / To sum up**, by staying off bottled water, and encouraging others to do so, you will be doing the planet an enormous favour and benefiting your own health as well.

Glossary

backlash noun [C]: negative, angry reaction
urge verb [T]: strongly advise
vast adj: very big

swell verb [I]: fill up
landfill noun [C]: hole in the ground for waste
hazardous adj: dangerous

incinerator noun [C]: machine that burns waste
decay noun [U]: gradual deterioration

How much bottled water do you drink every day?

Reading

1 **Work with a partner. Read the statistics about food waste in the UK and guess which is the correct number in each case.**

1 The percentage of dumped food that is thrown away untouched:
a) 6% b) 16% c) 60%.

2 The value of avoidable food waste in the UK each year:
a) £900,000 b) £9 million c) £9 billion.

3 The percentage of food purchased which is thrown away by families with children:
a) 7% b) 17% c) 27%.

4 The number of whole chickens thrown away in the UK every day:
a) 1,500 b) 3,500 c) 5,500.

5 The number of unopened yoghurt pots that are disposed of each day:
a) 13,000 b) 130,000 c) 1.3 million.

Read the article and check your ideas.

What a waste. Throwaway Britain wastes £9bn of food every year

A new study has exposed the alarming amount of food thrown away by the British public. According to research, a staggering 3.6 million tonnes of food is needlessly thrown away each year in England and Wales.

5 The study, conducted by the Waste & Resources Action Programme (WRAP), found that salad, fruit and bread were most commonly wasted and 60% of all dumped food was untouched.

Environment Minister Joan Ruddock said: 'These
10 findings are staggering in their own right, but at a time when global food shortages are in the headlines this kind of wastefulness becomes even more shocking.'

Value of food

The dustbins of 2,138 British households were analysed,
15 and the study revealed that £9 billion of avoidable food waste was disposed of in England and Wales each year.

Most of the food could have been consumed if it had been better stored or managed, or had not been left uneaten on a plate.
20 WRAP estimated that the average UK household needlessly throws away 18% of all food purchased. Families with children throw away 27%.

The study also suggested £1bn worth of food wasted in the UK was still 'in date'.
25 Nearly a quarter of that total amount was disposed of because the 'use by' or 'best before' date had expired.

Yoghurts and chickens

The study also found that:
- the two most significantly wasted foods that could
30 have been eaten were potatoes and bread. Bakery goods made up 19% of avoidable food waste. 220,000 loaves of bread are thrown away every day. Vegetables contributed 18%, with 5.1 million potatoes discarded daily.
35 - meat and fish also made up a large proportion – 18% of the total money wasted on food. WRAP said 5,500 whole chickens were thrown away each day in the UK.
- 'mixed foods' like ready meals made up 21% of the total cost of waste, with 440,000 thrown away each
40 day.
- yoghurt was a commonly abandoned product, with an estimated 1.3 million unopened pots disposed of each day.

Launching *The Food We Waste* report, WRAP's chief
45 executive, Liz Goodwin, described its findings – which mean that one in three shopping bags is dumped straight in the bin – as 'shocking'.

She said: 'People aren't really aware that we are wasting so much food; do we think it's acceptable to throw so
50 much away when people around the world are starving?'

2 **Work in groups. Discuss the questions.**

a) Do you think the amounts of food wasted in your country are similar or different to those in the UK?

b) What kinds of food do people throw away and what happens to the waste?

c) How much food does your own family throw away in a typical week?

Grammar

Passives review

be + past participle

It**'s being wasted.**
It**'s been thrown away.**
It **could have been recycled.**

1   Use the words in the box to complete the information from the article on page 62.

> bread   date   day   plate   year

WRAP found that …
a)   people most commonly <u>wasted</u> salad, fruit and _____ .
b)   people <u>disposed of</u> £9 billion of avoidable food waste in England and Wales each _____ .
c)   people <u>could have consumed</u> most of the food if they <u>had stored or managed</u> it better or <u>had not left</u> it uneaten on a _____ .
d)   people <u>disposed of</u> nearly a quarter of the food because the 'use by' or 'best before' _____ had expired.
e)   people <u>threw away</u> 5,500 whole chickens each _____ .

Rewrite the information using passive structures for the underlined verbs. Check your ideas in the article. Why are passive structures preferred in the article?

2   Read the review of the children's film *Wall-E*, about a robot whose job it is to clean the Earth. Why does it read unnaturally?

Wall-E

Pixar Animation Studios produced **the film** *Wall-E* and Andrew Stanton directed **it**. It follows the story of a robot called Wall-E (Waste Allocation Load Lifter Earth-Class) **who** somebody has programmed to clean up the polluted planet. Rubbish has so overrun **Earth** that it has forced **the planet's population** to take a vacation on a holiday resort spaceship where somebody does **everything** for them. The corporation Buy n Large run **the holiday resort**. Into this scenario pops Eve, another robot **who** somebody has sent to Earth to find plant life. Wall-E falls in love, but at first she doesn't reciprocate **his feelings** because she has no feelings. Pixar have aimed *Wall-E* at children, but it won't disappoint **adults**.

3   Rewrite the review so it reads more naturally.
   • Make the objects in bold into the subjects of passive verbs.
   • Use *by* + agent if you need to mention the 'doer' of the action.

4   **Grammar *Extra* 6, Part 2** page 136. Read the explanations and do Exercise 3.

Pronunciation & Vocabulary

Numbers review

Cardinal: **1,234,567**
Ordinal: **42ⁿᵈ**
Fraction: **¹/₂**
Decimal: **0.125**
Date: **11/09/2001**
Telephone: **0773 5576401**

Ways of saying *0*: **love, nil, nought, oh, zero.**
Years: **2009** (two thousand and nine OR twenty oh nine). BUT 2010 = two thousand and ten OR twenty ten.

1   Say the numbers in the box and categorise them in the table.

> 01/01/1901   99.9   ⁴/₅   246,813,579   020 7278 2332   53ʳᵈ

Cardinal numbers	Ordinal numbers	Fractions	Decimals	Dates	Telephone numbers

🔊 2.13 Listen, check and repeat.

2   🔊 2.14 Listen and write one more number in each column in the table in Exercise 1. Practise saying them.

3   🔊 2.15 Listen and write down five different ways of saying *0*. Match each way of saying *0* to an appropriate situation (1–5).
   1   the temperature   3   a year   5   a tennis score
   2   a football score   4   a speed

Useful phrases

1 **What sort of things do people complain about in restaurants? Match the items (a–e) with words from the box. Use your dictionary if necessary.**

a) The service
b) The lighting
c) The wine
d) The food
e) The other customers

bland	bright	(not) chilled
corked	dark	(un)helpful
noisy	off	over-cooked
over-done	rude	slow

🌐 **2.16** **Listen to the conversation and notice any of the complaints you thought of.**

2 **Complete the useful phrases with words from Exercise 1.**

a) The service is very _____ this evening.
b) It's so _____ in here that we can't read the menu.
c) Can we have the wine _____ , please?
d) I'm afraid this steak is _____ .
e) I think the prawns are _____ .

🌐 **2.17** **Listen and repeat. Have you ever complained about anything in a restaurant? Tell your partner about it.**

3 **Replace the underlined phrases (a–f) with the idioms (1–6) from the conversation.**

a) He's an important person in the hotel industry.
b) If you're really nice to him, he'll give you a nice big tip.
c) He thinks he's the greatest.
d) I feel like I need to be really careful.
e) It's all going very wrong now.
f) You have to give it all less importance.

1 you butter him up
2 take it all with a pinch of salt
3 I'm walking on eggshells
4 the best thing since sliced bread
5 a big cheese
6 pear-shaped

Check your answers in the Recordings on page 149.

4 **Work with your partner. Read the conversation below between the waitress (W) and her friend Helen (H). Choose the correct word to complete seven more idioms (1–7).**

H: How was work tonight?
W: Mad as usual. Over-booked with two waiters off sick.
H: Oh no, sounds like (1) a **recipe / dish** for disaster.
W: Exactly. Then I dropped a whole tray of glasses.
H: Oh poor you. I bet you felt really embarrassed.
W: I did. I (2) went as red as a **beetroot / tomato**.
H: Was Chef his usual bad-tempered self?
W: No, actually he was (3) as nice as **sugar / pie**. I think he's got a new girlfriend.
H: Oh, come on, (4) spill the **soup / beans**. Who is she?
W: Well, there's this new waitress. She's just finished university and wants to earn some money to go travelling.
H: Well, she'll have to earn some good tips because the restaurant (5) pays **peanuts / parsnips**.
W: I know – but she's (6) a smart **soufflé / cookie**. She'll be fine. Anyway, last week …

🌐 **2.18** **Listen and check.**

5 **Tell your partner about …**

- someone who's a big cheese in your world.
- a time when you had to butter someone up.
- the last time you felt really embarrassed.
- the sort of thing that makes you go as red as a beetroot.
- someone you know who's a smart cookie.

Vocabulary *Extra*

Exploring synonyms

1 Work with a partner. Look at these ways of saying that you're hungry. Order each expression from *least* hungry (1) to *most* hungry (5).

☐ 'I'm absolutely ravenous.'
☐ 'I'm a bit peckish.'
☐ 'I'm hungry.'
☐ 'I'm famished.'
☐ 'I'm really starving.'

Read the dictionary extract to check your ideas.

2 Which two verbs in the box collocate with all six noun phrases (*a–f*)?

chew   eat   grab   have   munch   nibble

a) _____ breakfast   c) _____ dinner   e) _____ something to eat
b) _____ lunch   d) _____ a snack   f) _____ a bite (to eat)

Which verb would you use to suggest that you only have a short time to eat?

3 Think of three …

a) items of food you would never have for breakfast.
b) places nearby where you could grab a bite if you were in a hurry.
c) items of food you can nibble.
d) items of food you can chew.
e) items of food you can munch.
f) times of year when some people might 'stuff themselves'.

Compare your ideas with your partner.

4 Think of other ways of saying *fat* and *thin*. Complete the table based on the information in the dictionary extracts.

FAT		THIN	
positive	negative	positive	negative
plump	big, large	slim	skinny
___	___	___	___
___	___	___	___
___	___	___	___

5 Work with your partner. Decide which word or words in the table in Exercise 4 you might use to describe …

a) a healthy baby.
b) an extreme medical condition.
c) somebody who looks good because of exercise.
d) somebody who looks extremely thin because of illness or lack of food.

6 Check your own dictionary. Which synonyms does it give for *hungry*, *eat*, *fat* and *thin*? Look for other ways of saying *cook*.

Other ways of saying **hungry**

peckish quite hungry: used especially to talk about feeling hungry when it is not a mealtime: *I often start to feel a bit peckish around mid-morning.*

starving or **starved** (informal) very hungry and wanting to eat immediately: *Have you got any bread? I'm starving!*

ravenous extremely hungry, especially because you have not eaten for a long time or you have been doing a lot of physical work: *The children are always ravenous after swimming practice.*

famished extremely hungry, especially because you have not eaten for a long time: *Can we order now? I'm famished.*

Other ways of saying **eat**

have breakfast/lunch/dinner to eat a particular meal: *Have you had breakfast yet?* ♦ *He phoned while we were having lunch.*

have something to eat to eat something or to have a meal: *We'll stop and have something to eat when we get to Newcastle.*

snack/have a snack to eat something small between your main meals: *We usually have a drink and a snack around 11.* ♦ *No snacking, now!*

grab a bite (to eat) (informal) to eat a snack or small meal when you do not have much time: *Maybe we could grab a bite at Charlie's before the film.*

eat up to finish all the food you have been given: *Eat up! There's plenty more.*

nibble (at) to take very small bites from your food: *She nibbled at her sandwich politely, waiting for the others to arrive.*

chew (on) to use your teeth to break food up slowly in your mouth: *He was chewing on a piece of celery.*

munch or **munch at** to eat something noisily and enthusiastically: *The kids were munching crisps in front of the TV.*

stuff yourself (informal) to eat so much that you feel ill or uncomfortable: *I'm not surprised you feel sick, the way you stuffed yourself last night.*

Other ways of saying **fat**

plump slightly fat in a way that looks quite nice: *a plump friendly-looking man in his forties*

chubby used especially for describing babies and children who look fat in a healthy attractive way: *a chubby little boy*

big or **large** used for suggesting that someone is a bit fatter than they should be or than they usually are, especially if they are also tall: *The driver was a big man with bright red hair.*

dumpy short and fat: *But I look so plain and dumpy in the uniform!*

overweight fatter than doctors think is healthy for someone of a particular height: *You risk heart disease if you are overweight and don't take regular exercise.*

obese very fat, especially in a way that might be dangerous to your health: *In some parts of the country, 15% of the population is now considered to be obese.*

Other ways of saying **thin**

slim thin in an attractive way: *He was looking much slimmer after his holiday.*

slender thin in a graceful way: *a tall slender woman in her late 40s*

skinny (informal) too thin: *a skinny little boy of about eight*

anorexic extremely thin in a way that does not look healthy, also used by doctors to describe someone who has the illness ANOREXIA NERVOSA: *He must have been dieting – he was looking positively anorexic!*

lean thin and strong: *a lean man wearing a cowboy hat*

emaciated extremely thin because you have been ill or do not have enough to eat: *emaciated children holding out bowls for food*

trim thin in a way that suggests you are careful about what you eat and how much you exercise: *His trim figure made him look younger than he was.*

gaunt so thin that people can see your bones under your skin: *His face was gaunt with lack of sleep.*

bony so thin that people can see your bones under your skin: *long bony limbs that never seemed to fit his clothes*

Review B

▶ Grammar *Extra* pages 134–137

Grammar

1 **Underline the correct alternatives.**

Some friends and I (1) **were deciding / decided** to explore the forest on the north-east coast of Australia. I was the experienced one – I (2) **travelled / had travelled** around the world, and my friends (3) **were counting / had counted** on me. After all, I (4) **was living / had been living** in Australia for ages.

As soon as we arrived, I (5) **picked / had picked** up a long stick and marched purposefully into the rainforest. As I (6) **was cutting / had been cutting** my way through the forest I (7) **heard / had heard** the sound of a large animal. And it (8) **was coming / had been coming** towards me! Was it a wild pig? Or a crocodile!? Suddenly, it appeared – a giant lizard. My friend and I (9) **looked / had looked** at each other for one second. Our other friends, who (10) **put / had been putting** up the tent, (11) **were hearing / heard** me before they (12) **were seeing / saw** me. I came running out of the forest screaming like a baby, effectively ending my reputation as an intrepid explorer.

2 **Make true sentences about what you will be doing at these times tomorrow. Use the future continuous.**

a) 7.15 a.m.   d) 8.10 p.m.
b) 10.20 a.m.   e) 1.10 a.m. (of the following
c) 1.20 p.m.   day)

3 **Complete the sentences to make them true for you. Use the future perfect.**

a) By ten o'clock this evening I …
b) By the end of the week I …
c) This time next year I …
d) Five years from now I …
e) In ten years' time I …

Compare your sentences in Exercises 2 and 3 with a partner. How many of your sentences are the same?

4 **Tick the sentences in which the bold words are possible. Correct the sentences which are not possible.**

a) I'**ll** often go out for a drink with friends.
b) I'**d** have blond, curly hair when I was a baby.
c) Most days I **used to** work until 8.00 p.m. I'm always exhausted.
d) When I was younger I'**d** go out every evening.
e) I'**ll** like watching horror movies.
f) I **didn't use to** like spinach, but I do now.

Which sentences are true for you? Compare with your partner.

5 **Complete the sentences with the verbs in brackets in the gerund or infinitive form.**

a) I'll never forget (see) _____ the first moon landing.
b) I always stop (buy) _____ a newspaper before my English class.
c) I never forget (call) _____ my mum on her birthday.
d) I've tried (eat) _____ seafood but I really don't like it.
e) I'll never stop (love) _____ Elvis Presley.
f) I tried (pass) _____ my driving test, but after six attempts I finally gave up.

Tick the sentences that are true for you.

6 **Read the conversation between an interviewer (I) and Chef Louis (CL). Underline the correct uses of the present perfect continuous. Change the incorrect uses to the present perfect simple.**

I: Chef Louis, well done on your new restaurant.
CL: Thank you. (1) **I've been dreaming** of this day for a very long time. Yes, (2) **I've been working** for some of the best chefs in the world and now, finally, I have my own place.
I: When and where did you start your career?
CL: I started in a small restaurant in France when I was just sixteen. You know, (3) **I've been cooking** for a very long time.
I: Tell me: what's the worst accident that (4) **has been happening** to you in all that time?
CL: Well, nothing disastrous fortunately, but (5) **I've been cutting** my finger more times than I can remember!
I: Tell us about your life in England.
CL: Well, (6) **I've been living** here since 1992. And in that time (7) **I've been having** some wonderful experiences. I'm very happy here.
I: And so tell us about your restaurant.
CL: (8) **I've always been loving** food. It's my passion. In my restaurant we have food from all over the world. I have a new chef, Yoshi Ikeda. (9) **He's been teaching** me some techniques from Japan. And (10) **I've been having** lessons from another fantastic chef from Thailand. Come and try our new dishes!
I: I'd love to. Chef Louis, (11) **I've been enjoying** our chat today. Thank you for your time.

7 **Write the sentences in the passive.**

a) In the past people used salt as payment for work. In the past salt _____ .
b) In France people eat 700 million snails every year. In France 700 million snails _____ .
c) People have produced chocolate for 2,000 years. Chocolate _____ .
d) Half the world's population eats rice. Rice _____ .
e) People are throwing away 88,000 kilos of food right now. 88,000 kilos of food _____ .

Vocabulary

1 Match each word part with the prefix *self-* or the suffix *ible/able* to form words.

self-
- a) conscious
- b) reason
- c) employed
- d) vis
- e) do
- f) unbear
- g) discipline
- h) ed

ible / able

2 Complete the sentences with the verbs in the box in the correct tense.

> call   get   keep   let   pick   take

a) It took Neil a long time to _____ over his illness.
b) I was counting on him, but he really _____ me down.
c) I'm going to _____ up tennis. I need to get fit again.
d) I hate it when you leave someone a message and they don't _____ you back.
e) I never had formal guitar lessons. I just _____ it up.
f) I'm getting old. I can't _____ up with the new fashions.

3 Put the words in the correct order.
a) have / I'd / on a / love to / Harley-Davidson / a go
b) at / have / surfing / a go / love to / I'd
c) the go / every day / 9–6 / I'm / from / on
d) wouldn't / I / yoga / mind / giving / a go
e) a glass of whisky / one / couldn't / in / drink / I / go

Tick the sentences which are true for you and compare with a partner.

4 Complete the words associated with weddings.
a) b r _ d _ _
b) g r _ _ _ m
c) b _ s t m _ n
d) c _ n f _ t t _
e) v _ _ l
f) h _ n _ y m _ _ n
g) b r _ d _ s m _ _ _ d
h) v _ w s
i) p r _ p _ s _ a t _ _ s t
j) w _ d d _ n g c _ k _
k) b _ _ q _ _ t _ f f l _ w _ r s

5 Underline the correct verbs.
a) **Raise / Stick** your tongue out.
b) **Hold / Clench** your hand up.
c) **Stick / Bend** your knees.
d) **Bend / Shake** your head.
e) **Clench / Stick** your fist.
f) **Shake / Raise** your eyebrows.

6 Cross out the incorrect adjective in each item.
a) I usually eat **gourmet / three-course / vegetarian** food.
b) I don't like food with a **bland / hard / strong** flavour.
c) When I travel I always like to try out the **local / regional / unmistakable** dishes.
d) I never eat **fast / ready-made / stodgy** meals. They're not very healthy!
e) I really hate eating from **organic / paper / plastic** plates.

Change the adjectives to make the sentences true for you. Compare with your partner.

7 Write an answer to each question.
a) When is your birthday? (*day/month/year*)
b) How many children do your parents have? (*cardinal number*) What position do you come in the family? (*ordinal number*)
c) What's your mobile number?
d) What's the population of your country?
e) As a fraction, what is the number of left-handed people in your family (eg 1 in 4 = ¼)? What is this as a percentage (eg 1 in 4 = 25%)?

Work with your partner. Read out your answers to each other.

Pronunciation

1 Look at some words from Units 4–6. Say the words and add them to the table.

> ~~candlelight~~   competition   expedition
> hazardous   however   invitation
> neighbourhood   organic   organised
> reception   superstitious   tomato

A: ☐□□	B: □☐□	C: □□☐□
candlelight		

2 Underline the stressed syllable.

🔊 2.19 Listen, check and repeat.

▶ 🔊 2.20 **Song**

7 Escape

Grammar Reporting verbs. Past modals. Articles
Vocabulary Word formation. Spoken discourse markers
Useful phrases Advice and recommendations

Reading & Vocabulary

1 **Work in small groups. Discuss the questions.**
   a) What words and images do you associate with the word *beach*?
   b) When was the last time you spent a day on a beach? Where? Who with?
   c) What sort of things might spoil a day at the seaside? Make a list.

   Read the extract from Bill Bryson's book, *Notes From A Big Country*. How many of the things you listed in *c* above does the author mention?

2 **Are the statements true or false? Compare your answers with a partner.**
   a) The author …
      1 enjoys the prospect of a day on the beach.
      2 is not very proud of his body.
      3 doesn't get bad sunburn.
   b) The author's wife …
      1 enjoys the prospect of a day on the beach.
      2 doesn't usually get her own way.
      3 says that Irish setters are very clean.
   c) The author's youngest child …
      1 is very demanding.
      2 is called Jimmy.
      3 said he needed to go to the toilet.

3 **Read the definition and complete the corresponding phrase from the extract. Check the text if necessary.**
   a) Walk in water that is not very deep = have a p_____
   b) Refuse very firmly to do something = put your f_____ d_____
   c) Look at the situation = survey the s_____
   d) A small boat you fill with air = an inflatable d_____
   e) Eat a sandwich by taking a lot of small bites = n_____ at a sandwich
   f) Have a short sleep during the day = have a little n_____

   Write your own example sentence for each phrase. Use a dictionary if necessary.

4 **Is your attitude towards beaches similar to a) the author's or b) the author's wife's attitude? Discuss with your partner.**

A day at the seaside

Every year, about this time, my wife wakes me up with a playful slap and says, 'I've got an idea. Let's drive for three hours to the ocean, take off most of our clothes and sit on some sand for a whole day.'

'What for?' I will say warily.

5 'It will be fun,' she will insist.

'I don't think so,' I will reply. 'People find it disturbing when I take my shirt off in public. I find it disturbing.'

'No, it will be great. We'll get sand in our hair. We'll get sand in our shoes. We'll get sand in our sandwiches and then in our mouths. We'll get sunburned and windburned. 10 And when we get tired of sitting, we can have a paddle in water so cold it actually hurts. At the end of the day, we'll set off at the same time as 37,000 other people and get in such a traffic jam that we won't get home till midnight. I can make interesting observations about your driving skills, and the children can pass the time sticking each other with sharp objects. It will be such fun.'

15 The tragic thing is that because my wife is English, and therefore beyond the reach of reason where saltwater is concerned, she really will think it's fun. Frankly, I have never understood the British attachment to the seaside.

So when, last weekend, my wife suggested that we take a drive to the sea, I put my foot down and said, 'Never – absolutely not,' which is of course why we ended up, three 20 hours later, at Kennebunk Beach in Maine.

On arrival, our youngest – I'll call him Jimmy in case he should one day become a lawyer – surveyed the scene and said, 'OK, Dad, here's the situation. I need an ice cream, a Li-Lo, a deluxe bucket and spade set, a hot dog, some candy floss, an inflatable dinghy, scuba equipment, my own waterslide, a cheese pizza with extra cheese and a toilet.'

25 'They don't have those things here, Jimmy,' I chuckled.

'I really need the toilet.'

I reported this to my wife.

'Then you'll have to take him to Kennebunkport,' she said serenely from beneath a preposterous sun hat.

30 By the time we found a toilet, little Jimmy didn't need to go any more, so we returned to the beach. By the time we got there, some hours later, I discovered that everyone had gone off for a swim, and there was only one half-eaten sandwich left. I sat on a towel and nibbled at the sandwich.

'Oh look, Mummy,' said number two daughter gaily when they emerged from the surf 35 a few minutes later. 'Daddy's eating the sandwich the dog had.'

'Tell me this isn't happening,' I began to whimper.

'Don't worry, dear,' my wife said soothingly, 'It was an Irish setter. They're very clean.'

I don't remember much after that. I just had a little nap and woke to find that Jimmy 40 was burying me up to my chest in sand – which was fine, except that he had started at my head – and I managed to get so sunburned that a dermatologist invited me to a convention in Cleveland the following week as an exhibit.

We lost the car keys for two hours, the Irish setter came back and stole one of the beach towels, then nipped me on the hand for eating his sandwich, and number two 45 daughter got tar in her hair. It was a typical day at the seaside in other words.

'Lovely,' said my wife. 'We must do that again soon.'

And the heartbreaking thing is she really meant it.

Glossary

slap noun [C]: sharp hit with the palm of your hand
warily adv: cautiously, nervously
chuckle verb [I]: laugh quietly
preposterous adj: silly or absurd
whimper verb [I]: say something in a pained voice
Irish setter noun [C]: large dog with long, dark red hair
dermatologist: noun [C]: skin doctor
tar noun [U]: thick oil

Vocabulary & Grammar

1 Look at this summary of the book extract on page 69. Put the lines in the correct order.

6 me that I'd have to take him to Kennebunkport, miles away. On return I was hungry but lost my appetite when my daughter casually **mentioned**

1 Every year, about the same time, my wife would wake up and **announce**

4 that I couldn't imagine anything worse, she always **reassured**

6 me to go, and three hours later we arrived at the beach. Almost immediately, my son **insisted**

3 driving all the way to the ocean. When I **explained**

2 that she had an idea. She'd **suggest**

7 on going to the toilet. Too busy sunbathing, my wife calmly **informed**

10 that, as we'd all had such a good time, we should do it again soon!

9 that I was eating the sandwich the dog had had. The dog then bit me, we lost the car keys and I ended up with severe sunburn. So imagine the shock when my wife **suggested**

5 me that we'd have a great time. This particular year, it didn't take her long to **persuade**

2 All of the verbs in bold in Exercise 1 are used to report messages. Divide them into list *A* and list *B* according to the headings.

A 'tell' verbs': where the hearer is usually the direct object	B 'say verbs': where the hearer is not usually the direct object
… persuade me to …	… mentioned that …

3 Add more reporting verbs from the box to the appropriate column in the table in Exercise 2. Check the verb patterns in your dictionary if necessary.

> admit   advise   assure   claim   confirm   convince   encourage

🌐 **2.21** Listen to five people talking about their favourite beach. Notice how the verbs in the box are used and confirm your answers.

Speaking: anecdote

You are going to tell your partner about a family holiday you went on as a child.

- Ask yourself the questions below.
- Think about *what* to say and *how* to say it.
- Tell your partner about the family holiday.

a) Where did you go?
b) Who chose the holiday destination?
c) Had you been to the same place before?
d) Who went on this holiday with you?
e) How did you get there and how long did it take?
f) Where did you stay?
g) Was it a good place for a holiday? Why? / Why not?
h) How did you spend your time there?
i) Who enjoyed the holiday most?
j) Have you been back to the same place since you were a child?

Listening & Grammar

1 Work with a partner. Look at the photos of three different holidays and discuss what sort of things might go wrong on holidays like these.

▲ Sarah and Paul in the French Alps

▲ Amy and Josh in Guatemala

▲ Rachel in Andalucia

🔊 **2.22–2.24** Listen to the three experiences and compare your ideas with what actually happened. Answer the questions.

a) Who shouldn't have ignored expert advice?
b) Who should have checked the weather forecast?
c) Who should have double-checked their travel itinerary?

Past modals

We **ought to have booked** earlier.
We **had to go** via Rome.
We **couldn't take** much luggage.
You **didn't need to fly**.
You **should have come** by train.
We **weren't allowed to change** our tickets.

2 Work with your partner. Underline the two modal verbs or phrases (*a, b* or *c*) which are appropriate to complete each sentence. Cross out the answer which is not appropriate.

1 Sarah and Paul _____ go skiing on the black pistes.
  a) couldn't b) weren't allowed to c) didn't need to
2 Sarah and Paul _____ get up early to go skiing.
  a) weren't allowed to b) didn't have to c) didn't need to
3 Amy _____ go on holiday to Guatemala alone.
  a) wasn't allowed to b) couldn't c) didn't have to
4 Amy and Josh _____ return to North America before they could fly to Guatemala.
  a) needed to b) could c) had to
5 Rachel didn't think she _____ buy a pair of padded cycling shorts.
  a) was allowed to b) had to c) needed to
6 Rachel _____ have listened to the man in the bike shop.
  a) should b) ought to c) shouldn't

Listen again and check. Tick the modal verb or phrase (*a, b* or *c*) that is actually used in the recordings.

3 Which modal verbs or phrases in Exercise 1 and 2 can you use to say it was …

a) necessary for you to do something?
  I had to / needed to …
b) not necessary for you to do something?
c) permitted for you to do something?
d) not permitted for you to do something?
e) wrong for you to do something?
f) wrong for you not to do something?

4 Think about a recent travel experience. Make as many true sentences as you can using the following prompts.

Think about …

a) something you had to do.
b) something you couldn't do.
c) something you didn't have to do.
d) something you could do.
e) something you shouldn't have done.
f) something you should have done.

Tell your partner.

5 Grammar *Extra* 7, Part 1 page 138. Read the explanations and do Exercise 1.

Reading

1 **Work with a partner. Discuss the questions.**

a) When was the last time you sent or received a postcard?

b) Which of the postcards (1–5) would you be most likely to buy/send?

c) If you had to send these particular postcards, who would you send each one to? Why?

2 Read the article below and match the character types (A–E) to the postcards (1–5) in Exercise 1.

EVERY POSTCARD TELLS A STORY

Did you know that the type of postcard you choose, together with the message you write, reveals more about your personality than the place you're describing? Flowery, long-winded descriptions often come from the indecisive person who loves the sound of their own voice and is incapable of summarising. On the other hand, short, sharp phrases – often illegible – are probably the work of the impatient, time-conscious no-nonsense-taker. Then there's the choice of card itself. Do you choose something jokey, or a historical monument or a tasteful water-colour by a local artist? Look at the examples on this page and choose the type that fits you best.

A: The culture vulture Sightseeing is a way of life for the sender of this card. This traveller takes life – at home and away – rather seriously. A bookish sort of person who likes to be well-informed about the places he visits. Can be a little humourless at times.

B: The joker This sort of card is bound to raise a smile but it gives no idea at all of what the holiday is really like. The sender is a cheerful sort of person, more interested in having fun than soaking up the local lifestyle and culture.

C: The indecisive type This card combines lots of different postcards in one, with a view to pleasing everyone. The sender is thoughtful and caring, but through their desire to please everyone, they run the risk of being unadventurous or even uninteresting.

D: The arty type The sender of this tasteful scene is a style guru, even on holiday. Image-conscious and stylish (some may say snobbish), they're often dissatisfied with the usual selection of postcards, and will go out of their way to find unusual ones. This traveller does not want to be mistaken for one of the crowd.

E: The totally tasteless type The irresistible tacky postcard is a genuine, unself-conscious choice. This holiday maker has a sunny, positive outlook and is happy to share it with friends back home.

Answers: A3, B4, C5, D2, E1

3 Think of people you know who fit the character types in the article. Tell your partner about them.

Vocabulary

Word formation

ful suffix with this quality: used with many nouns: *careful, cheerful, doubtful, helpful, painful, stressful, tasteful, tearful, thoughtful, useful*

ish suffix with this quality: used with some nouns: *bullish, childish, devilish, foolish, hellish, selfish*

less suffix without this quality: used with many nouns: *careless, childless, doubtless, endless, helpless, homeless, humourless, painless, relentless, selfless, tasteless, thoughtless, useless*

1 Reread the article on page 72 and underline all the adjectives with the suffixes *ful*, *less*, or *ish*. Which suffix means: (1) has this quality; (2) doesn't have this quality?

2 Which suffix (*ful*, *less*, or *ish*) can combine with *all* the words in each list (a–c) to form adjectives?
- a) care / end / home / relent / taste / use
- b) bull / child / devil / fool / hell / self
- c) doubt / help / pain / stress / tear / thought

Check your ideas in the Word formation panel. Tick the adjectives you know. Choose three more to learn. Write your own example sentences.

3 Look again at the article on page 72 and find ten negative adjectives beginning with the prefixes in the table. Add each adjective to the correct column.

dis	il	im	in	ir	un
			indecisive		

Complete the table with the negative version of the adjectives in the box. Use your dictionary if necessary.

> adequate   appropriate   divided   honest   legal   literate   logical   loyal
> mature   moral   obedient   polite   rational   relevant   responsible   willing

4 Read the story carefully. Use the words in bold at the end of some lines to form words that fit in the gaps on the same lines.

Never AGAIN!

I hate travelling. It's not that I'm (1) _____ . It's just that I've got a problem. **willing**
Four problems actually, and they're called Freddie, Charlie, Ella and Jack.
Ranging in age from five down to six months, they're (2) _____ when they're **resist**
asleep. But when they're awake they're (3) _____ . Individually they're hard **relent**
work; in twos they're a handful; all together, they're a nightmare. More often
5 than not, they're (4) _____ and seem to have endless competitions to see who **obedient**
can behave in the most (5) _____ way. On top of that, they all want my (6) _____ **devil   divide**
attention at the same time.
   Under these (7) _____ circumstances, you may think that it would be **stress**
foolish of me to even consider travelling alone with my children. Well, I know
10 now that it wasn't just foolish, but downright (8) _____ . **response**
   I wanted to visit my parents. My husband couldn't come, so I set off on
the five-hour train journey with a bagful of toys, a pocketful of sweets and a
headful of songs, stories and games.
   But regardless of my (9) _____ preparations, it was a (10) _____ **care   hell**
15 journey. In fact, it was one of the worst experiences of my life. The final straw
was when I arrived, exhausted and (11) _____ , at my parents' house. Instead of **tear**
being sympathetic, they took great delight in telling me how awful I had been as
a child. Thanks, Mum and Dad, that was really (12) _____ ! **help**

🎧 2.25 **Listen and check.**

5 Did you enjoy travelling as a child? Tell your partner.

Listening & Speaking

1   Have you ever met anybody on holiday and then stayed in touch with them?

2   ⊕ 2.26 Listen to Angela talking about her holiday romance and answer the questions.

    a)   What was Angela doing when she met Brad?
    b)   Why did she return to England?
    c)   Where does Brad live now?

3   Listen again and complete the extracts with a single word.

    a)   I have **actually** … many years _____ .
    b)   **Come to think of it**, he did look a bit like a film _____ .
    c)   **Anyway**, we met through a mutual _____ .
    d)   **In fact**, I really thought I'd met my _____ .
    e)   **Do you know what I mean?** I thought we may end up _____ .
    f)   **Basically**, our relationship wasn't strong _____ .
    g)   Well, **in the end** he met somebody _____ .
    h)   And **to be honest**, I was _____ .

4   Match each of the discourse markers in bold in Exercise 3 with its interpretation below.

    1   the final result was   5   To be more precise
    2   Do you understand?   6   Let's get back to the subject
    3   although this may surprise you   7   I really am telling the truth
    4   I've just remembered this   8   To put it simply

5   Gill's holiday romance was more successful than Angela's. Complete her story by underlining the appropriate discourse markers from Exercise 3.

Tony: You're not the type to have a holiday romance, are you, Gill?
Gill: (1) **Actually / Basically**, I am. In fact, I met my husband on holiday.
Tony: No!
Gill: Yes, it's true. I went on a camping holiday in Scandinavia with some university friends, and Ash came along at the last minute.
Tony: Camping in Scandinavia? Not exactly tropical ...
Gill: No, (2) **in the end / come to think of it**, it was a bit cold at times. (3) **To be honest / Anyway**, as soon as I saw him I thought, 'Yes, this one's for me.' (4) **Do you know what I mean? / Come to think of it**.
Tony: Oh yes, I do ... I do.
Gill: But then I found out he had a girlfriend back home.
Tony: Oh no!
Gill: (5) **Basically / Actually** I had two weeks to impress him – so I used my best weapon: I put on my little black dress ...
Tony: I thought you said it was cold ...
Gill: Yes, it was, but, (6) **anyway / to be honest** I didn't notice the temperature. And anyway, it was worth it because it worked – he resisted for a few days, which felt like years! But eventually he surrendered, and we spent the rest of the holiday together. (7) **In fact / Actually**, we were inseparable.
Tony: What happened when you got home?
Gill: Well, that was a horrible time because we knew we wanted to be together, but we both had other relationships to sort out.
Tony: That must have been difficult.
Gill: It was, but it all worked out well (8) **in the end / to be honest**. I mean, it's our fifth wedding anniversary in June.

    ⊕ 2.27 Listen and check. Practise the conversation with a partner. Concentrate on the correct stress and intonation. Take it in turns to be Gill.

6   Work with your partner. Write a similar conversation about meeting somebody on holiday. Include as many discourse markers as you can. Practise your conversation and perform it for the rest of the class.

'Our relationship wasn't strong enough,' says Angela Kenny.

'We're happily married,' says Gill May.

Reading & Grammar

Articles

The indefinite article
a/an:
a tourist, **a** man, **an** idea

The definite article *the*:
The tourist was from
the USA.
The man was from Africa.
The idea wasn't very good.

1 Complete the story with *a*, *an*, *the*, or put a dash (–) if no article is necessary.

Gone fishing

(1) ___ tourist in (2) ___ Africa was walking by (3) ___ sea when he saw (4) ___ man in (5) ___ simple clothes dozing in (6) ___ fishing boat. It was (7) _____ idyllic picture, so he decided to take (8) ___ photograph. (9) ___ click of (10) ___ camera woke (11) ___ man up. (12) ___ tourist offered him (13) ___ cigarette.

'(14) ___ weather is great. There are plenty of (15) ___ fish. Why are you lying around instead of going out and catching more?'

(16) ___ fisherman replied, 'Because I caught enough this morning.'

'But just imagine,' (17) ___ tourist said, 'If you went out there three times every day, you'd catch three times as much. After about (18) ___ year you could buy yourself (19) ___ motorboat. After (20) ___ few more years of (21) ___ hard work, you could have (22) ___ fleet of (23) ___ boats working for you. And then …'

'And then?' asked (24) ___ fisherman.

'And then,' (25) ___ tourist continued triumphantly, 'you could be calmly sitting on (26) ___ beach, dozing in (27) ___ sun and looking at (28) ___ beautiful ocean.'

🔊 2.28 Listen and check your answers. What is the moral of the story?

2 Here are some general rules for using articles. Find an example of each rule in the text in Exercise 1.

a/an
a) Use the indefinite article to introduce new information.
b) DON'T use the indefinite article with plurals or uncountable nouns.

the
c) Use the definite article to refer to things that have already been introduced.
d) Use the definite article when the listener knows the answer to 'which one?'
e) Use the definite article when there is only one.
f) DON'T use the definite article with continents, most countries, cities, lakes and mountains.

3 You do not use articles when talking about 'things in general'. Write three interesting generalisations, each of which combines a word from box *A* with a word from box *B*.

Travel is the best way to gain experience.   *Men are a mystery to women.*

A	death	gold	health	humour
	men	music	time	travel
	war	wisdom	youth	

+

B	experience	happiness		
	intelligence	life	love	money
	peace	silver	women	

Discuss your statements with a partner and the rest of your class.

4 Grammar *Extra* 7, Part 2 page 138. Read the explanations and do Exercises 2 and 3.

Pronunciation

1 🔊 2.29 Listen and repeat the place names. What is the difference between the pronunciation of *the* in box *A* and box *B*? Why?

A	the Danube	the Dead Sea
	the Himalayas	the Thames
	the Urals	

B	the Andes	the Eiffel Tower
	the Empire State Building	
	the Indian Ocean	the Orinoco

2 Have you ever seen, visited or travelled through any of these places? Add your own examples to boxes *A* and *B*. Find the English pronunciation in your dictionary.

8 Attraction

Grammar Passive report structures. *have/get something done.* Unreal conditionals
Vocabulary Appearance and character. Compound adjectives. Word-building
Useful phrases Body idioms

Listening & Vocabulary

1　Work in small groups and discuss these questions.

    a)　Who do you think is the most handsome man in the world?
    b)　Who do you think is the most beautiful woman in the world?
    c)　What makes them more attractive than other men and women?

2　Five people were asked to describe what features make a face attractive. Complete the collocations (*a–l*) to describe some of the facial features they mention. Choose the most suitable words from the box. Sometimes more than one answer is possible.

> bone structure　cheekbones　eyebrows　eyes　eyes
> in the cheeks　jaw　lips　nose　skin　smile　teeth

    a)　smooth _____
    b)　good _____
    c)　white _____
    d)　sparkling _____

    e)　a square _____
    f)　big _____
    g)　full _____
    h)　a big _____

    i)　a turned-up _____
    j)　high _____
    k)　arched _____
    l)　dimples _____

🔵 2.32　Listen and check. Do you agree with any of their opinions?

3　Look at these computer images of male and female faces. What do / don't you like about them? Tell a partner.

The perfect **face**

In a survey, ten thousand British men and women were asked about what they thought represented perfect male and female faces. When the data was processed by computer, these were the results.

4　Think about people that you know with interesting faces. Describe them to your partner. Try to use collocations from Exercise 2.

Reading

1 **Work with a partner. Look at the statements (*a–f*) about the nature of beauty. Decide whether you agree or disagree.**

a) Beauty is 'in the eye of the beholder'.

b) Most film stars and supermodels don't have ideal features.

c) People find exaggerated features attractive, such as larger than normal eyes.

d) Most women prefer men with gentle features.

e) There is more pressure on men to be perfect than there is on women.

f) People from different cultures have completely different views about what is beautiful.

Read the article and find out whether, according to the research, the statements are true or false.

Is **beauty** in the eye of the beholder?

▲ Julia Roberts

Is there such a thing as the perfect face? Is beauty something you can measure?

Recent scientific evidence suggests that the answer is 'yes'. A new science, the science of attraction, has come to the conclusion
10 that beauty is objective and quantifiable and not, as the romantics believe, in the eye of the beholder.

For more than a century it
15 was thought that a beautiful face was appealing because it was a collection of average features. Using his computer system, Dr David
20 Perrett of the University of St Andrews has challenged the theory. In a key experiment, photographs of women were ranked
25 for their attractiveness by a number of volunteers. Two composite pictures were then created: one, the average of all the pictures,
30 the other made from those rated most attractive. Although the faces looked very similar at first glance, a significant number said they
35 preferred the composite of most attractive faces.

'The conclusion I reached,' said Dr Perrett, 'was that the most attractive
40 face was not average. If you look at famous film stars and supermodels, most of them have ideal features – larger than normal eyes,
45 higher arched eyebrows, slightly smaller noses, cheekbones are a little more prominent. Even popular cartoon characters such as
50 Betty Boop, Yasmin from *Aladdin* and Bambi have big eyes, small turned-up noses, big mouths and small chins. And if these
55 features are exaggerated, the attractiveness rating goes up even more. Julia Roberts is a good example of this.'

But what do scientists
60 make of men's faces? Do men with large eyes, high cheekbones and a small chin have the same irresistible appeal? Researchers were
65 a bit shocked at the top-ranking male face. They expected it to have the classic square jaw and strong cheekbones, but
70 instead, women seem to prefer men with gentle faces.

Although there is more pressure on females to be
75 perfect, research suggests that men and women look for many of the same things: for example, expressive features such as arched
80 eyebrows and a big smile were associated with attractiveness in men.

Dr David Perrett puts forward an evolutionary
85 reason to explain why so many women now go for baby-faced stars such as Leonardo DiCaprio and Jude Law. Women like a
90 man with a feminine face because he is more likely to have higher levels of the female hormone oestrogen and therefore to
95 make a kinder and more trustworthy husband and father.

But do these ideals of beauty manage to cross
100 cultural boundaries? Are the same features considered to be attractive all over the world? A worldwide study carried out by
105 Professor Cunningham of the University of Louisville, Kentucky, concluded that there were only very subtle differences between ethnic
110 groups. In other words, although there might be a little truth in the old adage that beauty is in the eye of the beholder, by and large,
115 we all seem to be attracted to the same things.

▲ Jude Law

Glossary

a) _____ noun [C] *literary*: a person who sees sth

b) _____ verb [T]: put people/things into order from first to last

c) _____ phrase: on a first quick look

d) _____ noun [C]: well-known phrase commenting on life

e) _____ adj: impossible not to like

f) _____ adj: honest or reliable

g) _____ adj: not obvious, very small

h) _____ adj: sticking out

2 **Read the article again and underline words or phrases that you don't know.**

- Try to guess the meaning from context.
- Complete the glossary – how many of the words you underlined are included?
- Add any other words and write your own definitions. Use a dictionary if necessary.

Grammar

Passive report structures

Formal
It was thought that the world was flat.
Bananas are said to give you energy.

Informal
People thought that the world was flat.
They say that bananas give you energy.

1 **Look at an active and passive version of the same sentence. Answer the questions.**

1 *For more than a century <u>people thought that</u> a beautiful face was appealing because …*
   For more than a century <u>it was thought that</u> a beautiful face was appealing because …

2 <u>*Do people all over the world consider*</u> *the same features to be attractive?*
   <u>*Are the same features considered*</u> *to be attractive all over the world?*

a) Which structure – active or passive – is more formal?
b) Which structure is more likely to be found in written reports?
c) Which structure is used in the article on page 79?

2 **Put the missing word in brackets in the correct position in the sentence.**

a) Chocolate thought to be bad for your skin. (is)
b) It has suggested that you should drink at least two litres of water a day. (been)
c) It used to assumed that carrots were good for your eyesight. (be)
d) It said that reading in a dim light can damage your eyes. (is)
e) Shaving body hair widely believed to make it grow back thicker and faster. (is)
f) It often said that we only use 10% of our brains. (is)

3 **Rewrite the statements in Exercise 2 in a more informal style.**

a) People …   c) People …   e) Many people …
b) Some doctors … d) They …   f) They …

a) People say that chocolate is bad for your skin.

Work with a partner. Do people believe that the same things are true in your country?

Listening

1 **Look at the photos of three people who took part in a radio debate about cosmetic surgery. Match each person (*Jean, Rita* or *Michael*) with an opinion (*a–c*) you think they might have.**

a) 'I really don't think there's anything wrong with trying to improve on what nature has given us.'
b) 'I think we should be grateful for what God has given us.'
c) 'Personally, I'm dead against cosmetic surgery of any kind.'

▲ Jean Oldham, beauty editor

🔘 **2.33 Listen and check your ideas.**

2 **Complete the extracts from the radio debate with words from the box.**

ask	believe	frankly	have	point	trying

a) I _____ to say that the most beautiful women I know are not models.
b) I _____ that true beauty comes from within.
c) The _____ is, it's selfish and indulgent of people to spend vast amounts of money on superficial improvements.
d) Quite _____ , cosmetic surgery can do more for you than a holiday, because the benefits last longer.
e) I suppose what I'm _____ to say is that cosmetic surgery nowadays is almost as routine as going on holiday.
f) If you _____ me, what we need to accept is that we can't look young forever.

▲ Rita Taylor, cosmetic surgeon

Do you think cosmetic surgery is a good or a bad thing? Tell your partner.

3 **What are your opinions about the topics in the box?**

botox	piercing	size zero models	tattoos	testing cosmetics on animals

▲ Michael Hirst, religious journalist

Tell your partner about your opinions. Use as many of the highlighted expressions in Exercise 2 as you can.

Reading & Grammar

1 Look at the photos of Cindy Jackson. She has had extensive cosmetic surgery. Which parts of her face has she had changed?

Read her account and check your ideas. Complete the text with *had, have* or *having*.

Surgery changed my life!

'The features I wanted were the kind of feminine ideal that's embodied in plastic dolls like Barbie and Sindy. I wanted the wide eyes so I (1) *had* my eyes widened as much as I could. (2) _____ my eyes done made me
5 see that I really could change my face, so I decided to (3) _____ everything done that I possibly could.
    I wanted the pert, turned-up nose, so I (4) _____ my nose turned up. I wasn't happy with the first nose job – it only made it slightly smaller. So I (5) _____ it done
10 again, and they took more bone out and made the nostrils smaller. Now my nose is as 'Barbie' as it can

get for my face and the rest of my features.
    My chin bothered me a lot too, so I (6) _____ that moved back, so that it was in line with the upper lip.
15 Then there were my lips – I thought they were too thin, so I tried (7) _____ collagen put in. But that wasn't good enough, so I (8) _____ fat taken from my thighs and injected into my lips. Then I (9) _____ implants put into my cheeks to give me high cheekbones.
20   Before I had surgery, I was invisible. I have a genius IQ, and it never got me anywhere. Now I get lots of attention. Pretty girls just do.'

What does Cindy Jackson identify as the main change in her life after surgery? What do you think about her comments?

---

have/get something done

have/get + object + past participle
She**'s had** her hair **dyed**.
He**'s getting** his teeth **straightened**.

---

2 What is the difference in meaning between *I did my hair* and *I had/got my hair done*? When do you use the structure *have/get* + object + past participle?

3 Write the sentences in the correct order.
a) get / every six months / serviced / my car / I
b) redecorated / my house / four years ago / had / I
c) my hair / once a month / I / cut / get
d) installed / had / a burglar alarm / I've
e) last month / my blood pressure / checked / I / had
f) had / I've / my nails / never / done

Make questions based on the sentences (a–f) using *How often …?*, or *Have you ever …?*, or *When was the last time …?*, as appropriate.

Ask and answer the questions with a partner.

4 How well do you know the town or city you are in? Work with your partner and take it in turns to ask each other where the best place is to have / get things done. Use the verbs / objects in the box or your own ideas.

| clean / a winter coat   colour / hair   cut / a key   do / a tattoo |
| reheel / shoes   repair / a TV   take / a passport photo   test / eyes |

Where is the best place to get a winter coat cleaned?

5 Grammar *Extra 8*, Part 1 page 138. Read the explanations and do Exercise 1.

Reading & Speaking

1 Work in small groups. Discuss the questions.

a) What is the minimum time you need to know if you are attracted to someone?

b) What can you say about someone from what they wear and how they talk?

c) What would turn you off someone immediately?

2 Read the article on page 83 about a speed dating session. Make a note of each person's best and worst date, then answer the questions below.

a) Who were the most and least popular men?

b) Who were the most and least popular women?

c) Which two men had the same taste in women?

d) Which couple fell for each other?

Would you ever try / Have you ever tried speed dating? Tell a partner.

Vocabulary

1 Decide if these words usually have positive or negative meanings. Check your answers in the article on page 83.

a) self-centred (line 25) g) trustworthy (line 68)

b) enigmatic (line 40) h) open-minded (line 76)

c) down-to-earth (line 43) i) straight (line 80)

d) sensible (line 49) j) mature (line 91)

e) stand-offish (line 51) k) laid-back (line 94)

f) sensitive (line 68)

2 Choose words from the list in Exercise 1 which best replace the words in bold in these sentences.

a) My ideal partner would have to be someone **caring**, good-looking and **dependable**.

b) I think I'm quite a **level-headed** sort of person. I haven't done anything crazy yet, anyway!

c) I'd say I feel **relaxed** about work – I never let things worry me.

d) People think I'm **unfriendly**, but actually, I'm just really shy.

e) My parents are extremely **conventional**. I wish they were more **tolerant**.

f) I prefer to go out with people older than me. You can have more interesting conversations with somebody who's **experienced and grown-up**.

g) I know somebody who likes to think she's **mysterious**. In fact, she's very boring.

h) I know somebody who's very wealthy, but you wouldn't know it because he's so **unpretentious**.

i) I've got a friend who's rather **selfish** – probably because her parents spoilt her when she was a child.

Can you identify with any of the sentences above? Discuss with your partner.

Pronunciation

1 🔘 2.34 Mark the stress on each of the adjectives in the box. Then listen and check.

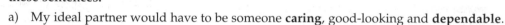

compatible   flexible   friendly   generous   happy   lively   mature   sad
sensitive   sexy   weak

2 Make the adjectives in Exercise 1 into nouns by adding the suffixes *ity* or *ness*. Use your dictionary if necessary.

🔘 2.35? Listen, check and repeat.

3 What is the effect on the word stress when you change the adjective into a noun ending in *ity*?

Your dream partner ... in five minutes!

The idea is simple – why devote a whole evening to one blind date when you can meet five potential mates in less than half an hour? Five men and five women are introduced by a master of ceremonies
5 or chaperone. Each 'couple' is given five minutes to get to know each other before moving on to the next candidate. At the end of the session, if the attraction is mutual, they can walk off together into the sunset (or at least swap telephone numbers).
10   We went along to a Speed dating night, where these five women and five men had signed up for the event, all hoping to meet their dream partner, safe in the knowledge that if they hate each other on sight, the suffering will last only five minutes or three
15 hundred excruciating seconds.

CRAIG, 21: a student

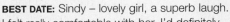

IDEAL DATE: I'm looking for someone who makes me laugh and someone I can learn something from. She has to be a brunette
20 though.
BEST DATE: Claire – she's a brunette with a great personality. She made me laugh, and I'd like to see her again.
WORST DATE: Erica – ugh! Awful manners and jokes. She
25 seems rather full of herself, a bit self-centred.

KEVIN, 31: a telecom salesman

IDEAL DATE: I've had a few serious relationships, but at the end of the day, nothing materialised. My ideal date is a lively,
30 pretty girl who is amusing and good to talk to.
BEST DATE: Sindy – bubbly and lively. I'd definitely like to see her again.
WORST DATE: Lara – didn't seem to be on the same planet as the rest of us. Too spaced-out for me.

35 ## MARK, 21: a party planner

IDEAL DATE: I broke up with my girlfriend of a year three months ago so now I'm after someone who is a good laugh but who you can get on a deeper level with.
40 **BEST DATE:** Karen – stayed very enigmatic, which I liked. Very attractive. I'd like to see her again.
WORST DATE: Erica – a bit dizzy. I prefer somebody a bit more down-to-earth.

JIM, 25: a computer consultant

45 **IDEAL DATE:** I didn't come into this thinking I was going to meet the ideal girl. I just wanted a bit of a laugh. I wouldn't use this technique to find my future girlfriend.
BEST DATE: Sindy – sensible and fun. The sort
50 of woman I'd take home to meet my parents.
WORST DATE: Claire – rather stand-offish and just not interested. She didn't ask any questions about me, and the five minutes went by very slowly.

TONY, 23: a journalist

55 **IDEAL DATE:** I rarely pull when I'm out and about unless I know the girl first as I'm quite shy. I'd like to meet someone who's good fun and easy to chat to.
BEST DATE: Sindy – lovely girl, a superb laugh.
60 I felt really comfortable with her. I'd definitely like to see her again. Name the date.
WORST DATE: Lara – rambled on too much about her home town in Ireland. A relief when the five minutes were up.

65 ## KAREN, 26: a student

IDEAL DATE: My ideal date is someone with intelligence, good looks, sexiness, a family man. He's got to be sensitive and trustworthy. In other words, I'm looking for the ideal man!!
70 **BEST DATE:** Craig – really cute, young, friendly and good-looking.
WORST DATE: Tony – harmless, but slightly boring and much too quiet.

LARA, 23: a piano tutor

75 **IDEAL DATE:** I like people who are open-minded and different.
BEST DATE: Mark – I found him charming, young and really sexy.
WORST DATE: Jim – he was polite, but a bit
80 too straight for me.

SINDY, 23: a florist

IDEAL DATE: My ideal man is someone interesting, amusing and full of life. I love being outgoing and friendly, so this was the perfect
85 dating game for me.
BEST DATE: Tony – wonderful, interesting and fun.
WORST DATE: Mark – a very cool bloke but not someone I'd date. Too young.

90 ## ERICA, 22: an actress and singer

IDEAL DATE: I like tall mature men who are quite a lot older than me.
BEST DATE: Mark – by far the coolest and most laid-back.
95 **WORST DATE:** Kevin – laddish and unambitious.

CLAIRE, 25: an editorial assistant

IDEAL DATE: I always manage to go out with very intense men who get very obsessive even
100 though I'm just looking for fun.
BEST DATE: Mark – sexy, exotic: a really pretty boy. Yes!
WORST DATE: Tony – sweet but not very inspiring. A bit drippy.

Reading & Speaking

1 Read the synopsis of a DVD entitled *The Secret*. Does it make you want to see it?

The Secret, described as a self-help film, is a documentary which claims to reveal a 'secret' which is so powerful, it can transform our lives and help us achieve all our desires. As explained by a number of experts in the film, this 'secret' is the 'law of attraction', a principle which suggests that our thoughts and feelings can influence the events in our lives. The film also implies that for centuries those in power have kept this central principle hidden from the public. In this film, the 'secret' is uncovered.

2 Read the sayings (*1–6*). Work with a partner and discuss the questions (*a–c*) below.

1 Like attracts like.
2 A leopard can't change its spots.
3 All that glitters is not gold.
4 What goes around, comes around.
5 You can't get blood out of a stone.
6 Be careful what you wish for …

a) What do you think the sayings mean?
b) Do you have any similar sayings in your language?
c) Which three sayings do you think describe the 'law of attraction'?

Listening

1 🔊 2.36 Listen to a radio programme about the 'law of attraction'. According to Dr Hudson, how is the 'law of attraction' similar to a genie?

2 Listen again. For questions *1–7*, choose the best option: *a*, *b* or *c*.

1 How many copies of *The Secret* have been sold on DVD to date?
   a) Two million.
   b) One and a half million.
   c) One million.

2 How old is the theory behind the 'law of attraction'?
   a) It has been around for ages.
   b) It's a new phenomenon.
   c) It has appeared in recent times.

3 How does Dr Hudson explain the 'law of attraction'?
   a) Positive thinking is less stressful than negative thinking.
   b) Positive thinking and negative thinking both exist in the universe.
   c) Positive thinking attracts good things. Negative thinking attracts bad things.

4 What everyday problem does Dr Hudson claim can be solved by positive thinking?
   a) Finding a parking space at a supermarket.
   b) Finding a supermarket with no other shoppers.
   c) Finding your way to a supermarket.

5 Where does Dr Hudson suggest you should start visualising your parking space?
   a) In the supermarket.
   b) On the way to the supermarket.
   c) In the supermarket car park.

6 What is a potential criticism of the 'law of attraction', according to the presenter?
   a) It might encourage people to buy really expensive houses.
   b) It might make people more materialistic and greedy.
   c) It might make people believe in genies.

7 Why does Dr Hudson say it's important to think big?
   a) Because it's better than being mediocre.
   b) Because there's no point in asking for something small.
   c) Because it will help improve things in the world.

Do you believe in the 'law of attraction'? Why? / Why not? Tell your partner.

Grammar

Unreal conditional structures

Imagine you were rich.
Suppose you had millions.
Assuming you were to make a will, who would you leave your money to?

1 Complete the questions with *would* or *were*.

a) If you _____ able to change three things in your life, what _____ they be?

b) Suppose somebody _____ to give you a cheque for any amount you liked – how much _____ you ask for and what _____ you do with it?

c) Imagine a genie _____ to grant you any wish you wanted – what _____ you wish for?

d) Supposing you could go out with anyone in the world, who _____ it be?

e) Assuming money _____ no object, what _____ be your ideal evening out?

f) If you _____ to have a film made of your life, which actor _____ you choose to play the part of you and why?

Work with a partner. Underline the words you can use instead of *if*.

Think about your answers. Ask your partner. How similar are your ideas?

2 Work with your partner. Complete the questions with your own ideas.

a) Imagine you were the President of your country, _____ ?

b) Suppose you could afford to have any car in the world, _____ ?

c) Imagine you could change places with a celebrity for a day, _____ ?

d) Suppose you could live anywhere in the world, _____ ?

e) Assuming your English were perfect, _____ ?

f) Supposing you could change your name, _____ ?

Use your questions to interview other people in the class.

3 Grammar *Extra* 8, Part 2 page 138. Read the explanations and do Exercise 2.

Speaking: anecdote

You are going to tell your partner about the most positive (or negative) person you know.

• Ask yourself the questions below.
• Think about *what* to say and *how* to say it.
• Tell your partner about the person.

a) Who is this person? A teacher? A boss? A member of your family? ...

b) What's his/her name and how old is he/she?

c) When and how did you meet him/her?

d) How did you get to know him/her?

e) What examples of his/her positive (or negative) nature can you give?

f) What do you think makes this person so positive (or negative)?

g) How does his/her positive (or negative) outlook affect you?

h) How often do you see this person?

i) When was the last time you saw him/her?

j) How positive (or negative) do you think *you* are?

Useful phrases

1 🔘 2.37 **Read and listen to the conversation. Underline eight phrases that are different from the conversation on the recording.**

Laura: Hey, Phil, how are you doing?

Phil: Oh hi, Laura – not too bad thanks. How are you?

Laura: Oh, extremely busy as usual. I'm on my way to my third meeting today. How's that lovely girlfriend of yours?

Phil: Oh, we split up three weeks ago. She's on holiday with her new boyfriend.

Laura: Oh no – trust me to say something to make you feel worse. I'm really sorry.

Phil: No, it's OK. I need to talk about it.

Laura: Who's her new boyfriend?

Phil: You wouldn't know him. He's not from around here.

Laura: How did she meet him?

Phil: Through work I think. He's one of those people who seems to be involved in lots of things. He owns several companies, including the one Mandy was working for.

Laura: Oh, Phil, I don't know what to say.

Phil: Yeah – it's hard. I mean, we were supposed to be going on holiday together in a couple of weeks.

Laura: So, what are you going to do?

Phil: I don't know – I haven't decided yet. I might go anyway, or I might not feel like it when the time comes. I don't know. I'll just have to see how I feel at the time.

Laura: Look Phil, I'm afraid I've got to run – but if you need someone to talk to, you know where to find me.

Phil: Thanks, Laura – I'll be fine.

2 **Work with a partner. Match the useful phrases (*a–h*) with the phrases you have underlined in Exercise 1.**

a) put my foot in it
b) play it by ear
c) a shoulder to cry on
d) get it off my chest

e) up to my eyes in work
f) this neck of the woods
g) made my mind up yet
h) have his fingers in a lot of pies

Listen again and check. Use at least three of the useful phrases to write example sentences about yourself or people you know.

Tell your partner about them.

3 **Work with your partner. You are going to write a conversation including some different expressions.**

brain eye foot hand head leg nose tongue

- Use a dictionary and find six expressions based on the body parts in the box.
- Write a conversation using the expressions you have found.
- Practise your conversation and perform it for the rest of the class.

Vocabulary *Extra*

Metaphor

1 Match each sentence (*a–f*) with an adjective or phrase from the box to describe the person's emotions.

angry	busy	happy	losing your temper	nervous	sad

a) She's on top of the world.
b) He feels really down about it.
c) She just flared up over nothing.
d) He's snowed under with work.
e) She's very wound up about it.
f) He nearly blew his top.

2 Underline the word or phrase in sentences *a–f* in Exercise 1 which illustrates each of these common metaphors.

1 BEING ANGRY = BEING HOT OR ON FIRE eg *flared up*
2 LOSING YOUR TEMPER = EXPLODING eg _____
3 BEING BUSY = BEING COVERED OR SURROUNDED eg _____
4 BEING HAPPY = BEING HIGH UP eg _____
5 BEING SAD = BEING LOW DOWN eg _____
6 BEING NERVOUS = BEING PULLED OR TIED eg _____

3 Decide which emotion from Exercise 1 can be described using these words.

a) drowning / swamped / inundated / buried
b) tense / strained / taut / uptight
c) burning / heated / blazing / boil
d) lifted / rise / over / high
e) blow up / outburst / go ballistic / erupt
f) low / depths / sink / dump

Find example sentences from the dictionary metaphor boxes to understand how the words are used. Choose one phrase for each metaphor that you would like to learn.

4 Underline the correct alternative to complete these statements.

a) The occasional blazing **row** / **discussion** is normal in a relationship.
b) The current economic outlook is very **gloomy** / **foggy**.
c) If you're good at time management, you never get **rained** / **inundated** with work.
d) Everybody needs to **let** / **put** their hair down once in a while.
e) People should cheer **up** / **away** a bit: the future is **shining** / **bright**!

Work with a partner. Check your answers in the metaphor boxes. Find out if your partner agrees or disagrees with the statements.

5 Work with your partner. Ask each other these questions.

When was the last time you …
a) lost your cool?
b) blew your top?
c) were up to your ears in work?
d) were over the moon?
e) were feeling blue?
f) let your hair down?

6 Check your own dictionary. How does it show information about metaphor?

Metaphor

Being angry is like being **hot** or **on fire**.
She burned with indignation. ♦ He has a fiery temper. ♦ Jack was a hot-tempered young man. ♦ Their parents were having a heated argument/debate about where to go. ♦ They were having a blazing/flaming row. ♦ She often flares up over nothing. ♦ It made my blood boil. ♦ I lost my cool. ♦ Alison was getting very hot under the collar.
Losing your temper is like an **explosion**.
When she told him, he nearly exploded. ♦ He blew up at her. ♦ Steve couldn't contain his anger any longer. ♦ It was an explosive situation. ♦ I'm sorry I blew my top. ♦ There was another angry outburst from Chris. ♦ Alex was bursting with anger. ♦ She'll blow a fuse/a gasket if she finds out. ♦ Bob went ballistic when he saw what they had done. ♦ A major row erupted at the meeting.
→ CRITICIZE, LOVE

Metaphor

Being very busy at work is like being **covered with things** or **surrounded by** something such as water or the ground, so that you cannot move easily.
They keep piling more work on me. ♦ I'm up to my eyes/ears/eyeballs/neck in work. ♦ I'm drowning in paperwork. ♦ I have got a lot of work to wade through. ♦ I'm snowed under with work. ♦ I don't have time to turn around. ♦ We're absolutely swamped at the moment. ♦ We've been inundated with phone calls. ♦ They buried/immersed themselves in their work.
→ RESPONSIBILITY

Metaphor

Feeling happy and hopeful is like being **high up** or like **moving upwards**. Feeling sad and unhappy is like being **low down** or like **falling**.
The news lifted her spirits. ♦ Things are looking up. ♦ Cheer up! ♦ My spirits rose when I got her letter. ♦ I've been walking/floating on air ever since. ♦ I was over the moon when they told me. ♦ I felt as high as a kite. ♦ She's on top of the world/on cloud nine. ♦ I was in seventh heaven. ♦ I feel really down/low about it all. ♦ He's in very low spirits. ♦ He's in the depths of despair. ♦ My heart sank when I saw him. ♦ They looked very down in the mouth/down in the dumps.
Happiness and hope are like **bright light** or **bright colours**. Sadness and lack of hope are like **darkness** or **dark colours**.
The future looks very bright/rosy. ♦ She brightened up when she heard the news. ♦ His face lit up when he saw them. ♦ They had shining eyes and beaming/dazzling smiles. ♦ The bride looked radiant. ♦ You have to look for the light at the end of the tunnel. ♦ He was in a black mood. ♦ I was feeling blue. ♦ There's no point in having these dark thoughts. ♦ His face darkened. ♦ They led a grey empty existence. ♦ I'm afraid the outlook is very gloomy/bleak/dismal. ♦ The news cast a shadow over the evening.

Metaphor

When you feel nervous it is like being **pulled, tied** or **stretched tightly**. When you relax, it is like becoming **loose** again.
I was feeling a bit tense. ♦ I find running is a good way to release tension. ♦ Her voice was high and strained. ♦ There's no need to get so wound-up about it. ♦ I've been really strung out lately. ♦ She's so highly-strung, she needs very sensitive handling. ♦ I felt taut and tense with nerves. ♦ I don't know why he gets so uptight about things. ♦ Her stomach seemed to be tying itself in knots. ♦ You should try to loosen up a bit. ♦ It's good to unwind at the end of the day. ♦ Just let go of all your worries. ♦ I told her to hang loose and stop worrying. ♦ It's a place where people can let their hair down.
→ FEELING

9 Genius

Grammar Past modals of deduction. *look*, *seem*, *appear*
Vocabulary Describing places. Time expressions. Collocations. Word families
Useful phrases Explaining how something works

Reading & Vocabulary

1 **Work with a partner. Who do you consider to be a genius? Try to name somebody (dead or alive, from your country or elsewhere) for each of these categories.**

- architecture
- art
- film
- literature
- maths
- music
- science and technology
- sport
- theatre

2 **Look at the photo on page 89 of the Guggenheim Museum in Bilbao, Spain. Which of the words in the box could you use to describe it? Use your dictionary if necessary.**

> contemporary   eccentric   hideous   important   metallic   19th century
> post-industrial   post-modern   run-down   semi-derelict   shiny
> space-age   sprawling   tough   urban

Read the article on page 89 and check your ideas. Classify the words in the box as follows.

a) Words to describe the Guggenheim Museum (Tick them.)
b) Words to describe the city of Bilbao (Circle them.)
c) Words to describe the area around the museum (Underline them.)

3 **Work with your partner. Explain the connections (*a–f*) from memory.**

a) Thomas Krens + jogging
b) The Guggenheim Museum + urban sprawl
c) The Basque government + Bilbao's global reputation
d) Bilbao city council + a wine-bottling warehouse
e) Thomas Krens + the Pompidou Centre and the Sydney Opera House
f) Frank Gehry + the waterfront site

Read the article again and check your ideas.

4 **Replace the underlined words and phrases in the sentences (*a–g*) with words and phrases from the article.**

a) To get from the airport to Bilbao you <u>meander</u> through the green hills of northern Spain.
b) As you approach Bilbao, the Guggenheim <u>is just visible</u> in the distance.
c) In some parts of the city you can find examples of <u>nasty, unplanned development</u>.
d) Recently, some famous architects were <u>paid</u> to design important new buildings.
e) The semi-derelict waterfront zone is the <u>perfect place</u> for a big new building.
f) The Guggenheim Museum <u>is impossible to miss in</u> Bilbao. It can be seen from everywhere.
g) The Bilbao Guggenheim is an incredible art museum and <u>deserves</u> a visit.

Work with your partner. Adapt each sentence to describe your own city or a city you know well.

FRANK GEHRY is one of the most respected architects of the 20th century. His designs include major civic and company buildings all over the world. One of his most famous buildings is the Guggenheim Museum in Bilbao in the Basque region, Northern Spain.

Where to go to see a
MASTERPIECE

If Thomas Krens, the newly-appointed director of the Solomon R Guggenheim Foundation, had not gone jogging one April evening in 1991, his brainchild, the Bilbao Guggenheim – a metallic,
5 post-modern, space-age museum – would almost certainly never have been built.

From the moment you leave the airport and wind through the green hills of Northern Spain towards the ochre-brown 19th century city of Bilbao,
10 the Guggenheim Museum can be glimpsed in the distance, like a shiny, modern toy surrounded by hideous urban sprawl.

What on earth possessed the Guggenheim Museum to come to a place like Bilbao? The story
15 goes something like this.

Bilbao is Spain's fourth largest city: a tough, sprawling, former shipbuilding community that faces out onto the Bay of Biscay. In the 1980s, the Basque regional government began a redevelopment
20 programme for the city. They commissioned the best and the brightest in the international architectural world to design a new subway system, a new airport terminal, a new congress and music hall, and a new railway station. But, in order to cement the city's
25 growing global reputation, they wanted an art museum.

In 1991 Basque officials approached the Guggenheim Foundation and met Thomas Krens, the fourth director in the museum's six-year history.
30 Krens was eager to establish a European base for the Guggenheim and with this ambition in mind, he came to Bilbao.

But there was a problem. Krens could see at once that the site chosen by the city council for its new
35 art museum, a former wine-bottling warehouse in the centre of town, was a non-starter. Krens had two models in his head – the Pompidou Centre and the Sydney Opera House. Both buildings had demanded an extraordinary amount of space, and Bilbao, an
40 over-crowded riverside city, did not seem to have the space.

Then, by chance, Krens found the ideal site. An athletic man, he went out running one evening. His route took him past the Jesuit University
45 overlooking the River Nervion, and it was here that he noticed, at one of the many curves of the river, a semi-derelict waterfront zone which was perfect for what he wanted to achieve.

The site was approved in a week, and Californian
50 architect, Frank Gehry, was chosen to realise the project.

Gehry immediately fell in love with the eccentric Basque city and the place Krens had found for him on which to build the most important building of the
55 century.

He says now, with affectionate laughter, 'What is it? A dirty river and a bunch of run-down buildings.' Yet he revelled in the chaos and dirt of the post-industrial environment, and was determined
60 not to change anything about the waterfront site.

The Bilbao Guggenheim dominates the city at every turn. It is a contemporary art museum like no other, and a building that must rank as one of the eight wonders of the modern world. It's well worth
65 a visit – and there are some interesting works of art inside too.

Glossary
cement verb [T]: make stronger
eager adj: very keen or enthusiastic
warehouse noun [C]: big building for storing things
non-starter noun [C]: idea with no chance of succeeding
curve noun [C]: smooth bend
revel in sth phrasal vb [T]: enjoy very much

Listening & Vocabulary

1   **Work with a partner. Look at the photo, picture and map showing Stonehenge and guess the correct answers (*a*, *b* or *c*) to the questions (1–6).**

1   How long has Stonehenge been standing?
    a) 5,000 years.   b) 50,000 years.   c) 5,500 years.
2   How many stones were there originally?
    a) Over 60.   b) Over 116.   c) Over 160.
3   What makes the bluestones turn blue?
    a) The sun.   b) The rain.   c) The cold.
4   How were the Sarsen stones transported?
    a) They were carried.   b) They were pushed.   c) They were dragged.
5   How far were the bluestones transported?
    a) 20 miles.   b) 250 miles.   c) 215 miles.
6   Why was Stonehenge built?
    a) It's a mystery.   b) It's a secret.   c) It's a work of art.

3.01 **Listen to an architect and an archaeologist talking about Stonehenge in a radio documentary. Check your ideas and underline the correct answers.**

2   **Find two synonyms in the box for each underlined word or phrase in sentences (*a–e*). Use your dictionary if necessary.**

alluring	draw (noun)	drizzling	enchanting	endures	enigmatic
incentive	intriguing	just	a mere	spitting	survives

a)   '… The sky is overcast and it's <u>raining lightly</u>.'
b)   '… it's been standing there for 5,000 years – and it <u>continues to exist</u>.'
c)   '… it remains such a <u>mysterious</u> and <u>captivating</u> place.'
d)   '… the inner circle is made up of bluestones and they weigh <u>only</u> four tonnes each.'
e)   '… Something was such an important <u>attraction</u> that they had to bring all these materials to here.'

Listen again and tick the word from the box that was actually used in the documentary.

What is the oldest building that you have ever visited? Tell your partner about it.

Grammar

Past modals of deduction

It **must have taken** ages.
They **may/might/could have** used slaves.
It **can't have been** easy.

1   3.02 **Listen to five visitors answering the question, 'What do you think Stonehenge was built for?' Underline whether they are 'almost certain' or 'uncertain' about the theories (a–e) they suggest.**

     a)   It was a kind of temple, a religious place.   **almost certain / uncertain**
     b)   It wasn't only a calendar.   **almost certain / uncertain**
     c)   It was a place where important ceremonies took place.   **almost certain / uncertain**
     d)   It was a landing site for spacecraft from other planets.   **almost certain / uncertain**
     e)   It was a healing place.   **almost certain / uncertain**

Use *can't, could, may, might* or *must* to rewrite the sentences (1–3).

     1)   I'm almost certain it happened. → It _____
     2)   I'm almost certain it didn't happen. → It _____
     3)   I'm uncertain whether it happened or not. → It _____ / It _____ / It _____

2   **Complete the second sentence so that it has a similar meaning to the first sentence. Use between two and five words, including the word given in bold.**

     a)   It's possible that the stones for Stonehenge were moved by a system of levers.
        might
        The stones for Stonehenge _____ by a system of levers.

     b)   It is almost certain that the material to build the Sphinx of Giza was transported down the Nile.
        must
        The material to build the Sphinx of Giza _____ down the Nile.

     c)   The construction of the Great Pyramid of Giza probably involved up to 50,000 workers.
        could
        The construction of the Great Pyramid of Giza _____ up to 50,000 workers.

     d)   Perhaps the Nazca Lines in Peru were a map of underground water supplies.
        may
        The Nazca Lines in Peru _____ a map of underground water supplies.

     e)   The Easter Island statues obviously didn't come from outer space.
        can't
        The Easter Island statues _____ from outer space.

     f)   Machu Picchu was almost definitely built as a fortress against powerful enemies.
        been
        Machu Picchu _____ as a fortress against powerful enemies.

What other theories do you know about the origin of these (or other) ancient ruins? Which do you think are the most / least likely? Tell a partner.

3   Grammar *Extra* 9, Part 1 page 140. Read the explanations and do Exercise 1.

Speaking: anecdote

You are going to tell your partner about your favourite historic place (building, monument or ruin).

*   Ask yourself the questions below.
*   Think about *what* to say and *how* to say it.
*   Tell your partner about the place.

     a)   What kind of place is it and what is it called?
     b)   Where is it located?
     c)   What does it look like?
     d)   What are the surroundings like?
     e)   How old is it?
     f)   What is it used for now?
     g)   When did you first see it?
     h)   What do you like most about it?

Grammar & Listening

1 Work with a partner. Look at the three paintings by Frida Kahlo and discuss what you think the story might be behind each painting.

🌐 3.03 Listen to a museum guide's descriptions and compare your ideas.

▲ Frida and Diego Rivera, 1931   ▲ Self-portrait with Cropped Hair, 1940

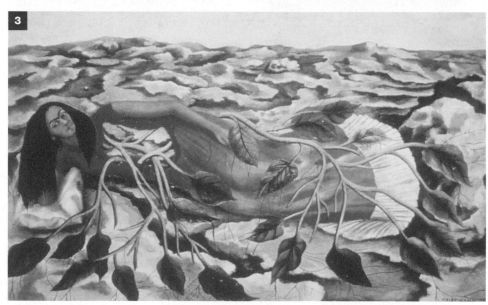

▲ Roots, 1943

look, seem, appear

look/seem + adjective
look like + noun
look/seem as if/though
+ verb phrase
seem/appear + *to be*

2 Match the sentence beginnings with the sentence endings from the museum guide's decriptions. Then match each sentence to a painting (*1–3*).

a) She looks like   quite comfortable.
b) She looks   if she's floating next to her husband.
c) She looks as   a man.

3 Listen again and read the recording script on page 152. Find sentences that include examples of the different verb structures for *look*, *seem* and *appear*.

4 **Grammar *Extra* 9, Part 2** page 140. Read the explanations and do Exercise 2.

5 What is your memory like? Look at the three paintings again for thirty seconds. Then go to the Additional material on page 128 and answer as many questions as you can.

Reading & Vocabulary

1 Read the following summary of Frida Kahlo's life. With a partner, discuss any aspects of her life that you can see depicted in the three paintings on page 92.

Frida Kahlo

FRIDA KAHLO was born in Coyoacán, Mexico in 1907. However, she claimed her birth date as 1910, the year of the Mexican Revolution, saying that she and modern Mexico had been born together.

5　When she was six she contracted polio and spent nine months confined to her room. As a result, her right leg was very thin and made her walk in a strange way. When she returned to school, the children teased her. From then on, she always concealed her right leg.

10　When she was eighteen, she was seriously injured in an accident between a streetcar and a bus: a metal handrail pierced her body. Over the years she underwent thirty-two major operations and suffered enormous pain for the rest of her life.

15　It was while she was convalescing from the streetcar accident that she took up painting.

She married a famous muralist, Diego Rivera, when she was twenty-two. He was forty-two and had been married twice before. She told a journalist, 'When I was seventeen
20　(subtracting three years from her age) Diego began to fall in love with me. My father didn't like him because he was a Communist and because they said it was like an elephant marrying a dove.'

Soon after she met Rivera, Kahlo began to dress in
25　traditional Mexican clothes. In particular, she chose the regional costumes of the Tehuana women of southern Mexico. The full skirts, shawls, braided hairstyles, and heavy jewellery that she adopted were worn partly to please Rivera, and partly to conceal her thin leg and
30　scars from her terrible accident. Yet it was also a political statement in support of her Mexican heritage.

Frida and Diego had a stormy relationship. Her husband was often unfaithful and even had an affair with Cristina, Frida's younger sister. Frida also had extramarital affairs,
35　including one with Leon Trotsky when the Russian revolutionary was exiled from the Soviet Union.

In January 1939 she travelled to Paris where she met Picasso. The Louvre purchased one of her self-portraits.

In April, on her return to Mexico, Frida and Diego
40　began divorce proceedings. Frida was devastated and for a while stopped wearing the traditional Mexican dresses that Diego loved so much. Ironically, she painted some of her most powerful works during her separation from Diego. The couple remarried in December 1940.

45　Frida was never able to have children. She said, 'My painting carries within it the message of pain.' And when asked why she painted herself so often,
50　she replied 'Because I am so often alone.' She died in
55　July 1954, barely two weeks after taking part in a Communist demonstration.

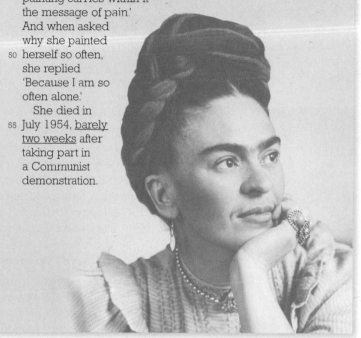

2 Look at some possible alternatives to the time expressions underlined in the text. In each case one is correct and has a similar meaning to the original. The other one is incorrect – cross it out.

a) At the age of six / ~~With six years~~ (line 5)
b) After that / At that moment (lines 8–9)
c) During the years / During her life (line 12)
d) during her convalescence / throughout her convalescence (line 15)
e) earlier / previously (line 19)
f) as soon as she returned / by her return (line 39)
g) while she was separating / while she was separated (line 43)
h) just two weeks / during two weeks (line 55–56)

3 Think about a famous person you know something about (an artist, a musician, a politician …). You are going to write a few lines about their life.

- Do not reveal their identity. Use *he* or *she*.
- Use at least three of the time expressions from Exercise 2.
- Read your partner's sentences and guess who they are describing.

Speaking & Listening

1 Work in groups. Look at the photos of six products (*a–f*) that have been invented over the last five hundred years. Discuss in what order you think they were invented and guess a date for each one.

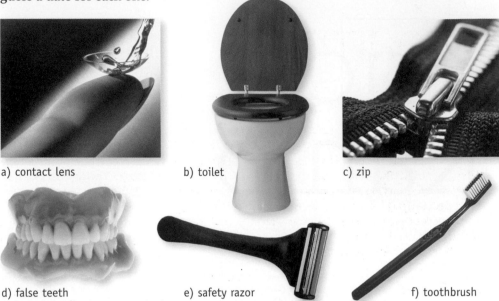

a) contact lens   b) toilet   c) zip

d) false teeth   e) safety razor   f) toothbrush

Go to page 129 to check your answers. Now discuss the questions.

- Which of the above inventions is the most/least important for society?
- Which of the above inventions could you / couldn't you live without?
- What do you consider to be the three most important inventions of all time?

2 🌐 3.04 Listen to an interview with Trevor Baylis about his invention, the clockwork radio. Put the questions in the order in which they are asked.

a) How many radios are produced each month?
b) How easy was it to find a backer and set up production?
c) What advice would you give to someone who had a good idea?
d) What gave you the idea for the clockwork radio?
e) How long did it take you to design a prototype?
f) How long was it then before the production of the radios started?

3 Match Trevor Baylis's responses (*1–6*) to the questions (*a–f*) in Exercise 2.

1 '… Don't go down the pub and tell everyone about it.'
2 '… it would have taken me two to three months, I guess …'
3 '… I'm sure they must be doing 200,000 a month.'
4 '… I was actually watching a programme about the spread of AIDS in Africa …'
5 '… Well, the important thing was funding.'
6 '… I was given a chance through the BBC World Service to meet up with the guys from the BBC *Tomorrow's World* programme …'

Listen again and check your answers.

Vocabulary

1 Look at the collocations from the Trevor Baylis interview. Underline the verb in brackets which best collocates with the noun to give a similar meaning. Use your dictionary if necessary.

a) form a company (set up / do)
b) do some experiments (make / carry out)
c) have an idea (find / come up with)
d) file for a patent (apply for / look for)
e) start production (begin / make)
f) design a prototype (develop / do)
g) do a search (conduct / make)

2 Work with a partner. Arrange the 'stages of production' in Exercise 1 in the most logical order.

TREVOR BAYLIS'S passion is inventing – especially products that might help people with physical disabilities. In 1993 he invented the clockwork radio.

Reading

1 Work with a partner. What do you remember about the story of Trevor Baylis and the clockwork radio? Complete the summary with appropriate words.

Dream invention

One evening in 1993, Trevor Baylis was watching a programme on television about the AIDS (1) *epidemic* in Africa. The programme explained that the only way to stop the (2) s_____ of AIDS was to educate people about the disease.
5 However, broadcasting the information was extremely difficult. Most people didn't have a radio, as there was no (3) e_____ , and batteries were too expensive. At this point Trevor Baylis dozed off and had a (4) d_____ . When he woke up, he had dreamt up the concept of the clockwork radio.

10 It took him just two to three months to develop a (5) p_____ and decide that his idea could really work. He filed for a (6) p_____ , and then the problems began. He wanted to find a backer for his idea, but every British company he contacted turned him down. However, his unexpected TV appearance
15 on the BBC programme, *Tomorrow's World*, changed everything. Trevor Baylis was approached by a South African businessman, and soon money was found to (7) s_____ up a company with a factory based in Cape Town. The company was called Baygen, which stands for Baylis Generators. Today
20 200,000 radios are made in Africa each month, with demand outstripping supply.

According to Trevor Baylis, you do not need to be a genius to be an inventor. His advice to anybody who has a good idea – keep the idea to (8) y_____ until you've filed a patent, and
25 never give up.

2 What do you think of the clockwork radio? Which electrical appliance would you miss most if you lived in an area of the world where there was no electricity?

Vocabulary & Pronunciation

1 Complete the table with word families and underline the stressed syllable in each word. Use a dictionary if necessary. Practise saying the words.

Noun (subject)	Noun (person)	Adjective + example collocations	
a) bi<u>o</u>logy			weapons
b)	<u>che</u>mist		reactions / weapons
c)		eco<u>no</u>mic	growth / research
d) ge<u>ne</u>tics			engineering
e)	mathema<u>ti</u>cian		equations / research
f) <u>sci</u>ence			advances / research
g)	tech<u>no</u>logist		advances / research

🔘 3.05 Listen and repeat the words in the table.

2 Complete these sentences taken from newspaper reports. Use appropriate adjective-noun collocations from the table in Exercise 1.

He was working on a series of (1) _____ and the page was crammed with numbers written in his tiny handwriting.

The latest (2) _____ suggests that seaweed-based treatments could cure all manner of medical conditions.

Scientists have used (3) _____ to protect tomatoes against the effects of freezing.

(4) _____ is projected at only 2% in the coming year.

UN inspections of other weapons of mass destruction – such as (5) _____ – will continue as planned.

(6) _____ over the past decade have drastically reduced the prices of computers and other electronic products.

The British Antarctic Survey said (7) _____ that cause ozone destruction had increased since last year's eruption of Mount Pinatub.

3 Use your dictionary. Find at least one more noun collocate for each adjective in the table in Exercise 1. Choose five new collocations to learn and write an example sentence for each one.

Useful phrases

1 🌐 **3.06** **Listen to a conversation between two friends. Brigit is going to stay at Alice's house while Alice is away. Match each object (*a–f*) with its function (*1–6*).**

a)	a small key	1	for switching the television on and off
b)	a dial	2	for turning the coffee machine on
c)	a silver remote control	3	for opening the front door
d)	a black remote control	4	for turning the cooker fan on
e)	a red button	5	for changing channels
f)	a switch	6	for controlling the thermostat

What surprise does Brigit get at the end of the conversation?

▲ Alice   ▲ Brigit

2 **Complete the useful phrases from the conversation by adding the word *it* in the correct position in each sentence.**

a) You need to turn twice anti-clockwise. *You need to turn **it** twice anti-clockwise.*
b) You turn until it clicks.
c) Make sure you turn down again.
d) You use the silver remote control to switch on and off.
e) Press the red button above the cooker to turn on.
f) Plug in at the wall.
g) Put water into the thing above.

What does *it* refer to in each case?

Listen again and check.

3 **Read Alice's description of how to use the coffee machine. Compare her spoken instructions with the written instructions. Underline the written (or formal) equivalents of the highlighted words and phrases.**

Spoken instructions	Written instructions
You put a filter into the filter holder and put the coffee into the filter. Put water into the thing above it, and make sure the lid's on tight. Then put a cup under the place where the coffee comes out. The machine will warm the water up to the right temperature, so you just have to wait a few seconds. When the cup's full, take it off and your coffee's ready.	Insert a filter into the filter holder. Place the coffee in the filter. Pour water into the water tank. Ensure that the lid is secure. Place a cup under the spout. The machine will heat the water to the correct temperature. When the cup is full, remove it immediately and your coffee is ready to drink.

4 **Think about a machine or a gadget in your house. Explain how to use it to your partner using spoken instructions.**

Writing *Extra*

Narrative

1 Read about the invention of the 3M® Post-it note. Complete the text with time expressions from the box.

> a few months previously
> Each Sunday
> In 1977
> One Sunday
> The following day

(1) _____ , Art Fry was a product designer with the huge 3M Corporation in the USA. (2) _____ , as a member of his local church choir, he would check which hymns he was to sing during the service, and mark them with bits of paper in his hymn book. Inevitably, just as a hymn was about to start, the paper would drop out, and Fry would have a frantic search for the right page. (3) _____ he was listening to the sermon when his mind began to wander. He remembered that (4) _____ , a research colleague had made a glue which had been discarded when it proved to have poor sticking power. (5) _____ he managed to obtain some of this failed glue and started making his bookmarks with it. Post-its are now a billion-dollar business.

2 Read about the invention of the microwave oven. Underline the most appropriate verb structures to complete the description.

In 1946, Dr Percy LeBaron Spencer (1) **worked** / **was working** on a radar-based research project when he (2) **felt** / **was feeling** something sticky in his pocket. It turned out to be a melted peanut bar. Spencer guessed that it (3) **had been affected** / **was affected** by high frequency radio emissions from the magnetron – a key component in radar. He (4) **heard** / **had heard** stories of partially cooked birds being found at the base of early radar installations but had, until now, dismissed them. Intrigued, he sent a boy out to buy a packet of popcorn. When he placed it close to the magnetron, the popcorn exploded. By the end of that year, the first prototype microwave oven (5) **was installed** / **had been installed** in a Boston restaurant.

3 You are going to write the story of another clever innovation, the social-networking site Facebook. Complete the sentences below by expanding the notes provided. Pay particular attention to tenses.

Mark Zuckerberg founded Facebook while studying psychology at Harvard University.
He had already developed ... including ...
In February 2004, …
Within 24 hours, ... and after one month …
The site became 'Facebook' in August 2005 when …
Previously, the site was only available to university students, but since September 2006 …
In 2007, rumours that Prince William …
In 2008, four years after three Harvard classmates …
Today, Zuckerberg is one of the youngest billionaires in the world.

Notes – the story of Facebook

- Mark Zuckerberg - founder of Facebook.
- Studied psychology at Harvard University.
- Developed a number of social-networking sites for fellow students.
- eg Facemash - a site for rating people's attractiveness.
- February 2004 - launched 'The Facebook'.
- In one day, 1,200 students signed up.
- Half the student population of Harvard set up profiles in the first month.
- August 2005 - Zuckerberg purchased the name 'facebook.com' for $200,000.
- September 2006 - Facebook became available to anyone over thirteen.
- 2007 Prince William - said to have signed up, but not true.
- Three of Zuckerberg's classmates accused him of stealing the idea for Facebook. Four years later, Zuckerberg settled out of court.
- Zuckerberg now one of the youngest billionaires in the world.

▲ Mark Zuckerberg

Review C

▶ Grammar *Extra* pages 138–141

Grammar

1 Underline the correct alternative.

Kate: Excuse me. Could you give me some information? Your airline just (1) **announced us** / **announced** that all your flights are cancelled today.

Airl: I'm afraid that's true, but I can (2) **assure you** / **assure** that we will find you another flight as soon as possible.

Kate: So can you (3) **confirm me** / **confirm** that we will fly today?

Airl: I must (4) **admit you** / **admit** I can't make any promises. However, I will (5) **inform you** / **inform** as soon as we have any further information.

Kate: Well could you at least (6) **explain us** / **explain** why this has happened?

Airl: I'm sorry. I (7) **suggest you** / **suggest** that you take a seat and wait for our next announcement, which is due soon.

2 Complete the text with the words in the box.

allowed	didn't	had	need	ought	should

Recently I travelled from London to Paris on business. I didn't (1) _____ to fly but foolishly I did! First, I (2) _____ to take off most of my clothes at security. Then I wasn't (3) _____ to use my phone during the flight. After an uncomfortable two hours, it took another hour to get out of the airport, only to learn my meeting had been cancelled. I know I (4) _____ have to fly back the same day. I know I (5) _____ to have stayed the night to see more of beautiful Paris but I just wanted to go home! Unfortunately, the return journey was even worse. I (6) _____ have taken the train! It would have been quicker and easier.

3 Complete the sentences with *a/an* or *the*, or leave blank where an article is not necessary.

a) I wish I had _____ curly hair.
b) I've never owned _____ expensive car.
c) I'd love to spend a week cruising on _____ Nile.
d) I've been to _____ New York a few times.
e) I'd really love to take _____ holiday in the Caribbean.
f) I've been to the top of _____ Eiffel Tower.
g) I wouldn't climb _____ Mount Everest, even for money.

Which statements are true for you?

4 Complete each sentence so that it means the same as the one above it.

a) We expect that the rate of inflation will rise sharply.
   The rate of inflation …
b) People think the Prime Minister will resign soon.
   It …
c) Scientists say that the world's climate will become more extreme.
   It …
d) They think vast oil reserves exist under the Arctic ice cap.
   Vast oil reserves …
e) People used to think that the Earth was the centre of the universe.
   It used to …
f) Some people say that the Mafia were involved in the assassination of JFK.
   It …

5 Write the questions in the correct order.

a) won / you / £10 million, / If / all / keep / you / it / would / ?
b) could / someone famous, / Supposing / be / it / who / you / be / would / ?
c) what / able to do / you / dream job, / do / would / you / Imagine / your / were / ?
d) would / time / like / new skill / no object / to learn / were / you / what / Assuming / ?

Answer the questions and compare with a partner.

6 Write sentences for each of the situations using *might have*, *must have* or *can't have*.

a) Amy isn't here yet and it's 9.30.
b) Will's got a terrible hangover this morning.
c) Daniela didn't answer her doorbell.
d) Kenji's arm is in plaster.
e) Paula keeps yawning.
f) Sam looks particularly happy today.

7 Complete the statements with the words in the box. Change the form if necessary.

as if	~~look~~	look like	seem	though	to be

a) My best friend always *looks* worried.
b) My mother _____ a model when she was young.
c) I never feel as _____ I have enough time.
d) When I was young my father always _____ to be busy.
e) It looks _____ tomorrow is going to be sunny.
f) My teacher never seems _____ happy with my homework.

Which sentences are true for you? Discuss with your partner.

Vocabulary

1 Add suffixes *ful*, *ish* or *less* to make adjectives.

a) bull_____ d) fool_____ g) self_____
b) cheer_____ e) home_____ h) stress_____
c) end_____ f) relent_____ i) tear_____

2 Put each adjective in the box into the correct column.

> adequate adventurous appropriate capable
> decisive divided honest legal legible
> literate logical loyal mature moral
> obedient patient polite rational relevant
> resistible responsible satisfied usual willing

dis-	il-	im-
____	____	____
____	____	____
____	____	____
____	____	____

in-	ir-	un-
____	____	____
____	____	____
____	____	____

3 Complete the text with facial features.

It is believed that to qualify as 'beautiful' you have to have a big (1) m_____ , full (2) l_____ and high (3) c_____ . Other desirable qualities are smooth (4) s_____ , white (5) t_____ , big, sparkling (6) e_____ and (7) d_____ in the cheeks. Surprisingly, women appear to prefer a softer face on a man than the classic 'square (8) j_____ ' look.

Discuss with your partner which features you think make a person attractive.

4 Match each adjective (*a–k*) to its synonym (*1–11*).

a) down-to-earth 1 unfriendly
b) enigmatic 2 unpretentious
c) laid-back 3 selfish
d) mature 4 caring
e) open-minded 5 mysterious
f) self-centred 6 conventional
g) sensible 7 level-headed
h) sensitive 8 relaxed
i) stand-offish 9 dependable
j) straight 10 experienced / grown-up
k) trustworthy 11 tolerant

Choose three adjectives to describe yourself. Compare with your partner.

5 Complete the adjectives.

a) c_nt_mp_r_ry e) p_st-m_d_rn
b) _cc_ntr_c f) r_n-d_wn
c) h_d_ _ _s g) s_m_-d_r_l_ct
d) m_t_ll_c h) spr_wl_ng

6 Complete the text with the words in the box.

> After As Barely During Soon When
> While

Audrey Hepburn was born in Belgium in 1929. (1) _____ she was ten, war broke out. (2) _____ the war, she lived with her mother in the Netherlands. (3) _____ the war she went to London and started acting. (4) _____ she was filming in France, she met the novelist Colette, who insisted she play the role Gigi in her Broadway play. (5) _____ after she finished on Broadway she starred in her first film, *Roman Holiday*, with Gregory Peck. (6) _____ soon as the film came out she was nominated for (and later won) an Oscar. She went on to enjoy a distinguished career. (7) _____ four months after being diagnosed with colon cancer, in 1992, Audrey Hepburn was dead. She was only sixty-three.

Pronunciation

1 Look at some words from Units 7–9. Say the words and add them to the table.

> ~~attractive~~ company cosmetics drizzle
> encourage genius genuine lively
> meander physics traveller urban

A: ☑☐	B: ☐☑☐	C: ☑☐☐
	attractive	

2 Underline the stressed syllable.

🔊 **3.07** Listen, check and repeat.

▶ 🔊 3.08 **Song**

10 Sell

Grammar Relative clauses. Emphasis (cleft sentences)
Vocabulary *look at* and *see*. Sales & Marketing collocations. Spoken discourse markers
Useful phrases Using emotive language

Reading & Vocabulary

1 Work with a partner. Look at 'Know Your Logos!'. Identify the brand in each case and circle the correct version of each logo. Check your answers on page 129.

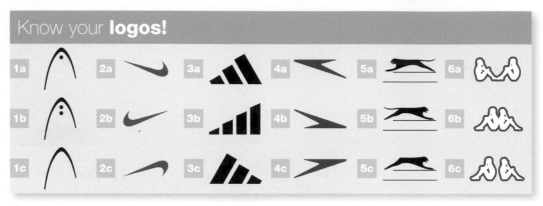

Know your **logos!**

2 Discuss the questions.
a) Which of these brands are popular in your country?
b) How many more logos can you draw? See if your partner can identify them.

3 Read the book extract from *Bonfire of the Brands* by Neil Boorman on page 101. Which three objects started the author's obsession with designer labels?

In what ways were you the same as or different from Neil Boorman when you were at junior school? Tell your partner.

4 Look at these different ways of saying *look at* and *see*. Complete the tables with four more examples of verb phrases from the book extract on page 101. Use the infinitive form. Discuss the differences in meaning with your partner.

| look at | = | gaze at | stare at | g_____ _____ | e_____ _____ |

| see | = | spot | make out | n_____ | c_____ _____ _____ |

5 Underline the appropriate verb phrases to complete this description.

I'm addicted to designer labels! I spend hours (1) **glancing at / gazing at** photos in fashion magazines, and I can't walk past a designer shop without (2) **eyeing up / spotting** the handbags and shoes in the window. I can't stand fake designer goods – in fact, if you show me two handbags, one a designer and one a fake, I can usually (3) **spot / catch sight of** the fake without even picking it up. I think about my clothes a lot, and I like to look perfect. I always (4) **stare at / glance at** my reflection in shop windows as I go past. Most of my friends wear casual clothes, so when I go out people (5) **stare at / gaze at** me because I look different. But I don't care. I like to be (6) **noticed / made out** and I know that as soon as they (7) **stare at / catch sight of** my designer mobile phone, they'll be jealous.

How would you describe your own attitude towards brands and designer labels? Tell your partner.

Bonfire of the BRANDS

JOURNALIST, Neil Boorman, was obsessed with designer brands but realised that the more he spent on expensive branded goods, the more miserable he became. So he decided to burn all
5 his branded possessions and live a brand-free life for a year. He then wrote a book, *Bonfire of the Brands*, about his experience. The following is an extract from his book.

If you and I met at a party, you would
10 probably ask me what I do for a living, what town I live in, perhaps the school I went to – the kind of questions that would help you to build a picture of who I am. I might ask the same of you, but probably I wouldn't be listening. It's more
15 likely I'd be looking at the label on your jeans, glancing at your shoes, eyeing up your mobile phone. These are the things that really tell me who you are. And considering the amount of time and money I spend on choosing the clothes I
20 wear and the objects I carry, I sincerely hope you would notice the same things about me. Well, that's the way it was a year ago.

I began to behave like this at a very early age. I remember the first day of junior school, standing
25 alone in the playground, desperately wanting to make friends. I headed straight for what seemed
30 to be the most promising group of boys. They were talking to girls, trading football cards, eating luminous green sweets – all the things I wanted to do. As I attempted to mingle, one boy asked me, 'Do you support Tottenham Hotspur?' Another, 'Do you have any Scalextric?' A third, 'Are you into Michael Jackson?' I answered *yes* to them all, even though the truthful answer was *no*.

35 Things seemed to be going well until one of the boys caught sight of my trainers. I'd never thought too much about them before. They were just plain blue sports shoes that Mum had bought, for playing in the back garden. At once, a roar of
40 disapproval broke out among the group. 'Where did you get those from? Oxfam?'

Looking at the boys in bewilderment, I noticed for the first time that they all had similar shapes on the sides of their trainers-ticks and stripes,
45 like the ones on footballers' boots on television. It wasn't just their shoes: crocodiles, eagles and tigers sat on the breasts of their T-shirts, and every single boy seemed to have the same school bag, a blue plastic holdall with a leaping puma
50 in silver on the side. I slunk away, dejected and confused. From that day on, I resolved to be like them, if not more so.

Glossary
luminous adj: very bright
mingle verb [I]: mix with / talk to other people
roar noun [C]: the noise that a crowd makes
Oxfam noun [U]: a charity that raises money to fight poverty
bewilderment noun [U]: confusion
slink away verb [I]: leave quietly so that no one notices you
resolve verb [I]: decide

▲ Joe Smedley, marketing executive

▲ Sally McIlveen, headteacher

Listening & Vocabulary

1 **You are going to listen to these two people giving their opinions about children and advertising. Guess which person is likely to have made each statement (a–f).**

a) '… children are being brainwashed by all the advertising that goes on around them.'

b) 'Brands give children a sense of identity and help them fit in with a peer group.'

c) '… it's time the government put a stop to all this aggressive television advertising.'

d) 'Companies donate free computers and in exchange they can advertise their brands on book covers and posters. I think it's fantastic – the kids benefit and the companies get brand loyalty from a very early age.'

e) 'I'd love to be a child today. They really know what they want …'

f) 'I don't think all this choice is liberating for children – it just means that they're encouraged to be materialistic …'

🌐 3.09–3.10 **Listen and check your answers. Work with a partner. Do you agree or disagree with the statements?**

2 **Work with your partner. Student A look at page 129, Student B look at page 131.**

Reading & Vocabulary

1   Look at the photo on page 103 taken from a classic TV advert. Discuss possible answers to these questions.

   a)   What was the commercial advertising?
   b)   In which country and in what decade was the action set?

   Read the first paragraph of *Commercial breakdown* and check your answers. Then read the rest of the article and match each paragraph (*A–E*) with the appropriate part of the photo (*1–5*).

2   Work with a partner. Without looking back at the article, try to remember the significance of the names and numbers in the box.

501	1985	Marlon Brando	1950s	Elvis Presley	Marvin Gaye
1968	Barbara Nokes	Nick Kamen	Madonna		

   Check your ideas in the article.

3   Look at the words and phrases highlighted in the article. Discuss their possible meaning with your partner. Then complete the glossary at the bottom of the article.

4   Work in groups. Go to the Additional material on page 129.

Grammar

Relative clauses

1   I bought a new coat, **which is unusual for me.**
2   I bought the coat **that you suggested.**
3   The coat, **which cost me a fortune**, is really stylish.

1   Look at the sentences that begin on lines 19, 35 and 59 in the article on page 103. Underline the relative clauses in each sentence. Then choose the description that best defines the function of each relative clause.

   1   It comments on the whole of the main clause (*non-defining*).
   2   It identifies something in the main clause (*defining*).
   3   It gives extra information about something in the main clause (*non-defining*).

   What punctuation is used to show that a relative clause is non-defining?

2   Work with your partner. Look at the sentence pairs (*a–h*). Decide which is the most suitable follow-up (*1* or *2*) for each sentence.

Main sentence	Follow-up sentence
a) She offered me some cigarettes that were very strange. b) She offered me some cigarettes, which was very strange.	1 They were red and blue. 2 She knows I don't smoke.
c) He's going out with Julie, who I can't stand. d) He's going out with Julie, which I can't stand.	1 He should be going out with me! 2 She's such a gossip.
e) She bought me an expensive tie that I didn't like. f) She bought me an expensive tie, which I didn't like.	1 Why waste money on ties? 2 It was a horrible orange colour.
g) My brother who lives in Rome is a model. h) My brother, who lives in Rome, is a model.	1 My other brother is an accountant. 2 He absolutely loves his job.

3   Look again at the main sentences in Exercise 2 and the type of relative clauses in Exercise 1. Answer the questions.

   a)   What type of relative clause does each main sentence contain: 1, 2 or 3?
   b)   Which relative pronoun (*who, which* and *that*) cannot be used with non-defining relative clauses?
   c)   Which relative pronoun is always used to introduce a comment on the whole main clause?

4   **Grammar *Extra* 10, Part 1** page 140. Read the explanations and do Exercises 1 and 2.

A GOOD-LOOKING young man walks into a small-town American launderette. He strips off and waits for his jeans to wash. Not much of
5 a storyline, but this remains one of the most popular TV adverts that has ever been made. Made to promote Levis 501s, the ad was a massive success the minute it
10 hit British TV screens in 1985. It epitomises everything that was, and perhaps still is, cool. Set in 1950s America, with its associations with Marlon Brando
15 and Elvis Presley (both of whom had been photographed wearing Levis), the advert was making a clear statement: this is genuine, original, authentic. It represented

COMMERCIAL **BREAKDOWN**

20 youthful rebellion, radical chic and sex appeal, which was perfect for Levis' intended positioning of their brand in the market. Interestingly, although the commercial
25 conjures up an authentic American scene, it was in fact made by a British creative designer for a British advertising agency with British actors.

30 **A** Even though we can't see her face, it's clear that the woman with the washing basket is more than a little interested in the scene that is taking place in front of her. But
35 what is she looking at? Her eyes are directed at the jeans that are hanging out of the machine. She wants them, not him. And she's fussy – it's not any old pair of
40 jeans, but a pair of 501s.

B The old washing machines are the biggest clue to 1950s America. Every period in history likes to look

back nostalgically to a mythical
45 past when life was simpler and less complicated. And the 1950s, with the birth of rock and roll, have always had a special place in the history of what is cool. But
50 for cool music, turn to the 1960s. The soundtrack, Marvin Gaye's *I Heard It Through the Grapevine*, was released in 1968. A haunting soul classic, it's the story of a man who
55 learns that his girlfriend is seeing someone else. A man, perhaps, who goes to the launderette now that his girlfriend has left him?

C Unlike the majority of adverts,
60 this ad was created by a woman, Barbara Nokes, who was creative director of the London-based agency, Bartle Bogle Hegarty. In the fiercely male-dominated
65 world of advertising, this advert established new ground by making a man into an object of sexual

desire. It was perhaps the first time that we had seen a man take his
70 clothes off on screen. However, this 'revolution' seems to have had little lasting effect.

D Do you recognise the face? Is it James Dean? A young Elvis?
75 Actually, the actor was Nick Kamen, who went on to become a successful pop star with a hit that was written by Madonna. He had a 1950s face and was considered such
80 a heart-throb that even now there are websites devoted to him.

E Completely uninterested in the scene taking place in front of his eyes, the old man is the antithesis
85 of everything the ad stands for. This is all about the young rebel – the rugged individual who couldn't care less about conventions. The presence of an old guy in a
90 straw hat lets us know exactly who the commercial is aimed at.

Glossary

a) _____ phrasal vb [T]: make you think of
b) _____ phrase: not be at all interested in
c) _____ verb [T]: be a typical example of
d) _____ adv: extremely
e) _____ adj: very concerned about details

f) _____ adj: sad but beautiful
g) _____ noun [C]: *informal* a very attractive man
h) _____ adv: remembering the past in a happy way
i) _____ adj: strong or tough
j) _____ phrasal vb [I]: *spoken* take off all your clothes

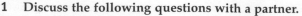

Listening & Speaking

1 Discuss the following questions with a partner.
- Who are the most photographed celebrities in your country?
- Which magazines devote themselves to celebrity news and gossip?
- What do you think are the pros and cons of being constantly in the public eye?

2 🔘 3.11 Listen to a radio programme discussing truth and accuracy in tabloid newspapers. Who do you sympathise with most: the celebrity or the editor?

Work with your partner. Use the words in the box to explain why the actress is unhappy.

co-star	bath	hotel room	good friend	champagne	divorce

▲ Shelley Russell

3 Read the sentences below taken from the interview. Who said each sentence: the presenter (P), the celebrity (C) or the tabloid editor (TE)?
a) The tabloid press have been criticised yet again, this time for their apparent lack of respect for truth and accuracy.
b) … before you were famous, you were urging us to write articles about you.
c) Take last week – your paper wrote this story about me and my co-star, who, by the way, happens to be married to a very good friend of mine.
d) I am sick of the tabloid press making up stories just so that they can put sensational headlines across the front page.
e) I think we need to address the cause of the problem.
f) If a newspaper prints something shocking or embarrassing about a famous person, they'll almost certainly deny it.

▲ Jim Falmer

Replace the highlighted words with the words that were actually used in the interview. Choose from the words in the box. Listen again and check your answers.

begging	're bound to	disregard	features	gutter
incidentally	root	scandalous	splash	under fire

4 Use the words in the box to complete the phrases used by the speakers in the radio discussion in Exercise 1.

but	but	finish	here	is	is	is	on	question	saying	was

a) Sorry, _____ …
b) If you would just let me _____ …
c) But the thing _____ …
d) Hang _____ , …
e) Anyway, to get back to what I was _____ …
f) The point I'm trying to make here _____ …
g) What you didn't say _____ …
h) If I could just come in _____ …
i) If you would let me answer the _____ …
j) The problem _____ …
k) I'm sorry to interrupt you, _____ …

Look at the recording script on page 154 and check your answers.

5 Use the following table to categorise the phrases according to their function.

Interrupting	Responding to an interruption	Introducing a point
Sorry, but …	*If you would just let me finish …*	*But the thing is …*

6 Work in small groups. Think of points for and against each statement. Discuss the statements and take it in turns to agree or disagree.
a) For celebrities, any publicity is good publicity, the more sensational the better.
b) It is a newspaper editor's job to increase circulation, not to worry about accuracy.
c) The public have a right to read articles about the private lives of famous people.

Grammar

Emphasis (cleft sentences)

I don't understand why I'm always poor.
What / The thing I don't understand is why I'm always poor.
Money doesn't make you happy. Friendship does.
It isn't money that makes you happy, it's friendship.

1 Work with a partner. Sentences *A* and *B* are two ways of saying the same thing. How does the emphasis change in sentence *B*?

A *Yes, but you didn't say what the inaccuracies were ...*
B *Yes, but what you didn't say was what the inaccuracies were ...*

Which sentence did Shelley Russell use in the radio programme on page 104?

2 Change the emphasis of these sentences using the sentence beginnings provided.

a) I don't understand why I never seem to have any money.
   What I don't understand is ...
b) I like weekends because I can go shopping with my friends.
   The thing I like about weekends is ...
c) People who only talk about money really annoy me.
   What really annoys me is ...
d) I really feel like going to the cinema tonight.
   What I really feel like doing tonight is ...
e) I hate winter because it gets dark so early.
   The thing ...
f) I'd really like to live and work abroad in the future.
   What ...

How many of the sentences are true for you?

3 Work with your partner. Which one of the statements about celebrities is true?

a) George Bush was the Republican candidate in the 2008 US Elections.
b) Jude Law replaced Piers Brosnan as James Bond.
c) Kate Moss used to go out with Johnny Depp.
d) John Grisham wrote *The Da Vinci Code*.
e) Brad Pitt plays Captain Jack Sparrow in *Pirates of the Caribbean*.
f) Juliette Binoche is married to Nicolas Sarkozy.

Use the information in the box and correct all the false statements beginning with
It isn't ... / It wasn't ...

| Dan Brown | Carla Bruni | Daniel Craig | Johnny Depp | John McCain |

It wasn't George Bush who was the Republican candidate, it was ...

▲ Juliette Binoche

4 Grammar *Extra* 10, Part 2 page 140. Read the explanations and do Exercises 3 and 4.

Pronunciation

1 Practise saying the following sentences with the appropriate emphasis.
  • Underline the stressed words.
  • Mark with // where there is a slight pause.

a) What I love about Peter is his wicked sense of humour.
   What I <u>love</u> about <u>Peter</u> // is his <u>wicked</u> sense of <u>humour</u>.
b) The thing I can't stand about this country is the weather.
c) What I really hate about my job is having to work at weekends.
d) What I find annoying about politicians is that they never give a straight answer.
e) The thing I find most difficult about English is the spelling.
f) What I would <u>really</u> like to do is to take a year off.

🌐 3.12 **Listen, check and repeat.**

2 Work with your partner. Use the sentence beginnings in Exercise 1 to express your feelings about your family, your friends, your job, etc.

Reading & Vocabulary

1 Work with a partner. You are going to read an article about the role of advertising in James Bond films.

a) Name some of the James Bond films.
b) Name some of the actors who have played James Bond.
c) Name some of the cars, products or brands that have appeared in Bond films.

Read the article on page 107, ignoring the gaps. How many of your ideas are mentioned?

2 Seven sentences have been removed from the article on page 107. Choose from the sentences *A–H* the one which fits each gap (*1–7*). There is one extra sentence which you do not need to use.

A At the time, Arterton commented that Bond Girl 007 embodied the qualities of a Bond girl: it's sexy, empowering and iconic.
B The 60:40 male:female ratio among Bond audiences is also appealing to many advertisers.
C At first Aston Martin made it clear that they would be happy to sell a car to the makers of the film, but that they were not in the lending business.
D But when there is too much product placement clutter, the producer is the loser and, by default, the brand.
E Critics referred to the movie as one long advert – for vodka, watches and cars.
F At the time, this was a record for product placement in a feature film.
G After 40 years of Bond films, winning a place for products has become big business.
H Most people remembered Rolex, the brand Bond wore in previous films, and in the Ian Fleming novels.

3 Work with your partner. Put this summary of the article on page 107 in the correct order.

- [ ] in vast sums of money from product
- [ ] clear that they would only lend a car on
- [1] In the movie business, the Bond franchise is known as a cash
- [ ] privilege. Recently, the producers have cut
- [ ] hit but the producers can also rake
- [ ] condition that they got it back at the end of filming.
- [ ] placement. Those companies willing to strike a
- [ ] back on advertising partners but it's still a far
- [2] cow. Not only is each film a huge box office
- [ ] cry from the 1960s. Back then Aston Martin made it
- [ ] deal might pay several million dollars for the

4 Apart from James Bond, think of three famous fictional movie characters. Which one is your favourite? Tell your partner.

LICENCE TO SELL

HIS NAME IS BOND, James Bond. And he likes his martinis shaken, not stirred. Make that *Smirnoff* vodka martinis. A subtle difference? Not to Smirnoff, whose brand has been associated with Bond movies since Sean Connery first appeared as 007 in *Dr No* in 1962.

5 The Bond franchise has long been known as a cash cow for its producers, not least because of how much it grosses at the box office, but also how much revenue it rakes in from advertisers who want to have their brands strategically placed in the movies. ☐1☐

If there was an Oscar category for best use of advertising in a feature-length film, the award would go to a Bond movie. The franchise is especially popular with advertisers because of the films' appeal to both young and old. ☐2☐

10 Product placement is not subtle in Bond films. In fact, there is so much product placement in the film *Die Another Day* that people in the marketing industry called it 'Buy Another Day'. ☐3☐ Twenty different companies saw their products on the screen, having paid between them $70 million for the privilege. ☐4☐

Then there are the spin-offs. In 2008, the cosmetics company Avon released the first 15 fragrance to be inspired by a Bond girl. Bond Girl 007 is advertised by one of the stars of *Quantum of Solace*, Gemma Arterton. ☐5☐

When brands are associated with a box-office hit, product placement is usually guaranteed to pay off, but there are rare occasions where it doesn't have the desired effect. In *Casino Royale* Bond has a conversation with a fellow MI6 agent about the 20 brand of watch he's wearing. The brand is Omega, as is spelt out in the exchange between the two agents. But a study carried out into the effects of product placement found that only one in five people recalled the Omega brand. ☐6☐

The over-the-top product placement seen in *Die Another Day* is a far cry from the early days, when attracting investors was much more difficult. In 1964, 25 Aston Martin refused to lend a car for *Goldfinger*, the film in which Bond was introduced to his silver birch Aston Martin DB5 for the first time. ☐7☐ After much negotiating they struck a deal: Aston Martin would lend them a prototype car, but only on condition that they returned it at the end of filming.

30 How things have changed.

Glossary

cash cow noun [C]: business that earns a lot of money
gross verb [T]: earn
franchise noun [C]: formal agreement for someone to sell a company's products in a particular place
rake in verb [T] *informal*: earn a lot of money
feature-length adj: of a standard length
product placement noun [U]: use of a company's product in a film as a way of advertising it

spin-off noun [C]: new product based on something that already exists
embody verb [T]: be the best possible example of
pay off phrasal vb [I]: bring you benefit
over-the-top adj *informal*: so extreme that it seems silly
a far cry from phrase *informal*: very different from
strike a deal phrase: make a formal business agreement

Speaking: anecdote

You are going to tell your partner about a blockbuster movie you have seen.

- Ask yourself the questions below.
- Think about *what* to say and *how* to say it.
- Tell your partner about the film.

a) What was the name of the film?
b) Who was in it and who directed it?
c) When and where did you see it?
d) Who did you see it with?
e) What did you know about the film before you saw it?
f) What did you particularly like or dislike about the film?

g) Were there any characters you could identify with?
h) Were there any characters who annoyed you?
i) What was the best/worst part of the film?
j) Would you go and see another film by the same director?

Useful phrases

1 🔊 **3.13** Listen to six people describing how they feel about a film they are just about to see. Which film (*a, b, c* or *d*) is it?

2 Underline the word or phrase each person used to describe their feelings.

1 'A bit / Totally / Extremely nervous, actually.'
2 'Yeah, distinctly / utterly / a little uneasy, I must admit.'
3 'I'm looking forward to being scared / nervous / frightened to death.'
4 'To be scared / afraid / bored stiff – hopefully.'
5 'I feel completely / terribly / quite apprehensive.'
6 'I expect it to be absolutely / quite / very terrifying.'

Listen again and check.

Look at the two other options in the useful phrases above. Cross out the option that doesn't form a common collocation and tick the option that does. Use your dictionary if necessary.

1) '<u>A bit</u> / ~~Totally~~ / Extremely ✓ nervous, actually.'

3 Work with a partner. Look at the adjectives in the box and decide which ones fit sentence frame *A* and which ones fit sentence frame *B*.

> amazing   boring   brilliant   disappointing   dreadful   entertaining
> extraordinary   funny   good   interesting   ridiculous   spectacular

A (*gradable adjectives*): The film was quite, very, extremely _____ .
B (*absolute adjectives*): The film was quite, absolutely _____ .

How does the meaning of *quite* change in *A* and *B*?

4 🔊 **3.14** Listen to the six people from Exercise 1 being interviewed after the film. What was the general reaction?

5 The speakers use similar words to the ones in bold in these useful phrases. Try to remember the exact words used by the speakers.

a) (1) **Terribly** disappointing … it does not live up to (2) **expectations**.
b) (3) **Utter** rubbish.
c) it was a (4) **huge** letdown.
d) I feel (5) **thoroughly** disillusioned.
e) I don't think I've ever been so bored in my (6) **whole** life.
f) A (7) **complete** waste of time.

Listen again, check and repeat.

6 Work with your partner. Ask each other about the worst films, TV programmes, concerts or sports events that you've seen recently. Use the useful phrases above to describe your feelings about them.

Vocabulary *Extra*

Collocations

1 Work with a partner. Read the text and identify collocations with the key words in bold. Some words may have more than one collocate, eg *extremely important* and *important aspect*.

> Recognising and using collocations is an extremely **important** aspect of learning a language. Learners soon **realize** that particular words regularly and naturally combine with each other. However, deciding which words go with which can **cause** problems. Occasionally, difficulties **arise** when the wrong word is used. Fortunately, good dictionaries provide useful **information** to help learners make informed **decisions**. This page offers some practical **suggestions**.

Find at least one collocation for each of the following grammatical categories.

a) adverb + adjective: *extremely important*
b) adjective + noun: *important aspect*
c) verb + noun (as object): _____
d) noun (as subject) + verb: _____
e) adverb + verb: _____

Check your ideas in the dictionary extracts. Add any more collocations that you find to the categories above.

2 Using appropriate alternative collocations, rewrite the text in Exercise 1 so that the meaning stays approximately the same.

*Recognising and using collocations is a **particularly important part** of learning …*

3 Look at the collocation boxes for *information* and *decision*. Divide the verb collocates for each noun into two 'meaning' groups.

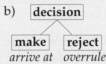

a) **information**
  give   **get**
  convey   *access*

b) **decision**
  make   **reject**
  arrive at   *overrule*

Choose two verb collocates for each noun that are new to you. Look them up in your dictionary. Write a definition and an example sentence for each one.

4 Look at the adjectives frequently used with *information* and *decision*. Find one or two alternative ways of expressing each of the following.

INFORMATION
a) correct information
  accurate information
b) extra or more information
c) secret information
d) new information
e) useful information

DECISION
a) a difficult decision
b) an historic decision
c) a decision based on facts
d) a decision where everybody agreed
e) a decision as part of a plan
f) a decision where not everybody agreed

5 Work with your partner. Look at the collocation boxes for *issue* and *problem*. In each case, arrange the verb collocates and the adjective collocates in different groups according to similarities in meaning.

6 Check your own dictionary. How does it show information about collocations?

Collocation
Adverbs frequently used with **important 1**
- crucially, extremely, most, particularly, terribly, vitally

Nouns frequently used with **important 1**
- aspect, element, factor, feature, issue, part, point

Collocation
Adverbs frequently used with **realize 2**
- belatedly, gradually, instantly, quickly, soon, suddenly

Collocation
Nouns frequently used as objects of **cause**
- alarm, concern, confusion, controversy, damage, distress, embarrassment, harm, problems, suffering, trouble

Collocation
Nouns frequently used as subjects of **arise 1**
- difficulty, issue, matter, need, opportunity, problem, question, situation

Collocation
Adjectives frequently used with **information**
- accurate, additional, available, background, classified, confidential, detailed, false, further, inside, new, relevant, up-to-date, useful, valuable

Verbs frequently used with **information** as the object
- access, acquire, collect, convey, disclose, divulge, elicit, extract, find, gather, get, give, glean, leak, obtain, provide, receive, retrieve

Collocation
Adjectives frequently used with **decision 1**
- controversial, difficult, final, informed, momentous, strategic, tough, unanimous

Verbs frequently used with **decision 1** as the object
- arrive at, come to, make, overrule, overturn, quash, reach, reconsider, rescind, reverse, take

Collocation
Adjectives frequently used with **suggestion 1**
- alternative, constructive, helpful, positive, practical, sensible, tentative

Verbs frequently used with **suggestion 1** as the object
- adopt, make, offer, oppose, reject, submit, volunteer, welcome

Collocation
Verbs frequently used with **issue 1** as the object
- address, cloud, complicate, confront, confuse, consider, dodge, duck, evade, examine, explore, fudge, raise, tackle

Adjectives frequently used with **issue**
- contentious, controversial, divisive, important, key, major, pressing, sensitive, thorny, unresolved

Collocation
Adjectives frequently used with **problem 1**
- big, fundamental, important, insoluble, intractable, major, pressing, real, serious

Verbs frequently used with **problem 1** as the object
- address, alleviate, cause, compound, create, encounter, exacerbate, experience, face, overcome, pose, resolve, solve, tackle

11 Student

Grammar Future forms. Future time clauses
Vocabulary Education. *is likely to / is expected to*. Exaggeration. Colloquial expressions
Useful phrases Using appropriate language in a job interview

Vocabulary & Reading

1 **Work with a partner and complete the tasks.**

a) Write a list of qualities that make a good teacher.
b) Compare your lists and agree on a class list of the three most important qualities.
c) Follow the same procedure to compile a list of qualities that make a good student.

2 **Match the two halves of these expressions to make some questions about education.**

a) How easy is it to **get a**	1 **in** another foreign language?
b) Have you ever **taken a course**	2 **low marks**?
c) What qualifications do you need if you want to **go**	3 **attention** in class?
d) What sort of things do you think it is best to **learn**	4 **on to further education**?
e) What time of day did you find it hardest to **pay**	5 **exam**?
f) How do you **apply for a place at**	6 **by heart**?
g) In which school subjects did you always use to **get**	7 **university**?
h) When was the last time you **failed an**	8 **bank loan** to pay your university fees?

Think about the questions. Then ask your partner and compare your answers.

3 **Read the article on page 111 about three people (*Romy, Ann* and *Henry*) who proved their teachers wrong. Answer the questions.**

a) Who was advised to just get married and raise a family?
b) Who followed the teacher's advice and didn't go on to university?
c) Who failed a maths exam at school but now does all the company accounts?

Read the article again and underline the expressions in bold from Exercise 2 that are used. Which expression is *not* used in the article?

4 **Find expressions in the article which mean the same as the underlined structures. Complete the sentences.**

Text A: It is inevitable that she will fail the exam. → She _____ .
Text B: It is improbable that she will go on to further education. → She _____ .
Text C: It is not thought that Henry will gain a place at university → Henry _____ .

5 **Complete these predictions about education in Britain, using the words in brackets. Do you think these things will happen in your country? When?**

a) Classrooms *are expected to* get less crowded as the birth rate decreases. (expected)
b) More eighteen-year-olds _____ take a gap year between secondary school and further education. (likely)
c) It _____ that classroom teachers will ever be replaced by computers. (highly unlikely)
d) Standards of spelling and grammar _____ get worse due to new technologies. (likely)
e) Students _____ rely more on websites than on books to do their homework. (bound)

Work with your partner. Write down three predictions about the future of education in your country. Find out if other students agree.

▼ The University of Oxford

Look at us now!

A **ROMY ADAMS** runs a catering company. She started off in
5 her own kitchen and now runs three catering teams from premises in North London and
10 caters mainly for conferences.

My maths teacher would die if she knew that I run my own company and do all the accounts myself. On my school report, she wrote, 'I see very
15 little point in entering Rosemary for maths GCSE. Judging by the consistently low marks she has been getting this term, she is bound to fail the exam'. She was right of course, but when I wanted
20 to set up my own company, I took an evening course in maths and accounting and I was one of the best in the class! A bit of motivation goes a long way!

B **ANN WATERMAN**
25 is a judge and has been an active member of parliament for the
30 last ten years.

I was sent to a rather old-fashioned boarding school run by nuns. I obviously didn't make much of an impression there,
35 because their final comment was, 'She has been a mediocre student and is unlikely to go on to further education. We think she is best suited to getting married and raising a family'. The first
40 thing I did when I left school was join the women's liberation movement.

C **HENRY WOODS** is an actor. He is at present
45 filming a series to be shown on television in the autumn.

History was the
50 only subject I was any good at. That's because the history teacher never made us learn lists of dates by heart – but would sit and tell stories and bring it all alive. But other teachers used to
55 say things like, 'Henry lives in a dream world. He needs to pay more attention' – that sort of thing. The worst one was at the end of secondary school. I was hoping to go to university, but then my
60 teacher wrote a comment on my report which took away all my confidence. He put, 'Henry is not expected to pass his A-levels with sufficiently high grades to gain a place at university. He would
65 do well to lower his expectations'. So I didn't apply for a place at university. I got a place at acting school, and the rest is history, as they say. I suppose it was fate, but I still feel angry with that
70 teacher.

Glossary
GCSE noun [C]: General Certificate of Secondary Education: an examination in a range of subjects taken at 16 in England and Wales

boarding school noun [C]: a school where students live during the school year
A-level noun [C]: an examination in a range of subjects taken at 18 in England and Wales

Pronunciation

1 🔊 3.15 Listen and repeat these common abbreviations. Tick the ones that you pronounce as words (acronyms). Underline the stressed letter for the ones you pronounce as individual letters.

1	AIDS	3	CV	5	FAQ	7	NATO	9	PhD	11	UNICEF
2	BSc	4	DIY	6	MBA	8	OPEC	10	PIN	12	VAT

2 Work with a partner. How many of the abbreviations in Exercise 1 do you know? What do the letters stand for? Which abbreviations are to do with education?

🔊 3.16 Listen and check your ideas. What are the equivalent abbreviations in your language?

Speaking: anecdote

You are going to tell your partner about your favourite (or least favourite) teacher at school.

- Ask yourself the questions below.
- Think about *what* to say and *how* to say it.
- Tell your partner about the teacher.

a) What was the teacher's name?
b) What did he/she look like?
c) What sort of clothes did he/she use to wear?
d) Was he/she strict or easy-going?
e) What subject did he/she teach?
f) Were you good at that subject?

g) Where did you sit in the classroom?
h) What sort of things did you use to do in class?
i) What characteristics did you most like (or dislike) about the teacher?
j) What did your classmates think about him/her?
k) When was the last time you saw him/her?

Listening & Vocabulary

1 Work in small groups. Decide at what age you think young people should ...

- make their own decisions. • be financially independent. • leave home.

▲ Mrs and Mr Barrington

2 🌐 **3.17** Listen to Mr and Mrs Barrington talking about their eighteen-year-old daughter, Saffron. Which of the following sentences best summarises their feelings?

a) They want Saffron to go to university but they're worried about the cost.
b) They think Saffron should get a degree before she tries to become a pop singer.
c) They think that it would be a waste of time for Saffron to go to university.

3 Choose the correct alternative in each of these extracts from the interview in Exercise 2.

a) 'Now she reckons she's going to **do** / **make** it in the pop world.'
b) '... once she gets a **taste** / **feel** of freedom, she'll find it harder to go back to college.'
c) 'At least if it doesn't work out she'll have a qualification **behind** / **under** her.'
d) 'We're just hoping that she'll get it out of her **body** / **system** ...'
e) '... and then come to her **thoughts** / **senses** and go back to her studies.'
f) '... we can't afford to pay for her to live in London, so it's **up** / **over** to her to make it work.'

Listen again and check your answers.

4 Work with a partner. Complete the following statements with an appropriate expression from Exercise 3. Change *her* to *you* / *your* as necessary.

a) If you want to go travelling, it's best to _____ before you start a career.
b) Once young people have had _____ , it's hard for them to live with their parents again.
c) The more qualifications you've got _____ , the better your chances are of getting a good job.
d) You don't need talent to _____ as a singer: just good looks and a good manager.
e) Whether or not you succeed in life is _____ . Nobody else can help.

Decide whether you agree or disagree with the statements. Would your parents have the same opinion?

Reading & Grammar

▲ Saffron

1 Work with your partner. Read a conversation between an interviewer (*I*) and Saffron (*S*) in which Saffron talks about her future. Think carefully about the context and choose the most appropriate future forms.

I: You're leaving school soon, aren't you?
S: Yes, (1) **my A-levels start / my A-levels'll start** next week, but I'm not too bothered about the results, because when I leave school (2) **I'm concentrating / I'm going to concentrate** on my music career. I'm the lead singer in a band and I don't need any qualifications to do that. I see my future very clearly – it's obvious that I've got what it takes to be successful. (3) **I'm going to be / I'm being** incredibly famous and fabulously rich.
I: So you've already got a contract then?
S: Er, no, not as such. Actually, we haven't got a manager yet, but the minute I've taken my last exam, (4) **I'm finding / I'm going to find** a really good one.
I: So, do you intend to continue living at home?
S: No way. (5) **I'll have moved / I'm moving** to London as soon as I've left school. London's where it all happens in the music industry.
I: Do you think (6) **you'll be able / you're able** to live off your music right from the start?
S: Well, if we don't make it straightaway, (7) **we're having to / we might have to** get part-time jobs for a few months or something. I know (8) **it's being / it's going to be** hard at first, but I bet you, by this time next year, (9) **we're having / we'll have had** a single in the charts.
I: And where do you see yourself in five years from now?
S: In five years' time (10) **I'm staying / I'll be staying** in posh hotels and won't be able to walk down the street without being recognised. In fact, (11) **I'll give / I'm giving** you my autograph now if you like – (12) **it'll be / it's being** worth a fortune in a few years' time!

2 🌐 **3.18** Listen and check your answers. Have your parents ever been against something you wanted to do? Tell your partner.

Grammar

Future forms and future time clauses

Future forms and future time clauses

I **start** / I**'ll start** / I **might start** / I**'m going to start** / I**'m starting** / I**'ll be starting** / I**'ll have started** tomorrow.

I'll do it **if I have** time.
I'll do it **when I've finished** this.
I won't do it **unless I'm feeling** OK.

1 Work with a partner. Complete the table of different future forms. Use examples from the conversation with Saffron on page 112 to illustrate each use.

Form	Use	Example
a) *will ('ll) +* infinitive	1 for prediction 2 to make an offer	1 _____ 2 *I'll give you my autograph now if you like.*
b) *might +* infinitive	for possibility	_____
c) _____	1 to talk about your intentions 2 to base a prediction on present evidence	1 _____ 2 *I'm going to be incredibly famous.*
d) Present continuous	for plans and arrangements	_____
e) _____	for fixed future events	*My A-levels start next week.*
f) Future continuous	to talk about something happening around a certain time in the future	_____
g) _____	to talk about something completed by a certain time in the future	*By this time next year, we'll have had a single in the charts.*

2 Look at sentences *a–c*. In each sentence underline the main clause, put the subordinate clause in brackets and circle the conjunction. Then answer questions (*1–3*) below.

... (⟨when⟩ I leave school), <u>I'm going to concentrate on my music career.</u>

a) ... the minute I've taken my last exam, I'm going to find a really good one. (line 14)
b) ... I'm moving to London just as soon as I've left school. (lines 16–17)
c) ... if we don't make it straightaway, we might have to get part-time jobs ... (lines 21–22)

1 In which clause (main or subordinate) can you use a future form?
2 What verb forms can you use after a conjunction?
3 When do you use a comma to separate the two clauses?

3 Complete the sentences about the future with an appropriate form of the verbs in brackets.

a) If I (fail) _____ my exams, my parents (kill) _____ me.
b) I (grow) _____ a beard as soon as I (leave) _____ school.
c) I (never read) _____ another poem once I (take) _____ my literature exam.
d) You (like) _____ the new teacher once you (get) _____ used to her.
e) He (not come out) _____ until he (do) _____ his homework.
f) When I (finish) _____ my business course, I (set up) _____ my own business.

4 Complete the sentences in any way that is true for you.

a) Once this lesson has finished, ...
b) The moment I get home today, ...
c) When I have enough money, ...
d) As soon as I have some free time, ...
e) When I'm next on holiday, ...
f) This time next year ...
g) In five years' time ...
h) By the time I retire ...

Compare your sentences with your partner.

5 **Grammar *Extra* 11,** page 142. Read the explanations and do Exercises 1 and 2.

Reading & Vocabulary

1 **Work in groups and discuss the questions.**

a) Is it common in your country for students to go backpacking in their summer holidays?

b) What do you think are the advantages and disadvantages of backpacking?

c) If you could go backpacking anywhere in the world, where would you go and what would you do?

2 **Read the first part of a newspaper article about students who go backpacking. Why should you always take travellers' tales with a pinch of salt?**

Why students love a journey to hell

THE summer holidays are approaching, and the buzz has already started in university bars across the land. Once again, students are competing with one another to see who can plan the toughest and most dangerous foreign trip this summer.

But travellers' tales should be taken with a pinch of salt. Everyone loves to exaggerate and embellish, to make things sound more dramatic. If you say

you did a bungee jump in Queensland of 44 metres, someone will say they did one of 98 at the Victoria Falls. If you got diarrhoea, they had amoebic dysentery or malaria. If you were stopped by police, they were dodging gunfire.

Part of the fun of travelling in your teens and twenties is the telling of tales afterwards. It's part of the rite of passage from child to adult, and there's nothing wrong with that.

3 **Find words and expressions in the text that mean ...**

a) exciting atmosphere.

b) stories.

c) to make a story more interesting by adding details which may be untrue.

d) avoiding.

e) something that marks an important stage in your life.

4 **Tom Griffiths is a university graduate. He recalls backpacking as a student. Read the two versions of his backpacking story. Which do you prefer and why?**

VERSION 1

'I was staying in this dirty hostel room which was full of big ants. One had already bitten my thigh, which had swollen up. So I was trying to kill them when I spotted one on the ceiling. I climbed onto the top bunk and hit it with my shoe. Then I fainted. The blades of the electric ceiling fan had hit my head and knocked me to the ground. I was taken to hospital where I had five stitches.'

VERSION 2

'I was staying in this filthy hostel room which was swarming with huge ants that looked like lobsters. One had already bitten my thigh, which had swollen up like a balloon. So there I was, going berserk trying to kill them all, when I spotted an enormous ant on the ceiling. Climbing onto the top bunk, I bashed it with my shoe. Then I blacked out. It turned out that the blades of the electric ceiling fan had dented my skull and knocked me to the ground. I had to be rushed to hospital where I had emergency surgery.'

Vocabulary

1 Read version 2 of Tom's story again on page 114. Did the ants really look like lobsters? Find ten more examples of language that has been exaggerated. Use your dictionary if necessary.

dirty ➔ *filthy*
full of ➔ *swarming with*

2 Work with a partner. Read two versions of Tom's second story. Combine elements from each version to rewrite the story as dramatically as possible.

VERSION 1

'While I was travelling, I got an incredibly painful tropical ear infection after I fell into a smelly latrine. I felt very ill and stayed in bed with a raging fever for a few days. Wracked with pain, I couldn't eat, and I lost so much weight that I looked like a skeleton. Eventually, I managed to get hold of some antibiotics which made me better.'

VERSION 2

'While I was travelling, I got an unpleasant ear infection after I fell into a stinking latrine. Feeling like death, I lay in bed with a high temperature for what felt like a lifetime. I was in pain so I couldn't face eating anything, and I lost a lot of weight. Finally, I got some antibiotics which brought me back from death's door.'

🌐 **3.19** Listen and check your ideas.

3 Match each of the informal exaggerated expressions (*a–j*) from column *A* with its meaning (*1–10*) in column *B*.

A	B
a) I was over the moon.	1 I thought it was really exciting.
b) I was at death's door.	2 I thought it was beautiful.
c) I burst into tears.	3 I was very happy.
d) I was scared stiff.	4 I started crying.
e) It was mind-blowing.	5 I was very tired.
f) I was at the end of my tether.	6 I was very worried.
g) It took my breath away.	7 I was desperate.
h) I was on my last legs.	8 I was very thirsty.
i) I was dying for a drink.	9 I felt very ill.
j) I was going out of my mind.	10 I was very frightened.

Choose three of the expressions from column *A* and use them in sentences describing the last time you felt like this.

The first time I saw Istanbul, it took my breath away. I thought it was the most beautiful place I'd ever seen.

Speaking

1 Work with your partner. Imagine that you recently came back from an exciting and eventful holiday including a traumatic six-hour boat journey. Prepare a story from the notes below. Make it as dramatic as possible and add some details of your own.

Story ideas	Useful linkers
It was a small fishing boat –	To begin with …
There were a lot of people on the boat –	Then …
The sea was calm when we left the harbour –	Later …
The sky turned black –	Suddenly …
A storm blew up –	Eventually …
We noticed there were no lifejackets or radio in the fishing boat –	To my horror …
The waves were big –	The worst thing was …
We thought we were going to die –	It turned out that …
I cried and then I fainted –	In the end …

2 Tell your story to another pair of students in the class.

Useful phrases

1 Work with a partner. You're going to listen to Sam being interviewed for a job. Put the interview questions (*a–g*) in the most logical order according to your ideas.

a) Do you have any questions you'd like to ask us?

b) What would you say your weaknesses are?

c) In your opinion, what are your greatest strengths?

d) What would you like to be doing in five years' time?

e) Tell us a little about yourself.

f) Why do you think you'd be right for a position in this company?

g) What are your long-term objectives?

🌐 3.20 **Listen and check. Do you think Sam will get the job?**

2 Look at the advice about how to do well in a job interview. In what ways do you think Sam could have improved his interview skills?

HOW TO DO WELL IN A **job interview**

- Don't waffle! Answer questions concisely, and stick to the point.
- Try to sound confident but admit your weaknesses or lack of experience in certain areas.
- Show some enthusiasm and keenness for the job.
- Do your homework before the interview: find out as much as you can about the company and think about the kind of questions you may be asked.
- Prepare your answers.

3 Match the model answers (*1–7*) to the questions (*a–g*) in Exercise 1.

1 I would say my greatest weakness has been my lack of proper planning in the past. However, since I've come to recognise that weakness, I've taken steps to correct it.

2 I graduated from university last year and since then I've been travelling. Now I'm ready to embark on my career and I'm very keen to work for a company like yours.

3 I'm highly motivated and conscientious. I'm a team-player, but equally I can work on my own.

4 I've always been interested in working in the media. I think I'm well-suited to this kind of work because I work well under pressure. I don't have much experience yet, but anything I don't know, I'm willing to learn.

5 Ideally, I'd like to be managing my own team.

6 I'd like to know a bit about the training opportunities in this job.

7 I'd like to gain some experience in this field for a few years, and then decide which area I want to specialise in.

🌐 3.21 **Listen to Layla being interviewed and check your answers. Which of the highlighted useful phrases could be used in other interview contexts?**

4 Work with your partner. Choose one of the jobs in the box or your own ideas, and write an interview. Use some of the highlighted useful phrases in Exercise 3. Practise your interview.

| bank clerk   estate agent   fitness trainer   flight attendant |
| gaming software engineer   interior designer   teacher |

Writing *Extra*

CV and letter of application

1. Arrange the following tips for writing a curriculum vitae under the headings *DO* and *DON'T*.

   a) be honest.
   b) mention your bad points or failures.
   c) try to be amusing.
   d) use a clear layout.
   e) use bold and italic for headings.
   f) include dates.
   g) check for spelling and typing errors.
   h) use family or friends as referees.

2. Read Sam Arnoldson's CV. Apply the tips in Exercise 1 above and identify where he has gone wrong.

3. Work with a partner. Look at Sam's 'Employment' and 'Skills'. Think about ways in which he could express this information in a more formal and positive way.

   ~~Worked in an office.~~ *Office assistant. Improved my computer skills.*

   Now look at page 130 for an improved version of Sam's CV and compare your own ideas.

4. Read Sam's application letter. Some parts of the letter are acceptable, and some parts are completely inappropriate. Cross out all the parts which you think are inappropriate in order to produce a good letter.

5. Write your own CV and letter of application for a job as a holiday representative.

Sam Arnoldson
311 Cowley Rd Oxford
telephone 0788 988789
e-mail SuperSam@hotmail.com

DOB 12.8.89
   Educasion
☺ English A level grade C
☺ Geography A level grade D
☺ History A level failed
☺ 8 GCSEs
EMPLOYMENT
☺ Worked in an office
☺ Did some babysitting
☺ Washed dishes in a French ski-resort
☺ Backpacked around France and Spain and did some fruit picking
☺ Worked in my mother's shop
SKILLS
☺ I can use a compUter.
☺ I can speak supermarket French and holiday Spanish
☺ Have failed driving test three times. Hope to pass next time.
PERSONNEL INTERESTS
Donating blood – 14 litres so far
Music

References : Mrs Beryl Arnoldson, 311 Cowley Rd, Oxford ☎ 01865 372 82

To whom it may concern
DO NOT PUT THIS LETTER IN THE BIN!!!!!

Dear Sir or Madam or Mademoiselle,
   I am writing to apply for the post of holiday representative advertised in The Times this week. As you can see from my curriculum vitae enclosed, I do not have a great deal of work experience and no experience whatsoever as a holiday rep. However, what I lack in experience I am willing to make up for in enthusiasm and hard work.
   Since I left college in June last year, I have been in continual employment. First of all, I worked as a shop assistant where I learnt a lot about the retail industry. But it was my mother's shop and we argued all the time, so I resigned. After that I worked in a ski resort in France where I enjoyed working as part of a team and improved my spoken French. I left because the pay was rubbish and I never had time to go skiing.
   Through the variety of posts I have held, I have learnt important interpersonal skills, improved my knowledge of European languages and have gained extensive computing skills. I feel the job you are offering will enable me to put these skills into practice.
   As I'm unemployed at the moment, I can be available for interview at your convenience.

Yours faithfully,

Sam Arnoldson ☺
Sam Arnoldson

12 Home

Grammar Participle clauses. Nouns and quantity expressions
Vocabulary Houses. Furnishings
Useful phrases Ways of saying hello and goodbye

Reading & Vocabulary

1 **Work with a partner. How do you imagine your dream house?**

My dream house ...
- is eco-friendly.
- is light and bright.
- is quiet.
- is in the middle of nowhere.
- has a terrace.
- has bedrooms with en suites.
- is on the coast.
- has amazing views.

Look at the photos on page 119 of two unique houses. Which features above do you expect each house to have? Read the article and check your ideas.

2 **Which house would you prefer to live in? Discuss your reasons with your partner.**

3 **Work with your partner. Try to complete each collocation with a suitable word. Then check your ideas by finding the collocations in the article on page 119.**
   a) What are some examples of fossil _____ ?
   b) In which month do people usually switch on their central _____ ?
   c) What kind of things can give young people street _____ ?
   d) On what occasion might you see a fireworks _____ ?
   e) How can you make a room pitch _____ ?
   f) For what kind of reason might you pop next _____ ?

   Discuss the answers to the questions.

Grammar

1 **Complete the table with the two appropriate sentences from the article on page 119.**

Two separate sentences	A single sentence with a relative clause	A single sentence with a participle clause
We're in a bungalow. It is covered in earth.	We're in a bungalow, which is covered in earth.	1) _____
You will see a ship. It is coming in.	You will see a ship, which is coming in.	2) _____

Participle clauses

The people **living next door** moved in last month.
(Defining clause: no commas needed.)

The house, **redecorated throughout**, took ages to sell.
(Non-defining clause: commas needed.)

2 **Rewrite each of the following as one sentence using the participle in brackets.**
   a) My apartment block is quite modern. It was built in the 1990s. (built)
      My apartment block, built in the 1990s, is quite modern.
   b) My own apartment is very light and airy. It is located on the top floor. (located)
   c) Every morning I am woken up by the sun. It streams through my window. (streaming)
   d) My bedroom is full of souvenirs. They have been collected on my travels. (collected)
   e) The neighbours are very friendly. They live opposite us. (living)

   Are any of these sentences true for you?

3 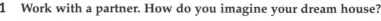 **Grammar *Extra* 12, Part 1** page 142. Read the explanations and do Exercise 1.

The earth shelter

Jerry Harrall, 46, lives with his wife, Kay, and their children, Penelope, 14, Royston, 12, and Molly, 10. Their home is an earth-sheltered eco-dwelling he built himself.

Jerry: `Although we have no heating, the temperature remains between
5 18 and 21°C. Occasionally we get called Teletubbies or Hobbits, but we're not underground – we're in a bungalow covered in earth. I think we've created an environment of serenity and tranquillity that demonstrates to the children how we can have a comfortable life without reliance on fossil fuels.

10 One side faces south with a lot of glass, so we have a high level of daylight. The rest, including the roof, is covered in two to ten feet of earth planted with ivy, which reduces the rate of heat loss and acts as sound-proofing.

I think the children are calmer here, with the chance to reflect and
15 contemplate.

They say their friends' homes are stuffy and dark – that's because they're covered in carpets, vinyl and plasterboard, which harbour dust mites and mould growth, and we've got high daylight levels. Whenever we go away, the children all ask if the central heating can be switched
20 off or windows opened. They can't sleep, and want to get out.

The children like the linear layout because they can run up and down – and they've been caught skateboarding down the corridor.'

The lighthouse

Frank and Danielle Sheahan run a guesthouse in an old lighthouse. They have two sons, Jed, 17, and Brodie, 14.

25 Frank: `At school, Jed and Brodie are known as the lighthouse kids and they say it gives them street cred. When the bed and breakfast is quiet, their friends think it's a cool place to stay over because all the rooms have en suites and TVs. When they were younger, we'd all go up into the lamp-room to watch electrical storms. They're amazing – like a fireworks
30 display. The view is fantastic. You can see right over the estuary to England.

The sea is about thirty feet away and, in 2004, a 40-tonne whale got stranded on a sandbank just outside. It was very sad. The children would never have experienced that in London.

There was a big storm once and the waves were spilling over. But
35 lighthouses are built to take a hammering. And there's a psychological aspect to living in a round structure: you feel protected. The closeness of the elements is part of the fun. At night, it's pitch dark out there but then you will see a ship coming in with all its lights on like a Christmas tree.

On the negative side, you can't simply pop next door to a mate's
40 house. Being in the middle of nowhere, the children are reliant on us to take them everywhere. And I think there are times when the children resent having paying guests. But it means that we can live in this unique building. And for Jed's 18th birthday, we're going to close the B&B and have his party up on the terrace. How cool is that?'

Glossary

dwelling noun [C]: place where someone lives
sound-proofing noun [U]: material that stops sound from entering or leaving
stuffy adj: too warm and smells because there is no fresh air

mite noun [C]: very small insect
mould noun [U]: green or blue bacteria that grow on things that are not clean or dry
stranded adj: left in a place with no way of going anywhere else
hammering noun [C]: rough treatment

Vocabulary

1 Work with a partner. List each item in the box under an appropriate heading to show where you would expect to find it. Use your dictionary if necessary.

> candlesticks   coat hooks   a doormat   a dustpan and brush   a fireplace
> an ironing board   a mantelpiece   ornaments   patterned wallpaper
> a shaving socket   a shower curtain   a sink   tea towels   a towel rail
> a tumble dryer   a washbasin

In the kitchen	In the bathroom	In the living room	In the hallway

2 With which part of a room would you associate these groups of items? Choose from: *a window*, *a wall*, *a door* or *the floor*.

a) fitted carpets, parquet, rugs, tiles

b) blinds, curtains, double-glazing, shutters, a sill

c) power points, light switches, radiators, shelves

d) a bell, a bolt, a knocker, a latch, a letterbox

Tick all the items in Exercises 1 and 2 that you have in your own home.

Speaking & Listening

1 Work with your partner. Compare the two photos and discuss these questions.

a) What kind of people do you think each of these rooms belongs to?

b) What kind of house do you think each room is part of?

c) Which room do you like best and why?

2 You're going to listen to a psychologist talking about what each room says about the people who live there. Before you listen, match each of his interpretations (*a–f*) to the room you think it applies to.

a) This is obviously a family room.

b) I imagine both parents go out to work and so they don't have much time to tidy up.

c) There's plenty of evidence to suggest that this is a successful career person.

d) This person wants to be ready to pack their bags and leave at short notice.

e) I think the people who live here are laid back, sociable people who enjoy entertaining.

f) I think this is someone who doesn't actually spend much time at home.

🔘 3.22–3.23 Listen and check your ideas. Do you agree with the psychologist's comments? Go to page 130 to find out if the people who live there agree.

Grammar

Read the explanations and do Exercises 2 and 3.

Nouns and quantity expressions

Countable nouns
Use: *none, not any, few, a few, several, some, many, a lot, loads, plenty*

Uncountable nouns
Use: *none, not any, little, a little, a bit, some, much, a lot, loads, plenty*

not enough = less than you need
too much/many = more than you need

1 Work with a partner. Complete the extracts from the room descriptions on page 120 with *There is* or *There are*.

a) _____ far too many cushions.
b) _____ very few clues.
c) _____ hardly any personal objects.
d) _____ loads of different colours.
e) _____ plenty of evidence.
f) _____ n't really enough furniture.

Arrange the highlighted quantifiers in a logical order from 'none' to 'a lot more than necessary'.

2 Work with your partner. Look at the sentence beginnings (*a–d*). Decide which is the most suitable ending (*1 or 2*) for each sentence.

a) My father speaks **a little** English
b) My father speaks **little** English

1 so he probably won't understand you.
2 so he'll probably understand you.

c) **A few** people can understand him,
d) **Few** people can understand him,

1 which he finds encouraging.
2 which he finds discouraging.

Which quantifiers in bold mean: a) *some*; b) *not much*; c) *not many*?

3 Complete the sentences so that they are true for you. Compare with your partner.

a) I try to find a little time each day for …
b) There are few people I know who …
c) If I met the president of the USA, I'd ask him a few questions about …
d) This year, I've had very little …
e) I have very little patience with people who …

4 Choose the correct verb form for these statements.

a) There **isn't** / **aren't** nearly enough nightlife.
b) There**'s** / **are** loads of traffic.
c) There**'s** / **are** very few tourists.
d) There**'s** / **are** no underground system.
e) There**'s** / **are** plenty of job opportunities for young people.
f) There**'s** / **are** plenty of space to park in the centre.

Change the statements as necessary to describe your home town or city. Add two more statements and then compare your answers with your partner.

5 Grammar *Extra* 12, Part 2 page 142. Read the explanations and do Exercises 2 and 3.

Speaking: anecdote

You are going to tell your partner about your favourite room.

• Ask yourself the questions below.
• Think about *what* to say and *how* to say it.
• Tell your partner about the room.

a) Which is your favourite room?
b) What do you use it for?
c) What size and shape is it?
d) How is it decorated?
e) What sort of furniture does it contain?
f) What kind of floor does it have?
g) What do the windows look out on to?
h) How much time each day do you spend in it?
i) What's the best thing about the room?
j) What – if anything – would you like to change about it?

Reading & Speaking

1 You're going to read an extract from *Sons and Lovers* by DH Lawrence on page 123. First, look at the photo of the kitchen and write three adjectives to describe the kitchen and three adjectives to describe the life of the people who might live here. Then compare with a partner.

2 Read the extract to find out if your ideas were correct. Then answer the questions.
   a) What time does Morel get up and what time does he go to work?
   b) What does he have for breakfast, and what does he have for lunch?
   c) How does he feel about having breakfast alone?

3 Put Morel's morning routine in the correct order. Then read the extract again and check your answers.

1	He got out of bed.		He made his lunch.
	He took his wife a cup of tea.		He took off his nightshirt.
	He boiled the kettle.		He read yesterday's newspaper.
	He put on his trousers.		He blocked out the draught under the door.
	He ate his breakfast.		

4 Work in small groups. Based on the extract, discuss the questions about Morel and his relationship with his wife.
   a) What sort of man do you think Morel is?
   b) What kind of lifestyle do you think he and his family have?
   c) Do you think Morel and his wife have a happy relationship? Why? / Why not?

Go to page 131 to read a summary of *Sons and Lovers* and check your ideas. Were you surprised by any of the information?

Listening & Vocabulary

1 How do people in the class start the day? Ask questions to find someone who ...
   • slept more than eight hours last night.
   • slept with the curtains or blinds open.
   • woke up naturally, without an alarm clock.
   • can remember what they dreamt about.
   • had something cooked for breakfast.
   • spent more than twenty minutes eating breakfast.

2 Work with your partner. The food and drink in the box is a mixture of breakfast items from around the world. Answer the questions.
   a) Is there anything in the box that you or your family normally have for breakfast?
   b) Is there anything you would find difficult to eat at breakfast?

bacon bread rolls cereal cheese coffee cold meat eggs green tea ham grilled fish jam miso soup orange juice omelette pancakes pickled vegetables rice seaweed tea toast

3 🌐 3.24–3.26 The food and drink in Exercise 2 are some breakfast items from the USA, Germany and Japan. Which items do you think belong to a typical breakfast from which country? Listen and check.

▲ Lizanne, USA   ▲ Nicola, Germany   ▲ Michiko, Japan

4 What's your perfect breakfast? Tell your partner.

A MINER'S BREAKFAST

He always made his own breakfast. Being a man who rose early and had
plenty of time he did not, as some miners do, drag his wife out of bed at
six o'clock. At five, sometimes earlier, he woke, got straight out of bed, and
went downstairs. When she could not sleep, his wife lay waiting for this
5　time as for a period of peace. The only real rest seemed to be when he was
out of the house.

　He went downstairs in his shirt and then struggled into his pit-trousers,
which were left on the hearth to warm all night. There was always a fire,
because Mrs Morel raked. And the first sound in the house was the bang
10　bang of the poker against the raker, as Morel smashed the remainder of the
coal to make the kettle, which was filled and left on the hob, finally boil.
His cup and knife and fork, all he wanted except just the food, was laid
ready on the table on a newspaper. Then he got his breakfast, made the tea,
packed the bottom of the doors with rugs to shut out the draught, piled a
15　big fire, and sat down to an hour of joy. He toasted his bacon on a fork and
caught the drops of fat on his bread; then he put the rasher on his thick slice
of bread, and cut off chunks with a clasp-knife. Then, in solitude, he ate
and drank, often sitting, in cold weather, on a little stool with his back to
the warm chimney-piece, his food on the fender, his cup on the hearth. And
20　then he read the last night's newspaper – what of it he could – spelling it
over laboriously. He preferred to keep the blinds down and candle lit, even
when it was daylight; it was the habit of the mine.

　At a quarter to six he rose, cut two thick slices of bread-and-butter, and
put them in the white calico snap-bag. He filled his tin bottle with tea. Cold
25　tea without milk or sugar was the drink he preferred for the pit. Then he
pulled off his shirt, and put on his pit-singlet, a vest of thick flannel cut low
round the neck, and with short sleeves like a chemise.

　Then he went upstairs to his wife with a cup of tea because she was ill,
and because it occurred to him.

Sons and Lovers, 1913

Glossary

hearth noun [C]: the floor of a fireplace

rake verb [T/I]: to use a tool to separate pieces of burning coal

hob noun [C]: the top part of a cooker that you put pans on

chimney piece noun [C]: mantelpiece

fender noun [C]: a low frame around a fireplace

calico noun [U]: heavy white cloth made of cotton

Useful phrases

1 Ann is saying goodbye to Bob after an evening at his house. Read the conversation and complete the 'goodbye' expressions using the words in the box.

> already   be   better   carefully
> for   Give   good   inviting
> Love   must   regards   Take
> too   will   you   yourself

Ann: I'd (1) _____ be going.
Bob: It was (2) _____ to see you.
Ann: Thank you for (3) _____ me.
Bob: Thanks (4) _____ coming.
Ann: I'll (5) _____ off then.
Bob: Give my (6) _____ to your family.
Ann: I (7) _____ .
Bob: (8) _____ me a ring.
Ann: Okay. I really (9) _____ be off now.
Bob: (10) _____ care.
Ann: See (11) _____ .
Bob: Drive (12) _____ .
Ann: (13) _____ you.
Bob: Me (14) _____ .
Ann: Take care of (15) _____ .
Bob: Missing you (16) _____ !

🔘 **3.27** Listen and check.

2 Work with a partner. Match each phrase (*a–j*) with an appropriate response (*1–10*). Which exchanges are ways of saying hello and which are ways of saying goodbye?

a) Fancy seeing you here!
b) You must come and stay again soon.
c) Good to see you again! You haven't changed a bit.
d) Safe journey.
e) Long time no see!
f) What have you been up to?
g) Thank you for everything.
h) Hi, how are you doing?
i) We must get together again soon.
j) Keep in touch.

1 Not much. The usual.
2 I will.
3 Oh, I come here all the time.
4 Yes, it must be over a year.
5 Absolutely, that would be lovely.
6 Thanks. I'll call when I get there.
7 Nor have you. As gorgeous as ever.
8 Fine thanks. How about you?
9 You're most welcome.
10 I'd love to.

🔘 **3.28** Listen, check and repeat the useful phrases.

3 Work with your partner. Choose two of the exchanges from Exercise 2. Invent a context and write a longer conversation, including the lines you've chosen. Consider some of these questions.

- Where does the conversation take place?
- What time of day is it?
- Who are the speakers?
- How old are they?
- What has happened just before?
- What will happen straight afterwards?

Practise your conversation.

Vocabulary *Extra*
Get it right

Based on evidence from the *Louvain International Corpus of Learner English*, the following exercises address some of the most common and persistent learner errors at this level. Test your knowledge and then check your answers in the dictionary extracts.

1 **FALSE FRIENDS** Complete the statements with *actual / actually* or *current / currently*.

a) The _____ economic situation is not very good.

b) Homeowners are _____ paying very high rates of interest.

c) The official number of unemployed is two million. However the _____ number is probably much higher.

d) The _____ government talk a lot but _____ have no idea what to do.

e) Saying you'll do something and _____ doing it are two very different things.

Do you agree or disagree with the statements?

2 **VERB PATTERNS** Which verb or verb phrase is the odd one out? Test your ideas by using sentence frames *A* and *B*.

afford / avoid / help / risk / spend time / suggest

A) He couldn't _____ to do it.   B) He couldn't _____ doing it.

3 **VERB + PREPOSITION** Underline the correct alternative.

a) I agree **my parents** / **with my parents** about most things.

b) I don't approve **children** / **of children** wearing make-up.

c) I don't like discussing **about politics** / **politics**.

d) I sometimes enter **into competitions** / **competitions** but I never win.

e) I use my credit card to pay **products** / **for products** I buy online.

Which sentences are true for you?

4 **COUNTABILITY** Are the nouns in the box usually countable or uncountable?

advice	behaviour	evidence	information	knowledge
news	progress	proof	research	work

Which of the nouns in the box can replace *advice* in the sentence 'Advice is important'?

5 **NOUN + PREPOSITION** What is the common error in these sentences from the *Louvain International Corpus of Learner English*?

a) ✗ The experiment has not led to the expected decrease of crime.

b) ✗ Women in those times were totally dependent of their husbands.

c) ✗ There is a big difference of grammar between Japanese and English.

d) ✗ Is gun ownership connected with the increase of violent crime?

e) ✗ The main reason of poverty is unemployment.

f) ✗ The role of the government is to find a solution of this problem.

Correct each sentence with *for, in, on* or *to*.

6 Check your own dictionary. Identify six errors that you sometimes make and find example sentences that show the correct usage.

Get it right: actual

Don't confuse **actual** with **current** or **present**. Actual is not used for referring to things that are happening now or that exist now. Use **current** or **present** to express these ideas:

✗ The ~~actual law~~ obliges every young man to do military service.
✓ The **current law** obliges every young man to do military service.
✓ The **present law** obliges every young man to do military service.
✗ They have to work together to improve ~~the actual situation~~.
✓ They have to work together to improve **the current situation**.
✓ They have to work together to improve **the present situation**.

Actual is used for referring to what is really true or exact:

The reports cites 554 AIDS cases, with 2600 persons infected with HIV. But officials concede that the actual number may be closer to 8000.

Got it right

afford is never followed by a verb in the **-ing** form. Use an infinitive.
avoid is never used with an infinitive. It is followed by a verb in the **-ing** form.
help: The **-ing** form is only used with **help** in the fixed expression **can't help doing something**.
risk is never followed by an infinitive. Use the pattern **risk doing something**.
spend: When you use **spend** with another verb use the **-ing** form of the verb, not the infinitive.
suggest: When **suggest** means 'to offer an idea or a plan', it is never followed by an infinitive. Use the pattern **suggest doing something**.

Get it right

agree: When you want to say that you approve of something or think it is the right thing to do, use the pattern 'agree **with** something' (not 'agree something').
approve: When **approve** means 'to have a positive feeling towards something or someone', it is followed by **of**, not by a direct object.
discuss is never used with the preposition **about**. It is simply followed by a direct object.
enter is usually a transitive verb, and it takes a direct object. It is not used with the prepositions **into** or **in**.
pay is never followed by a direct object that refers to the thing you are buying. We **pay for** a product or a service.

Get it right

advice is an uncountable noun
behaviour is usually an uncountable noun
evidence is an uncountable noun
information is an uncountable noun
knowledge is an uncountable noun
news is an uncountable noun
progress is an uncountable noun
proof: When **proof** means 'information that proves something', it is almost always an uncountable noun.
research is an uncountable noun
work: In most of its meanings, **work** is an uncountable noun.

Get it right

decrease: Don't use **decrease of** when you want to talk about what is decreasing. Use **decrease in**.
dependent: The usual preposition to use with **dependent** is **on**, not **of**.
difference: When you are talking about a way in which two people or things are different, use the pattern **a difference in** something (not 'difference of' or 'difference about').
increase: Don't use **increase of** when you want to say what is increasing. Use **increase in**.
reason: After **reason**, use the preposition **for**, not **of**.
solution: The usual preposition to use with **solution** is **to**, not **of**.

Review D

► Grammar *Extra* pages 140–143

Grammar

1 Complete the sentences with *which* or *who*.

a) This is Sandra, _____ is studying art.

b) He calls her 'sweetiepie', _____ I can't stand.

c) My sister, _____ lives in London, is a lawyer.

d) Oh, look. It's that strange man _____ came into the shop yesterday.

e) They gave me a brown jumper, _____ is absolutely hideous.

f) She came to my party, _____ was rude, because she wasn't invited.

2 Write the sentences in the correct order. The first and last words of each sentence are given.

a) **What** annoys / really / at / talk / me / is / who / the / people **cinema**.

b) **What** sense / I / like/ Connie / is / her / of / about **humour**.

c) **What** eating / and / feel / like / tonight / is / steak / I **chips**.

d) **The** I / summer / thing / can't / about / stand / the / is **mosquitoes**.

e) **What** like / really / to / do / is / watch / I'd **TV**.

f) **What** married / don't / I / is / why / he / understand **her**.

3 Underline the correct alternative.

At the moment, I'm working in an office, but I've always wanted to be a doctor. A few months ago, I applied for a place at medical school, and, guess what? I (1) **'ll have** / **'m having** an interview for a place to study medicine at university next Tuesday. I feel very nervous about it! It (2) **isn't going to be** / **isn't being** an easy interview. It's a very good university, and I (3) **won't get** / **might not get** a place. I (4) **'m not going to tell** / **don't tell** anyone at work about the interview, in case I don't get in. Another thing I'm worried about is that I might not be able to earn enough money to go back to full-time education. My parents have said they (5) **'re helping** / **'ll help** me, but they can't really afford to give me very much. I know I (6) **'m having to support** / **'ll have to support** myself while I'm studying. The course (7) **starts** / **will start** next September. And, if all goes well with the interview, by September (8) **I'm going to leave** / **'ll have left** my office job, and (9) **'ll be starting** / **'ll start** my course. Wish me luck!

4 Complete the conversation between May and Jim with the correct form of the verbs in brackets.

M: Could you do some photocopying for me today?

J: Of course. I'm just sorting the post, but I'll do the copying as soon as I (1 finish) *'ve finished*.

M: Thanks. And when you (2 do) _____ the photocopying, could you take these invoices to the accounts department?

J: OK. I'll do that once I (3 organise) _____ the papers for the conference tomorrow.

M: But I really need you to (4 do) _____ it now.

J: Well, Mrs Blunt said I shouldn't do anything until I (5 do) _____ the papers.

M: But if these invoices don't go to accounts, they (6 not be) _____ paid.

J: Well, if I (7 not get) _____ these papers done, Mrs Blunt (8 be) _____ furious!

M: But the invoices are urgent.

J: Everything (9 be) _____ always urgent here!

M: Are you OK, Jim? You seem a bit stressed.

J: Yes, I am stressed. The minute Mrs Blunt comes back, I (10 tell) _____ her I quit.

5 Complete each sentence so that it means the same as the two sentences above it.

a) My house was built one hundred years ago. It's situated in the middle of the town.
My house, *situated in the middle of the town, was built one hundred years ago*.

b) These ornaments are very valuable. They were given to me by my grandmother.
These ornaments, …

c) The cat had kittens last year. She's sitting on the windowsill.
The cat …

d) Those children are my brothers and sisters. They are playing in the photos.
Those children …

e) The people are very kind. They live around here.
The people …

6 Complete the sentences with the words in the box.

| enough   far too much   few   little   none |
| plenty of |

a) _____ of my friends have much money.

b) I never seem to have _____ time to sit and read.

c) I have _____ hobbies. I'm always busy.

d) There's very _____ food I won't eat.

e) There is _____ stuff in my home. I need to get rid of it.

f) I have very _____ new clothes.

Tick the sentences that are true for you.

Vocabulary

1 Complete the sentences with the correct form of the words in the box.

> catch sight   gaze   make out   notice   spot
> ~~stare~~

a) Stop *staring* at people. It's rude.
b) On holiday we spent many evenings on the balcony, _____ at the stars in the sky.
c) I just _____ of myself in that shop window. Why didn't you tell me I had chocolate on my chin?
d) Despite the big crowd, we managed to _____ Brad Pitt going into the hotel.
e) Through her binoculars, Penny could just _____ the island in the distance.
f) Did you _____ that advert in the shop window? It said, 'Kittens for sale'.

2 Underline the correct words.

Today, Adam Grant is one of the country's most successful businessmen, but he was not always a success. He had a troubled childhood, and was brought up in an orphanage. Moreover, he was dyslexic at school and found reading a problem. Because of that it was an effort for him to (1) **make / pay** attention in his lessons, and he often (2) **got / had** bad marks in his subjects. For most students like Adam, (3) **applying / going on** to further education was highly unlikely. It was generally expected that he would (4) **miss / fail** his exams and leave school at sixteen. But, luckily, Adam had a teacher, Mrs Phelps, who realised that he showed great talent in science. Mrs Phelps helped Adam with his reading, and encouraged him to think about university, an idea that Adam had never considered before. At the age of eighteen, Adam (5) **applied for / passed** and succeeded in getting a place at Sheffield University to (6) **take / follow** a course in mechanical engineering. He also (7) **passed / got** a full grant to pay for his studies.

3 Replace each underlined word or phrase in sentences (a–f) with an appropriate form of a word or phrase from the box.

> behind   come to (your) senses   make it
> ~~up to (you)~~   get it out of (your) system

a) I don't mind what colour we paint the kitchen. It's <u>your decision</u>.
   It's up to you.
b) Do you think Ken can really <u>be a success</u> in the acting world?
c) I wish Elaine would <u>be sensible</u> and leave Brian.
d) Every successful person usually has a supportive family <u>backing</u> them.
e) My son was obsessed with going bungee jumping. In the end we let him do it so that he would <u>stop thinking about it</u>.

4 Complete the sentences with the correct form of the expressions in the box.

> at death's door   at the end of (your) tether
> dying for a drink   on (your) last legs
> over the moon   ~~take (your) breath away~~

a) I loved their performance last night. It *took my breath away*.
b) They were _____ about their lottery win.
c) I've really had enough of the twins' behaviour. I'm _____ .
d) Is that car going to get us to London? It looks as if it's _____ .
e) Justin was _____ when he got malaria on his trip.
f) Let's stop here and buy some water. I'm _____ .

5 Label the picture with the words in the box.

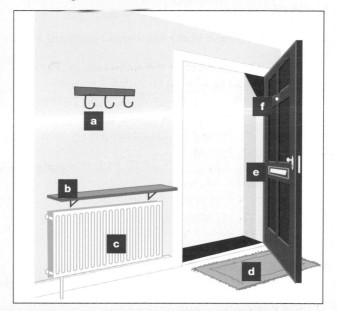

> doorbell   coat hook   doormat   letterbox
> radiator   shelf

Pronunciation

1 Look at some words from Units 10–12. Say the words and add them to the table.

> ~~absolutely~~   advertise   disappointing
> education   epitomise   evidence   experience
> extraordinary   nostalgically   ornament
> television   thoroughly

A: ☐☐☐	B: ☐☐☐☐☐	C: ☐☐☐☐
	absol<u>u</u>tely	

2 Underline the stressed syllable in each word.

🔊 **3.29** Listen, check and repeat.

▶  **Song**

Additional material

Unit 1 Grammar (page 7)

Follow these instructions to play Question Tag Bingo. You will need to use the sentences you wrote in Exercise 2 on page 7.

Instructions

a) Copy the Bingo card onto a separate piece of paper.

b) Take it in turns to read out one of your sentences from Exercise 2. If your partner can answer with a response on the Bingo card, cross out the square. If what you say is not true for your partner, you must wait for your next go to try another sentence.

c) The winner is the first person to cross out all the squares on the card.

So was I.	Nor do I.	So have I.
So would I.	Nor am I.	So did I.
Neither have I.	So am I.	Neither can I.

Unit 4 Listening & Vocabulary (page 41)

Work with a partner. Make sentences beginning *Find someone who …* by matching each verb with an appropriate noun phrase.

Find someone who …	burns off does feels gets goes goes for has cancelled is stuck wears works out	+	a brisk walk at the weekend a gym membership calories by cycling to work inside all day lycra gear at the gym out of shape plenty of fresh air running team sports at the gym

Find someone in the class who does (or has done) each of these activities.

Unit 4 Useful phrases & Pronunciation (page 44)

Student A

Work with Student B. Take it in turns to describe your problems. When you hear your partner's problem, react sympathetically or unsympathetically and then give some advice.

- You don't want to go out because you've got a huge spot on your nose – you ate too much chocolate yesterday.
- You think you've caught a cold – you can't stop sneezing.
- Your back is killing you. You did four hours of gym yesterday.
- You have trouble remembering people's names.
- Your teeth hurt when you eat something cold.

Unit 9 Listening & Grammar (page 92)

Test your memory. Answer these questions about the three paintings on page 92. Then look back and check your answers. Which painting did you remember best?

Frida and Diego Rivera, 1931

a) Describe Frida's clothes.
b) What jewellery is she wearing?
c) What is Diego holding in his right hand?
d) There's something above Frida's head – what is it?
e) What colour is Diego's shirt?

Self-portrait with Cropped Hair, 1940

a) Describe Frida's face.
b) What is she wearing?
c) What is she holding in her right hand?
d) She's sitting on a chair – what's it made of?
e) What's at the top of the painting?

Roots, 1943

a) Describe the landscape.
b) What is Frida leaning on?
c) Is her hair tied up or loose?
d) Which part of her body do the roots seem to be coming from?
e) What colour are the leaves?

Unit 9 Speaking & Listening (page 94)

Answers

Listed in the order in which they were invented

f) The toothbrush – the first mention of a toothbrush with bristles at right angles to the handle is in a Chinese encyclopaedia of 1498.

b) The water closet toilet – Queen Elizabeth 1 was delighted to add this new 'throne' to her collection when her godson Sir John Harrington invented it in 1597.

d) False teeth – before French pharmacist Alexis Duchateau perfected a set of porcelain dentures in 1770, it was common practice to use 'dead men's teeth' – particularly plentiful after the frequent wars at the time.

a) Contact lenses – the first workable pair were produced in 1887 by F. E. Muller, a glassblower from Wiesbaden in Germany.

e) The safety razor – US citizen King Camp Gillette patented this in 1901. He believed his fortune lay in inventing something that people used once and then threw away. He wasn't wrong. Within the first year he sold over twelve million of his disposable blades.

c) The zip – there were several attempts at this before the Swedish engineer Gideon Sundback finally got the zipper to work in 1913. It was later claimed that by replacing the buttons on trousers the new device would eliminate any risk of embarrassment. Sadly …

Unit 10 Reading & Vocabulary (page 100)

Answers

1a) Head   2b) Nike   3a) Adidas   4c) Speedo   5a) Slazenger   6b) Kappa

Unit 10 Listening & Vocabulary (page 101)

Student A

You are going to complete some lists of common noun collocations often used to talk about sales and marketing. Complete each list with a word from the box. Use your dictionary if necessary. Then check your answers with Student B.

advertising   bank   cash   consumer   finance   price   purchase

a) _____ choice / confidence / goods / groups / products / spending

b) _____ cut / index / list / rise / tag / war

c) _____ agency / campaign / executive / industry / revenue / space

Student B answers:
a) sales
b) brand
c) market

Choose six useful collocations from the lists and write an example sentence for each one.

Unit 10 Reading & Vocabulary (page 102)

Work in groups and discuss the questions.

a) What other interesting advertisements (TV, cinema, magazines) have you seen?

b) If you were making a TV advertisement for jeans, how would you do it? Consider the following questions.

- Who would the advertisement be aimed at?
- What storyline would you use?
- Which actors would you want to use?
- Where and when would the advert be set?
- What music would you use?

Compare your ideas with other groups.

Grammar *Extra*

Unit 1 Verb structures. Auxiliaries

Part 1: Verb structures

Present verb structures

You use the present simple to talk about habits and routines or things that are always true. *I usually **go** to bed around midnight. / The sun **rises** in the east.*

You use the present continuous to talk about activities that are in progress now, or to describe changing situations. *I'm **learning** Japanese as well as English. / The Earth **is getting** warmer.*

You use the present perfect to talk about present situations which started in the past and are continuing now, or which exist because of a completed past event, or which happened at an indefinite time in the past. *I've **been taking** English classes since last year. / Look, she's **changed** her hairstyle. / We've **seen** Madonna in concert nine times!*

▶ See page 136 for more on the present perfect simple and continuous.

Past verb structures

You usually use the past continuous in contrast with the past simple to talk about activities that were in progress when something happened. *He was **living** in London when he met her.*

You use the past perfect to show that one past event happened before another past event. *The film **had started** when I arrived.*

▶ See page 134 for more on the past perfect simple and continuous.

You can use both *would* and *used to* to refer to regular or repeated past actions. *When she lived with us, she **used to** get up at six o'clock and **would** always have coffee for breakfast.* You can also use *used to* – but not *would* – to refer to past states or situations. *I **used to** have a motorbike but I sold it.*

▶ **Now do Exercise 1.**

Part 2: Auxiliaries

so / neither (nor)

The auxiliary verbs *be*, *have* and *do* are used to form different verb structures. They are also used with *so* and *neither (nor)* in question tags and in short answers. You use *so* to mean 'also' in the structure *So + auxiliary + subject*. *'I'm American.' 'So am I.'*

You use *neither* or *nor* to mean 'also not' in the same structure. *'I can't swim.' 'Nor can my brother.'*

Both *so* and *neither* are used to show agreement between speakers. Note what happens when there is disagreement between speakers. *'I'm Irish.' 'I'm not.'* (NOT *'I'm not Irish.'*) */ 'He hasn't got a car.' 'She has.'* (NOT *'She's.'*)

Question tags

You usually use a negative question tag with a positive statement, and a positive question tag with a negative statement. *You're Irish (+), **aren't you** (–)? / You're not Irish (–), **are you** (+)?*

You use *they* to refer to *somebody, anybody/everybody* and *nobody*. ***Somebody** must have seen her, mustn't **they**?*

You use a positive question tag after *never, hardly, little*. *He **never** gives up, **does he**?*

You can use *will/would* or *can/can't/could* after imperatives. ***Get** me some milk from the shops, **would you**?*

Other cases: ***Let's** go out for dinner, **shall we**? / **There's** no time left, **is there**? / **Nothing** can go wrong, **can it**?*

▶ **Now do Exercises 2 and 3.**

Unit 2 Verb patterns (1)

verb + *to*-infinitive

These verbs *don't* typically take an object before the *to*-infinitive: *aim, arrange, attempt, can't afford, decide, hope, intend, manage, offer, plan, refuse, seem, tend, try.* *She **manages to stay** in shape.*

verb + object + *to*-infinitive

a) These verbs *sometimes* take an object before the *to*-infinitive: *expect, help, want.* *I **wanted her to go out** with me, but she said she was busy.*

b) These verbs *usually* take an object before the *to*-infinitive: *allow, encourage, force, remind, teach, urge, warned (not).* *My father **taught me to swim** when I was five.*

verb + gerund

You use the *gerund* after these verbs: *avoid, can't stand, don't mind, enjoy, fancy, finish, keep, miss, spend/waste time.* *I **can't stand being** the centre of attention.*

verb + object + gerund

These verbs sometimes take an object before the *gerund*: *avoid, don't mind, dread.* *I **dreaded** my parents finding out.*

verb + object + infinitive without *to*

Make and *let* take an object before the infinitive without *to*. *They **let me have** my own beliefs.*

▶ **Now do Exercises 1 and 2.**

Unit 1 Exercises

1 **Underline the most appropriate verb structure.**

a) I **'m remembering / remember** where I was when I **was hearing / heard** about Princess Diana's death.
b) Over the years, I **'ve seen / saw** the footage of JF Kennedy's assassination loads of times.
c) I **'ve watched / watched** the news about 9/11 live on TV.
d) I **'m thinking / think** that Bill Clinton **was / has been** a good president.
e) I **used to / would** love flying, but airport security checks **have changed / had changed** how I feel about it now.
f) The recent global recession **was affecting / affected** me personally.
g) I **never enjoyed / 'd never enjoyed** the Olympic Games until **I've seen / saw** the last one.

Are any of the sentences true for you?

2 **Write one response to show agreement and one response to show disagreement.**

a) I've been to New Zealand.   *So have I*   /   *I haven't*
b) I'm from South America.   _____ / _____
c) I don't like coffee.   _____ / _____
d) I was born in Europe.   _____ / _____
e) I've never smoked.   _____ / _____
f) I watched TV last night.   _____ / _____
g) I can't swim.   _____ / _____
h) I wouldn't like to be famous.   _____ / _____

Tick the statements that are true for you and compare with a partner.

3 **Complete the statements with a question tag.**

a) You're Polish, *aren't you?*
b) It's a lovely day, _____ ?
c) She can't swim, _____ ?
d) We don't have much time, _____ ?
e) He must be cold, _____ ?
f) They haven't been to the US before, _____ ?
g) Let's have a game of tennis, _____ ?
h) Answer the phone, _____ ?

Unit 2 Exercises

1 **Underline the correct form of the verb.**

Steve and I decided (1) **to get / getting** married when we were eighteen. Our parents warned us not (2) **to rush / rushing** into anything. I don't think any of them wanted us (3) **to go / going** through with it. But, to their credit, they helped us (4) **to buy / buying** our house, and they didn't mind (5) **to look / looking** after our children when they came along. Even though I dreaded my mother in law (6) **to come / coming** round, I must say she was fantastic. So now we feel that whatever our kids want (7) **to do / doing**, we're ready to let them (8) **make / to make** their own mistakes.

2 **Complete the sentences with the correct form of the verbs in brackets.**

a) My mother taught me (cook) _____ .
b) I can't stand (live) _____ at home but I can't afford (move) _____ out.
c) I enjoy (go) _____ shopping, as long as it's for clothes.
d) I've always wanted (have) _____ a large family of my own.
e) My father always made me (obey) _____ his rules, while my mum always let me (do) _____ what I wanted, as long as I avoided (get) _____ into trouble.
f) I don't intend (get) _____ married or (have) _____ any children.
g) My parents have always encouraged me (follow) _____ my dreams.

Which sentences are true for you? Discuss with a partner.

Unit 3 Reported speech. Unreal conditionals

Part 1: Reported speech

Reporting speech means using your own words to report what somebody has said. You usually use the verbs *say (that)* or *tell (someone that)* and *ask (someone if / whether)* for questions.

Tenses

There is usually a 'back-shift' of tense. Present simple, continuous and perfect change to past simple, continuous and perfect. Past simple and past continuous change to past perfect simple and past perfect continuous. Modal verbs *can* and *will* change to *could* and *would*. Some forms don't need to change: a verb already in the past perfect remains in the past perfect; modal verbs *could*, *might* and *would* remain in the same form.

Word order in reported questions

The word order in reported questions is the same as in statements (subject + verb). You don't use *do/does/did*. For *yes/no* questions you use *if* or *whether*.

'Do you have enough money?' ➜ *She asked me if / whether I had enough money.*

Pronouns

Pronouns and possessive adjectives may change.
Direct speech: '*I* like *your* ideas.'
Report 1: *My* boss told *me* that *she* liked *my* ideas.
Report 2: *His* boss told *him* that *she* liked *his* ideas.

Time references

Here are some common changes from direct speech to reported speech when referring to time: a few weeks ago ➜ a few weeks previously; now ➜ then; today ➜ that day; tomorrow ➜ the following day; this week ➜ that week; next week ➜ the following week. '*I'll see you tomorrow*' ➜ *He said he'd see me the following day*.

▶ Now do Exercise 1.

Part 2: Unreal conditionals

These sentences consist of an *if*-clause and a main clause and are used to refer to unreal situations in the present or past.

if-clause

The *if*-clause expresses the condition. To show that a situation is imaginary, the tense backshifts (present ➜ past; past ➜ past perfect).

Real situation		Imaginary situation
I'm not rich.	➜	*If I was/were rich, …*
I spent too much money.	➜	*If I hadn't spent so much money, …*

Main clause

The main clause expresses the outcome of the condition, and can either refer to the present (1) *would/n't + infinitive without to*, or the past (2) *would/n't + have + past participle*.

if-clause		Main clause
If I hadn't wasted all my money,	➜	*I wouldn't be poor now.* (1) *I wouldn't have lost my house.* (2)

▶ Now do Exercises 2 and 3.

Unit 4 Narrative tenses. Future continuous and future perfect

Part 1: Narrative tenses

Past simple and continuous

The past simple is usually used to fix events in the past. You can use it to describe the main events of a story. Most verbs are regular and end in *-d/-ed/-ied*, although the most common ones are often irregular. There is a fuller list of irregular verbs on page 159.

The past continuous is often used in contrast with the past simple. You can use it to describe an activity in progress when the main events of the story happened.
*When they **looked** back, the polar bear **was running** after them.*

Past perfect simple and continuous

The past perfect can be used when you want to refer to an event (simple) or activity in progress (continuous) which clearly took place before the time of the main events of the story. *When they made their first stop, they **had been travelling** for 12 hours. / He was just twenty-three and **had never been** on a polar expedition.*

▶ Now do Exercise 1.

Part 2: Future continuous and future perfect

You use the future continuous to talk about an action that will be in progress at a certain time in the future. *Don't phone at 8.00 – we'll be having dinner.*

You use the future perfect to talk about an action that will be completed before a certain time in the future. *I'll have finished work by 5.30.*

▶ Now do Exercise 2.

Unit 3 Exercises

1 **Complete each reporting sentence.**

    a) 'I was just thinking about you!' He said *that he was just thinking about me.*
    b) 'We went to Paris a few days ago.' She told us …
    c) 'When I get my bonus I'm going to spend it wisely.' He said …
    d) 'How do you manage to live on so little money?' He asked us …
    e) 'What will happen to us tomorrow?' She asked him …
    f) 'I think your work is excellent.' My manager told me …
    g) 'Can we afford a holiday this year?' I asked her …

2 **Make unreal conditional questions using the verb in brackets.**

    a) I can't speak English fluently. (do)
       If you could speak English fluently, what would you do?
    b) I didn't win the lottery. (buy)
    c) I'm not rich. (go)
    d) I can't afford an expensive car. (choose)
    e) I arrived on time this morning. (happen)
    f) I'm not the president of my country. (change)
    g) It rained yesterday. (do)
    h) I had to work last weekend. (go)

3 **Write full answers to the questions in Exercise 2. Compare with a partner.**

a)   *If I could speak English fluently, I'd become a teacher.*

'If I was married to you, I'd divorce you!'

Unit 4 Exercises

1 **Underline the correct form of the verb.**

Canadian explorer Jamie Clarke (1) **was climbing** / **climbed** Mount Everest when he (2) **was having** / **had** the idea to cross the Arabian desert. Two years later, Jamie and two friends, three Bedouin guides and twelve camels (3) **were setting off** / **set off** from Salalah in Oman on their desert crossing. They (4) **were following** / **had been following** the route British explorer Wilfred Thesiger (5) **took** / **had taken** fifty years earlier. Before starting their journey, Thesiger (6) **was advising** / **had advised** them to take good care of their camels. It (7) **was** / **has been** good advice because without the camels they wouldn't have survived. They (8) **were wearing** / **wore** the traditional clothes of the Bedouin and (9) **were eating** / **ate** bread and meat. They (10) **have never experienced** / **had never experienced** such temperatures, by day 49°C dropping to around 8°C by night. Thirty-nine days later they (11) **have arrived** / **arrived** in Abu Dhabi. They (12) **were travelling** / **had travelled** 1,000 km in that time. Throughout his travels he (13) **was keeping** / **had been keeping** a diary and a year after his return from Arabia, he (14) **published** / **had published** *Everest to Arabia*, an account of the challenges he (15) **has faced** / **had faced** on his two epic journeys.

2 **Complete the sentences to make them true for you. Use future continuous (action in progress) or future perfect (completed action).**

    a) This time next week, I'll … (in progress)
       be lying on a beach.
    b) By the end of the week, I'll … (completed)
    c) At 1pm on Sunday, I'll … (in progress)
    d) Two years from now, I'll … (completed)
    e) At 10am the day after tomorrow, I'll … (in progress)
    f) Five years from now, I'll … (completed)
    g) At 8pm this evening, I'll … (in progress)
    h) In ten years' time, I'll … (completed)

Compare your answers with a partner.

Unit 5 Present and past habits. Verb patterns (2)

Part 1: Present and past habits

will / would

To talk about habitual behaviour which is characteristic and predictable, you can use *will* for the present and *would* for the past.

He'll get up at seven o'clock and he *won't talk* to anyone until he's finished his breakfast. / I'*d walk* home every day unless it was raining.

Will and *would* are almost always contracted (*'ll*, *'d*). The full forms can make you sound angry. *She* **will insist** on opening all the windows.

used to

You can use *used to* to talk about past habits or past states or situations.

I *used to have* a pet rabbit called 'Dingbat'. / I *used to come* home from school every day at five o'clock.

I *didn't use to enjoy* sports lessons.

▶ Now do Exercise 1.

Part 2: Verb patterns (2)

A small group of verbs can be followed by both the *to*-infinitive and the gerund, each with a change in meaning.

1 try

With the *to*-infinitive the action of the verb is not completed successfully. *I tried to make* her understand my feelings, but she wouldn't listen.

With the gerund the action of the verb is completed successfully, but it doesn't have the desired effect. *I tried leaving* her messages, but she never replied.

2 stop

With the *to*-infinitive you are giving the reason for stopping. *She stopped to tell* me about her boyfriend when I saw her in town.

With the gerund you are saying that an activity has stopped. *She stopped talking* to him after they split up.

3 remember, (never/not) forget

With the *to*-infinitive you are referring to actions somebody is/was supposed to do. *I remembered to buy* her a birthday card. But I *forgot to post* it.

With the gerund you refer to definite events – things that people actually did. *I remember meeting* her in a bar. (= I met her and now I remember this meeting.) / *I'll never forget kissing* her for the first time.

NOTE It's uncommon to use the affirmative of *forget* + gerund (*He forgot meeting Bob.*). 'Don't remember' is more usual (*He didn't remember meeting Bob.*).

▶ Now do Exercise 2.

Unit 6 Present perfect simple and continuous. Passives review

Part 1: Present perfect simple and continuous

The present perfect always shows a connection between the past and the present. It describes actions or processes that have happened (*finished*) or have been happening (*unfinished*) in time 'up-to-now'.

The simple form usually describes *finished* actions. You don't say *when* they happened. *I've been to Rome.*

The continuous form usually describes *unfinished* actions or processes. You normally say *how long* for. *I've been going* to Rome since I was a child.

The continuous form can also describe an action which

has *just* finished, and which has present results. *My hair's wet because I've been swimming*.

⚠ Verbs describing single actions are unusual in the continuous form. *She's lost* her keys (NOT ~~She's been losing her keys~~).

⚠ Verbs describing states are very rarely used in the continuous form. *I've known* her for years (NOT ~~I've been knowing her for years~~).

▶ Now do Exercises 1 and 2.

Part 2: Passives review

In passive sentences the object of the active verb becomes the subject of the passive verb.

subject	active verb	object
Somebody	's eaten	my sandwich!

subject	passive verb
My sandwich	has been eaten!

subject	active verb	object
The police	are holding	two men.

subject	passive verb	by + agent
Two men	are being held	by the police.

In passive sentences the 'doer' of the action – known as the 'agent' – is either not mentioned at all, or mentioned at the end of the sentence after *by*.

▶ Now do Exercise 3.

Unit 5 Exercises

1 Rewrite the sentences describing habits and states using *will*, *would* and *used to*. Use contractions (*'ll, 'd*) where possible.

a) My father insists on smoking in the car. I hate it!
   My father will insist on smoking in the car. I hate it!
b) My family and I lived in a large house.
c) During the school holidays I spent all my time with my friends.
d) I didn't have dark hair when I was young.
e) During the week I don't go to bed until after midnight.
f) At school I took a lucky charm into exams with me.
g) My partner speaks for hours on the phone. It drives me crazy!

Which sentences are true for you? Compare with a partner.

2 Complete the conversation with an appropriate form of the verbs in brackets.

A: Did you know that Emily and Sam are splitting up? I'm not surprised. Emily is not an easy person. I tried (1) (get on with) _____ her but I couldn't.

B: What about Sam? He never stops (2) (flirt) _____ with other women. I'll never forget (3) (see) _____ him dancing with Alice at the Christmas party. It was outrageous!

A: I just remember them (4) (argue) _____ all the time. It's very sad. They wanted the marriage to work. They even tried (5) (have) _____ counselling.

B: Anyway, are you ready? Don't forget (6) (bring) _____ the keys and the camera.

A: Fine, oh, and we need to stop (7) (get) _____ some petrol. And I must remember (8) (buy) _____ a card. I think it's going to be a really nice wedding. Don't you?

B: Yeah. Let's hope that Emily's brother is luckier in love than she has been.

Unit 6 Exercises

1 Write sentences using the present perfect simple or continuous.

a) I /learn/ English/ for six years.
   I've been learning English for six years.
b) I /know/ my best friend since I was a child.
c) I'm exhausted. I /work/ hard all day.
d) I /not see/ my parents for ages.
e) I'm tired. I /not feel/ well lately.
f) I /not done/ any housework for weeks.
g) I /sit/ here for more than an hour.
h) I /think/ of changing my job lately.

Tick the sentences which are true for you. Compare with a partner.

2 Complete the sentences with *for* or *since*.

a) I've been in this town _____ 2001.
b) I haven't eaten _____ two hours.
c) I've been studying English _____ I was a child.
d) I haven't had a break _____ three hours.
e) I haven't seen my friend Tom _____ the beginning of the month.
f) It's been sunny here _____ more than two weeks.
g) I've been feeling great _____ last Sunday.

Replace the words in bold with information which makes the sentences true for you. Compare your new sentences with a partner.

3 Write passive sentences. Use *by* + agent if you need to mention the 'doer' of the action.

a) My brother made that chair.
b) Someone introduced us yesterday.
c) They could recycle more than 80% of our waste.
d) Someone is processing your application now.
e) Alexander Graham Bell invented the telephone.
f) Around 400 million people speak English as a first language.
g) The police have arrested a man in connection with the robbery.
h) They will make an announcement later on in the week.

'Hello... This is the police. If you are being attacked from behind by a mad axe-murderer, press "One"...'

Unit 7 Past modals. Articles

Part 1: Past modals

In addition to the nine 'pure modal verbs' (*can, could, may, might, will, would, shall, should, must*), there are some phrases which express similar functions, and so are classed as 'semi-modals': *be allowed to, have to, need to* and *ought to*.

Function	Affirmative	Negative	Structure
Expressing permission	*was/were allowed to* *could*	*wasn't/weren't allowed to* *couldn't*	+ infinitive (without *to*) (*go / do* etc.)
Expressing necessity	*had to* *needed to*	*didn't have to* *didn't need to*	
Talking about the 'right course of action'.	*should have* *ought to have*	*shouldn't have* *ought not to have*	+ past participle (*gone / done* etc.)

▶ **Now do Exercise 1.**

Part 2: Articles

No article

You don't use articles with proper nouns such as places, people and companies.
Ian Smith *is from* **Leeds**. *He works at* **IBM**.
Exceptions are when the article is part of a name (**The USA, The BBC, The Beatles**).
As the indefinite article means 'one', you don't use it with plurals or uncountable nouns. *He had lots of **ideas**, but not much **money**.*

Indefinite article *a/an*: introducing

You use *a/an* when you first mention new people, places or objects. *There was **a tourist** from the USA.*

Definite article *the*: referring or identifying

You can use *the* when referring back to a person or thing that has already been introduced.
***The** tourist took a photo of a fisherman.* (We have already been introduced to *the* 'tourist'.)
You can also use *the* when the person or thing is shared knowledge.
***The sun** shone brightly as he looked out at **the ocean**.* (It's obvious which sun and which ocean.)

Back reference and shared knowledge can combine. *He took **a photograph**. **The click** of **the camera** woke **the man** up.* (We know that to take a photograph you need a camera, and that most cameras go click.)

NOTE You don't usually use the definite article with plural or uncountable nouns. *Tigers are endangered. / Time is money.*

▶ **Now do Exercises 2 and 3.**

Unit 8 *have / get something done.* Unreal conditional structures

Part 1: *have / get something done*

You use *have something done* when someone does something for you. Compare the two sentences.
Mandy cut her hair last week. (= She cut it herself.)

Mandy had her hair cut last week. (= Someone cut it for her.)
NOTE *get something done* is more informal.

▶ **Now do Exercise 1.**

Part 2: Unreal conditional structures

You usually begin an unreal conditional clause with *if* when you are making questions. Here are some alternatives.

Conditional clause			Main clause			
If *Imagine (that)* *Supposing (that)* *Suppose (that)* *Assuming (that)*	subject	past simple past continuous *were to* + inf. *might* past perfect	*what* *where* *how* etc.	*would* *could* *might*	subject	infinitive? *be* + present participle? *have* + past participle?

***Imagine** you **were meeting** someone for the first time, how **would** you **introduce** yourself?*
***Assuming that** you **were to go** on another date, where **might** you **be planning** to meet?*

▶ **Now do Exercise 2.**

Unit 7 Exercises

1 Underline the correct past modals of obligation.

On my last holiday …
a) I **didn't have to / should have** get up early.
b) I **shouldn't have / didn't need to** speak a different language.
c) I **ought to have / had to** taken a good book to read.
d) I **wasn't allowed to / ought to have** use my mobile on the plane.
e) I **couldn't / shouldn't have** eaten so much.
f) I **had to / ought to have** pay for my in-flight meals.
g) I **shouldn't have / couldn't** relax.
h) I realised I **needed to / should have** gone to a different place.

Are any of the sentences true for you?

'Now, write one hundred times:
"I must not waste my time".'

2 Complete the list below with *the* or put a dash (-) if no article is necessary.
a) **Mountain ranges:** *the* Alps, _____ Himalayas
b) **Mountain summits:** _____ Mount Everest, _____ Mont Blanc
c) **Continents:** _____ Europe, _____ Asia
d) **Towns / cities:** _____ Prague, _____ Tokyo
e) **Parks:** _____ South Park, _____ Hyde Park
f) **Lakes:** _____ Lake Malawi, _____ Loch Ness
g) **Streets:** _____ Baker Street, _____ Hollywood Boulevard
h) **Months:** _____ January, _____ September
i) **Oceans:** _____ Pacific Ocean, _____ Indian Ocean
j) **Seas:** _____ Mediterranean Sea, _____ Black Sea
k) **Rivers:** _____ Nile, _____ Amazon
l) **'of' phrases:** _____ Statue of Liberty, _____ Houses of Parliament

3 Complete the story with *a, an, the* or put a dash (-) if no article is necessary.

(1) _____ elderly couple from (2) _____ USA were driving through (3) _____ Mexico and were approaching (4) _____ city named Oaxaca. They saw (5) _____ sign with (6) _____ name of (7) _____ city printed in (8) _____ capital letters: OAXACA. (9) _____ couple tried to figure out how to pronounce (10) _____ name – Wacks acka? Oaks-acer? They kept trying as they drove into (11) _____ city. As they were hungry, they pulled into (12) _____ place to get something to eat. At (13) _____ counter, (14) _____ man said to (15) _____ waitress: "My wife and I can't figure out how to pronounce (16) _____ name of this place. Could you tell us and say it very slowly so that we can understand?" (17) _____ waitress looked at (18) _____ him and said: "(19) _____ Buuurrrgerrr Kiiiinnnng."

Unit 8 Exercises

1 Make questions from the prompts. Use *Would you ever + have/get* something done.

a) shave head
Would you ever get your head shaved?
b) whiten teeth
c) colour hair
d) do a tattoo
e) wax legs
f) pierce ears
g) straighten teeth

Work with a partner. Ask and answer the questions.

2 Put the words in the correct order to make unreal conditional questions.

a) could take / what / do / Supposing / a year off work, / you / would you?
Supposing you could take a year off work, what would you do?
b) who / Imagine / with anyone in the world, / could / choose / you / have dinner / would you?
c) what / most of your money / you / would you / spend / Assuming / on / a millionaire, / were?
d) was late / Supposing / for your first date, / how long / someone / you wait / would?
e) went well, / your first date / before phoning / how long / Assuming / would you wait / him/her again?
f) do you think / a different job, / to do / Imagine that / you had / what / you'd have chosen?
g) until 3.00 a.m., / you hadn't / be feeling now / Supposing that / gone to bed / you'd / do you think / how?
h) Imagine that / of your character, / what / change one aspect / you / would / could / it be?

Work with a partner. Ask each other the questions and take it in turns to answer them.

Unit 9 Past modals of deduction. *look, seem, appear*

Part 1: Past modals of deduction

There are many ways of expressing degrees of certainty about something which happened in the past.

Degree of certainty	Past modal auxiliaries		Other phrases
99% certain it *WAS.* ✓		*must*	I'm almost certain it was …
	(It)	*may* *could* + *have* + past participle *might*	I'm uncertain …
99% certain it *WASN'T.* ✗		*can't*	I'm sure it wasn't …

Stonehenge **might have been** *a kind of temple. It* **must** *have taken a long time to move the huge stones.*
⚠ The opposite of *must have been* is *can't have been*: *It* **can't have been** *easy trying to move stones without wheels. They* **must have been** *really heavy.*

▶ **Now do Exercise 1.**

Part 2: *look, seem, appear*

look / *seem* + adjective
The verb **look** refers to the sense of sight and is followed by an adjective. *He* **looks** *great for his age.* The verbs for the other senses follow the same pattern (*She* **sounds** *nice. It* **tastes** *great. It* **feels** *cold. That* **smells** *good.*)
look like + noun
This means *resemble* and is usually followed by a noun. *He* **looks like** *Brad Pitt.* (= He resembles Brad Pitt.)

look / *seem as if* / *though* + verb phrase
We use this to describe what something seems like. The verb in the phrase can be in any tense. *It* **looks as if** *it's fallen over.* / *She always* **seems as though** *she's going to cry.*
seem / *appear* + to be
These verbs help to describe your understanding of a situation. They can be followed by an adjective or noun phrase. *She* **seems** *sad.* / *He* **appears to be** *in trouble.*

▶ **Now do Exercise 2.**

Unit 10 Relative clauses. Emphasis (cleft sentences)

Part 1: Relative clauses

Non-defining relative clauses
You use non-defining relative clauses for two main reasons. You can either comment on the whole of the main clause or you can give some extra, non-essential information about the person or thing you are talking about. Compare the following:
He's going out with Julie, **which I can't stand**. (= a comment on the whole of the main clause)
He's going out with Julie, **who I can't stand**. (= a comment or 'extra information' about Julie)
You always begin a non-defining relative clause with a relative pronoun, and you separate it from the main clause with commas.
You don't use *that* with non-defining relative clauses.
You always use *which* when introducing a comment on the whole of the main clause.

Defining relative clauses
You use defining relative clauses to identify exactly which person or thing you are talking about. When the relative pronoun (*who, that* or *which*) is the subject of the relative clause you *can't* leave it out. *I like friends* **who** *never let me down.*
However, when the relative pronoun is the object of the relative clause you *can* leave it out. *He's got a job* **that** *he's really interested in.* or *He's got a job he's really interested in.*
NOTE You don't need another object pronoun. *… he's really interested in.* (NOT *… he's really interested in it.*)

⚠ You can never leave out *whose. That's the man* **whose** *dog bit my son.*

▶ **Now do Exercises 1 and 2.**

Part 2: Emphasis (cleft sentences)

What structures (= The thing(s) that)
You can use *What … is/was …* to emphasise either the subject or the object of a sentence. *I don't understand* **why** *it's so cold.* → **What** *I don't understand* **is why** *it's so cold.*

You can replace *What* with *All* if you want to emphasise *The only thing that. I only want to play tennis.* → **All** *I really want to do is play tennis.*

It is / *was …* + relative clause
You can use this structure to emphasise almost any part of a sentence. *Carla Bruni married Nicolas Sarkozy in Paris in 2008.* **It was Carla Bruni** *who married …* / **It was Paris** *where Carla Bruni married …* / **It was in 2008** *that Carla Bruni married …*
You often use this structure when you are correcting what other people say. **It wasn't Juliette Binoche** *who married Nicolas Sarkozy, it was Carla Bruni.*

▶ **Now do Exercises 3 and 4.**

Unit 9 Exercises

1   **Make sentences using** *can't have, might / may / could have or must have.*

   a) It's possible that Albert Einstein was born in Austria.
      Albert Einstein may have been born in Austria.

   b) U.S. astronauts almost certainly didn't see the Great Wall of China from the Moon.

   c) Picasso most probably produced more than 5,000 paintings in his lifetime.

   d) There's a possibility Shakespeare didn't die on his birthday.

   e) It is very likely that Mozart wasn't very well known when he died.

   f) It is very likely that Walt Disney won more Oscars than any other entertainer.

   g) There is a possibility that Leonardo da Vinci had an affair with Mona Lisa.

**Work with a partner. Four of these speculative sentences are true and four are false.
Can you guess which is which?**

2   **Complete the sentences in a way that makes them true for you.**

   a) Today I look …
   b) The weather looks as if …
   c) My mother always seems as though …

   d) Lately my teacher has seemed …
   e) My best friend looks like …
   f) My progress in English appears …

Compare your sentences with a partner.

Unit 10 Exercises

1   **Write the words in the correct order to make defining relative clauses. In each case there is one word too many.**

   a) **a job** / in / that / it / interested / are / you
      a job that you are interested in ~~it~~

   b) **a bank account** it / out / never / that / runs

   c) **a boss** get / him / with / who / you / on

   d) **a car** it / that / down / never / breaks

   e) **a government** voted / that / them / you / for

   f) **a friend** who / you / she / down / lets / never

   g) **a home** in / there / happy / you / that / are

   h) **a partner** love / you / her / who / in / are / with

**In which of the defining clauses above can you omit the relative pronoun? Put items *a–h* in order of
importance for you in your life. Compare with a partner.**

2   **In each case make a single sentence containing a non-defining relative clause using the extra information in
brackets.**

   a) He bought me an expensive dress. (I didn't really like him buying me the dress.)
      He bought me an expensive dress, which I didn't really like.

   b) Adam turned up at 10.30 this morning. (Adam is almost never late.)

   c) That woman works in our shop. (She looks like my sister.)

   d) Mike's father is in advertising. (Mike's father lives in France.)

   e) There's a lift in the building. (You can use the lift to go to the top floor.)

   f) Ellen got me a really nice jacket. (Ellen getting me the jacket was a complete surprise.)

3   **Write the words in the correct order to make cleft sentences.**

   a) love / What / my country / weather / fantastic / is the / I / about

   b) like most / is their / person / The / humour / thing / sense of / I / in a

   c) enjoy / playing / What / is / I / most / tennis

   d) most / is / thing / studying / The / the tests / hate / I / English / about

   e) need / stress-free / What / is / in life / we all / a / most / job

   f) never / understand / What / I / enough / don't / time / is why / I / have / free

Which sentences do you agree with?

4   **Change the emphasis in these sentences by starting** *It is / was …*

   a) He met his wife in Paris.
      It was in Paris that he met his wife.

   b) I only understood how serious it was when he phoned.

   c) Ian didn't break that cup, you did.

   d) Ben stole the cake, not Amy.

   e) He wanted money, not love.

   f) Sam spends all her time on the computer, not the phone.

Unit 11 Future forms and future time clauses

Will ('ll), (be) going to, and the present continuous

These are the three most common future forms.

1 *Will* (*'ll*) is used for predictions or decisions reacting to circumstances such as offers, promises and requests. *It'll be worth a fortune in a few years' time.* / *I'll give you my photograph now.*

2 (*be*) *going to* is used for intentions or predictions based on present evidence. *I'm going to concentrate on my musical career.* / *Look at those clouds. It's going to pour down in a minute.*

3 The present continuous is used for arrangements. *I'm moving to London next month.*

The present simple

You can use this tense to talk about fixed future events: timetables, routines, schedules. *My exams start next week.*

might and *may*

If you want to speculate about a future possibility you can use *might* or *may*. *He might have to get a part-time job.*

The future continuous

You use this tense to talk about something happening around a certain time in the future. *This time next week I'll be trekking in Nepal.*

The future perfect

You use this tense to talk about something completed by a certain time in the future. *The builder will have finished the kitchen walls by the end of the week.*

Future time clauses (*if, when, as soon as ...*)

When it is clear from the main clause that the sentence is about the future you don't use a future form in the subordinate clause. *When I leave school, I'm going to concentrate on my music career.* (NOT *When I will leave school, ...*) / *It'll be a miracle if she's passed the exam.* (NOT *... if she will have passed the exam.*)

Other conjunctions which introduce subordinate clauses: *after, as soon as, before, once, the moment, the minute, unless, until.*

▶ Now do Exercises 1 and 2.

Unit 12 Participle clauses. Nouns and quantity expressions

Part 1: Participle clauses

When a present or past participle forms part of a relative clause, it is possible to leave out the relative pronoun (*who, which,* etc.) and auxiliary verb *be*. *We live in a house located in the centre of town.* (= We live in a house which is located in the centre of town.)
These are known as 'participle clauses' or 'reduced relative clauses'. As with other relative clauses, there are both defining and non-defining participle clauses.

Defining participle clauses: *The man walking down the street is my neighbour.* (= The man who is walking down the street is my neighbour.)
Non-defining participle clauses contain extra, non-essential information which is separated from the main clause using commas. *His house, built in the 1930s, needs redecorating.* (= His house, which was built in the 1930s, needs redecorating.)

▶ Now do Exercise 1.

Part 2: Nouns and quantity expressions

You use determiners (*every, most, no*) and quantifiers (*all of, most of, none of*) to express quantity.

1 Quantity expressions used with both **countable** and **uncountable** nouns: *none, not any, hardly any, some, a lot, loads, plenty.*

2 Quantity expressions used only with **countable** nouns: (*very*) *few, a few, several,* (*too/not*) *many.*

3 Quantity expressions used only with **uncountable** nouns: (*very*) *little, a little, a bit,* (*too/not*) *much.*

4 When there is the definite article (*the*), a possessive pronoun (*my, your,* etc.) or a demonstrative pronoun (*that, these,* etc.) before the noun, you use a quantity expression with *of: Several of my friends live in small villages.* (NOT *Several my friends ...*)

5 When you want to talk about small numbers or amounts you can use *a few / a little* to emphasise the positive (*some*), or *few / little* to emphasise the negative (*not many/much*): *We did it because we wanted to have a little fun. Please hurry up! There's very little time.*

Verb forms

You use a singular verb form if the noun after *of* is uncountable (U) or singular. You use a plural if the noun is countable (C).
There's lots of traffic (U) *in the centre.*
There are lots of tourists (C) *in summer.*

▶ Now do Exercises 2 and 3.

Unit 11 Exercises

1 Complete the second sentence so that it has a similar meaning to the first sentence. Use between two and five words, including the word given in bold.

1 There's a possibility she won't pass the exam.
might
She *might not pass* the exam.

2 I'm seeing the director at 3 pm.
arranged
I _____ the director at 3 pm.

3 When I've finished this test, I'm leaving.
soon
_____ I've finished this test, I'm leaving.

4 I intend to concentrate on my acting career.
going
I _____ concentrate on my acting career.

5 The builders are due to finish in a week.
have
By this time next week, the builders _____ .

6 We won't go if you can't come with us.
can
_____ come with us, we won't go.

7 When he's finished, he'll come out.
until
He's _____ he's finished his homework.

8 I predict a good result for the team today.
to
I think the team _____ win today.

'You'll be hearing from my lawyer'

2 Write three sentences about the future: one about you, one about your country and one about the planet. Compare with your partner.

Unit 12 Exercises

1 Rewrite the sentences using a defining participle clause.

a) That man who is speaking very loudly is my cousin. That man ...
b) The people who live in my street are very friendly. The people ...
c) We keep the glasses in that cabinet. They are very expensive. The glasses ...
d) The rooms that overlook the back of the house are the best. The rooms ...
e) That place sells pizzas. They are the best! The pizzas ...

2 Underline the correct alternative.

My hometown is small but there (1) **'s / are** loads of people out on a Saturday night. Sometimes there's so (2) **much / many** noise in the city centre, you'd think it was daytime. If you want to go out there are a (3) **few / little** really good nightclubs and (4) **plenty of / too much** pubs. But the pubs close early so you often have very (5) **few / little** time to finish your drink. (6) **Some / Some of** my friends and I go bowling, but (7) **hardly any / hardly many** of us are any good. It might not sound like we have (8) **a lot of / many** fun, but we do – it's my home and I love it!

3 Add an appropriate quantity expression from the box to make the sentences true for you.

| all of   most of   several of   not (very) many of   a few of   hardly any of   none of |

a) _____ my friends live in small villages.
b) _____ the people I know go to work by car.
c) _____ the shops near my home are open on Sunday.
d) _____ the houses in my street have big gardens.
e) _____ my neighbours keep pets.
f) _____ the buildings in my area are old.
g) _____ the people I work with smoke.
h) _____ these exercises are easy.

Compare your answers with a partner.

Recordings

Unit 1

💿 1.05

(W = Woman; M = Man)
W: Excuse me, is it OK if I sit here?
M: Sure, go ahead.
W: Thanks. … Sorry, but you're English, aren't you?
M: Yes. How did you know?
W: Oh, I heard your accent. … It isn't very busy here today, is it?
M: No, it isn't.
W: Are you on holiday?
M: No, I'm working here for a few months.
W: Oh, really? So am I. What do you do?
M: I work for the American Central Bank.
W: Oh. And do you like it here?
M: No. I can't stand it – especially the weather. It was so hot yesterday, wasn't it?
W: Oh yeah, you're right: the heat's terrible. But, you know, I love New York.
M: How long have you been here?
W: Oh, not long – a few weeks. How about you?
M: The same. What are you doing here?
W: I'm an artist, and I was asked to bring over some of my work to a small gallery just near here. I've just had my first exhibition there.
M: Wow – that's impressive.
W: Thanks. So where are you from?
M: I'm from London – Notting Hill.
W: Really? So am I! Don't tell me you went to Atkins School?
M: Yes, I did, actually – but I wasn't a very good student.
W: Me neither. What year did you leave?
M: 1989.
W: That's weird – me too. Do you remember Mrs Rivers?
M: The Maths teacher? Yeah. She was really horrible, wasn't she?
W: She's my mum.
M: Oh. … Look, I'm sorry. … I didn't mean to …

💿 1.07

(J = Journalist; R= Rick)
1
J: Excuse me.
R: Me?
J: Yes, hi there! I'm working on a feature for *CHAPS* magazine about men's personal style. Do you mind if I ask you some questions?
R: No, I suppose not.
J: Could you tell me what image you're trying to achieve?
R: Image? I don't really have an image. I wear clothes I feel comfortable in – I suppose you'd call it a casual look.
J: Do you think that you're aware of fashion?
R: Er, probably not, no. My style hasn't changed for years.

💿 1.08

(J = Journalist; M = Matt)
2
J: Hello! I'm doing some research for an article about the way men dress. Can I ask you some questions?
M: Yeah, no problem.
J: Do you mind telling me what you wear to go out in the evening?
M: In the evening? You mean clubs and that sort of thing?
J: Yes, when you go clubbing.
M: I dress exactly like this.
J: You don't dress up then?
M: Well, put it this way – I never put a suit on. The clubs I go to don't let men in if they're wearing suits.
J: Really!? How strange. Um, one more question? I'd just like to know if there's an item of clothing you couldn't live without.
M: Trainers. Definitely couldn't live without them. I've got about twenty-five pairs.

💿 1.09

(J = Journalist; C = Charles)
3
J: Excuse me! Hello.
C: Hello.
J: I work for *CHAPS* magazine and we're doing a survey about men's self-image. Do you mind if I ask you a couple of questions?
C: Oh. No, no, go ahead. What do you want to know?
J: Well, I'd like to know what your clothes say about you.
C: What do my clothes say about me!? Gosh – I suppose they say that I'm meeting a client this afternoon, and that means I've got to make the right impression. So I have to wear a suit.
J: Would you say that you care about your image?
C: Oh yes, I think I do. I like to look smart, even when I'm not working. Even when I wear jeans and a T-shirt, I like them to be clean and neat, and I think this says that I care about myself. It says that I've got good self-esteem.

💿 1.10

(J = Journalist; A = Adam)
4
J: Excuse me, sir. Is it OK if I ask you a couple of questions for an article I'm doing for *CHAPS* magazine?
A: Yes, that's fine. Are you going to take photos?
J: Er, yes, if you don't mind. But first I'd like to know whether your appearance affects your life in any way.
A: Oh yes, totally. The way I dress is my life really. It hasn't really affected my career so far, but I'm hoping it will. Basically I want to be noticed, and the reason I want to be noticed is that I

want to get on television.
J: Ah. And do you know what the last thing you bought was?
A: Oh yes, I adore shopping. Er, that would be a pink shirt I bought yesterday – oh, and a pink and black tie.

💿 1.12

(R = Rose; I = Ian; M = Mike)
R: Have you got the tickets?
I: No, I thought you had them.
R: Ian, honestly, I can't trust you to do anything.
I: Calm down – they're here.
R: Grr – you're so annoying.
I: You're so easy to wind up.
   Hey, look at that woman over there.
R: The one in the white jacket?
I: Yeah.
R: What about her?
I: Don't you think she's the spitting image of Gwyneth Paltrow?
R: No, she doesn't look anything like Gwyneth Paltrow.
I: Yes she does. She's got the same hair.
R: What – long and blond?
I: Not just that – I'd recognise that smile anywhere.
R: How often has Gwyneth Paltrow smiled at you?
I: I've seen enough films with her in. She's got a very distinctive smile.
R: It can't be her – she wouldn't come here to our local club. And actually, that woman bears absolutely no resemblance to Gwyneth Paltrow.
I: Oh.
R: Hey, there's Mike. Hi Mike – how's it going?
M: Very well – you'll never guess who I've been talking to.
I: Not Gwyneth Paltrow!
M: Gwyneth Paltrow?
R: Oh, ignore him – he's obsessed.
I: Sorry. You were saying?
M: Well, I was just at the bar, and I saw this amazing-looking woman walking towards me. I didn't recognise her until she was right in front of me. She's changed so much!
R: Who was it?
M: Sally – you know, my ex-girlfriend? Anyway, we …

Unit 2

🔘 **1.15**

(I = Interviewer; M = Mum; D = Dad)

I: You're going to meet Sarah's boyfriend tomorrow.

M&D: That's right.

I: How do you feel about that?

M: Well, we're looking forward to meeting Andy at last – we've heard a lot about him, because Sarah's been going out with him for a while now. Several weeks, I believe.

I: Does Sarah usually bring her boyfriends home to meet you?

D: Well, it's difficult to know with Sarah really – she changes boyfriends like other people change their socks. We've met some of them.

M: Yes, I'd say we've met half a dozen over the years.

I: Have you liked most of her boyfriends?

M: No, not really. I'm always amazed at how awful they are. She goes for very strange types. There was just one we liked, wasn't there?

D: Oh, yes – you mean Jeremy. Lovely chap. We were impressed with him.

M: But he didn't last long. As soon as we told her we liked him, she dropped him.

I: What sort of person would you like Sarah to go out with?

M: Well, I think it's essential for him to come from the same kind of background.

D: Yes, and it's very important for him to have some kind of qualifications – you know, some ambition.

M: He needs to be a strong character to stand up to Sarah – she'd soon go off somebody who lets her do what she wants all the time.

D: Oh anyway, we're not going to take it too seriously. She's far too young to get married or engaged or anything like that. And the poor chap is unlikely to last very long.

🔘 **1.16**

(I = Interviewer; A = Andy)

I: How do you feel about meeting Sarah's parents?

A: A bit nervous. I'm worried about making a bad impression because I'm quite shy. So I find it difficult to get on with people straight away.

I: But you're a DJ, aren't you?

A: Yes, but it's easy for me to hide behind my music decks at work. I'm not very good at making conversation, especially with older people.

I: What are you most nervous about?

A: Well, I gave up studying to become a DJ, and I don't think Sarah's parents will be very impressed with that. Also, I dyed my hair red last week, and they'll probably be a bit shocked by that.

I: How are you going to try to make a good impression?

A: Well, I'm going to wear clean clothes – not a suit or anything, I haven't got one. And I'll take her mum some flowers.

I: Why are you going to meet Sarah's parents?

A: Because Sarah fancies going to London for the day, and she feels like having Sunday lunch at home. And I always do what she wants.

🔘 **1.20**

(J = Jill; M = Marie)

J: Hello, Marie, come in. Did you have a pleasant journey?

M: Pleasant journey?

J: A good trip?

M: Oh yes, thank you. Very good.

J: Well, welcome to our home. I hope you'll be happy here. It's not very big, but I think you'll have everything you need.

M: Yes, thank you. It's very nice.

J: Oh good, I'm glad you like it. Let me introduce you to the rest of the family, and then I'll show you around.

M: OK, thank you Mrs Brown.

J: Oh, you must call me Jill. Now, this is Benjie.

M: Hello, Ben.

J: And this is Katy.

M: Hello, Katy.

K: Hello.

J: And this is Max – he's a baby so he can be a bit excited. Down, Max. Sorry. I hope you don't mind dogs.

M: No, I love dogs.

J: Oh good. So, this is the kitchen – we usually eat breakfast in here. Help yourself to tea and coffee. The fridge is here, look – and the cups and saucers are in this cupboard here. I'm afraid the microwave is broken, but we seem to manage without.

M: It's a lovely kitchen.

J: Yes, it's my favourite room actually. Now, this is the living room – excuse the mess, but Benjie and Katy have lots of friends around. This is the dining room – Max isn't allowed in here, are you Max? Down boy! Now, if you'd like to leave your bags here for a minute, I'll show you the upstairs.

M: Thank you.

J: Here's the bathroom. Sorry about the pink walls – that was Katy's idea.

M: Oh, I like pink. My bedroom walls are pink.

J: Really? How funny. OK, this is Katy's bedroom – we're not allowed to go into Benjie's room, but it's probably just as well. And this is your room. It's quiet in here because the window looks out on the garden.

M: Oh it's lovely – thank you.

J: Now, you make yourself at home, and if there's anything you need, just give me a shout, OK?

M: OK.

J: Oh, by the way, Benjie's vegetarian, so we don't usually eat meat because he gets upset. Is that OK with you?

M: Yes, I like vegetables.

Unit 3

🔘 **1.22**

During the gold rush, Sam Brannan became one of the most successful businessmen in California. He arrived in California in 1846, when San Francisco (then called Yerba Buena) was just a small community of a few hundred people.

When gold was discovered on John Sutter's land in 1848, Sam Brannan was running the only store between San Francisco and the gold fields. Quickly recognising a gap in the market, he bought up all the picks, shovels and pans he could find, and then ran up and down the streets of San Francisco shouting, 'Gold, gold on the American River!'

He had no intention of digging for gold! No, he was planning to sell shovels. And having cornered the market, he ended up with a lot more gold than the person who had to dig for it.

This was a man who keenly understood the laws of supply and demand. A metal pan that sold for twenty cents a few days earlier, was now available from Brannan for fifteen dollars. In just nine weeks he made $36,000. Within a few years he had become the first gold rush millionaire.

In the end, though, Sam Brannan lost his fortune and his health, as did many of those who first benefited from the gold rush. Alcoholism finally led to his downfall, and California's first millionaire died an unnoticed death.

🔘 **1.25**

(I = Interviewer; P = Patti; E = Eric; L = Lee)

I: It's impossible to have too much money – do you agree with that, Patti?

P: Yes. If you have dreams, money makes them possible. Personally, I can't imagine having too much money. I'm always broke. Anyway, if I ever felt I had too much money, I'd give it away to charity.

I: And Patti, would you prefer fame or fortune?

P: Being practical, I'd say fortune, but if I were single with no kids and no responsibilities, I'd go for fame.

I: Eric, were you given or did you earn pocket money as a child?

E: I was given two shillings a week by my father, but on condition that I behaved myself. If I didn't behave well, I didn't receive it. Parents were much stricter in those days.

I: And Eric, what was the first thing you saved up for and bought yourself?

E: A set of toy soldiers. Not the plastic ones you get nowadays, but little metal ones, beautifully hand-painted. It took me nearly a year to save up for them. If I'd known that they would become valuable antiques, I would've kept them. They'd probably be worth a fortune now.

I: Tell me, Lee, if you could buy yourself a skill or a talent, what would it be?

L: Well, there are lots of things I'd like to be better at, but if I had to choose one, it would have to be football – I'd like to be a brilliant football player!

I: And finally Lee, what can't money buy?

L: Happiness. I tend to think that once I have enough money to buy some new clothes or get a better car, then I'll be happy. But it never works out like that.

🌐 1.27

1 Chris

I suppose you'd call it a vintage camera now. It's a Zeiss Contaflex and I bought it in South Africa 50 years ago. It cost £50 which was a lot of money for me then, but it was still a lot less than I would have paid back home in England. So I was delighted – it was the best camera you could get at the time and it was a bargain. Unfortunately, I had to pay nearly £40 in tax at customs when I arrived back in the UK, so in the end it was less of a bargain. But I've certainly had my money's worth out of it. It's been everywhere with me and all our family photographs were taken on this camera. Last year, for my 70th birthday, my children bought me a wonderful, and very modern, digital camera. It takes much better photographs than my old Zeiss, but I can't use it I'm afraid. I'm too old-fashioned.

🌐 1.28

2 Katie

I know it sounds a bit stupid, but this is the thing I would least like to lose. It's not because it's worth anything, although it is quite an expensive one because it's got GPS – you know, satellite navigation – on it too. But the main thing is that if I lost this, I'd lose the addresses and numbers of practically everybody I know. It contains the details of about three hundred people.

🌐 1.29

3 Heather

This is my most precious possession because it saved my life when I got caught in an avalanche in Johnson Pass in Alaska's Chugach Mountain Range. It had been snowing for four days, and the temperature rose that morning – perfect avalanche conditions. When the first person in our group of snowboarders leaped off the cornice, the rest of us decided to follow his tracks – no traversing and no hard turns, so as not to disturb the snow. When it was my turn, I made it down the first pitch safely and thought I was out of danger. But the person behind me started before I was at a safe distance and nervously made a hard right turn. I heard a loud crack, and then WHOMPH! The snow hit me really fast in the back of the neck. I pushed my neck-warmer over my face, which kept the snow out of my mouth and nose, allowing me to breathe as the avalanche swept me up. I began frantically swimming and tried to stay aware of which way was up. When the snow finally settled I had managed to get part of my glove up through the surface. It took the others a few minutes to find me, but I knew they would. Luckily, my neck-warmer allowed me the extra air to wait out those few minutes.

🌐 1.30

(J = John; C = Cara; SA1 = Ship assistant 1; SA2 = Shop assistant 2)

J: Thanks for doing this. I really don't know where to start.

C: Right, first you need to tell me what you're looking for. Do you have any ideas?

J: Well, diamonds are always good.

C: OK. And do you prefer gold or silver or platinum or white gold?

J: Whoa, hang on. Say that again.

C: Does Julia wear more gold or more silver?

J: Gold, I think.

C: And what's your budget?

J: My budget? I don't know. This is only the second time I've done this.

C: What? You were engaged before?

J: Yes, it was a mistake. We were too young.

C: And did she keep the ring?

J: Yeah, but it wasn't worth much – I was really hard up at the time so I just got something cheap and cheerful.

C: Well, you have to be prepared to splash out this time. It's a once-in-a-lifetime thing. Well, twice-in-a-lifetime for you, I suppose.

J: OK – my budget is … two or three hundred pounds.

C: Hmm. OK, well, you may have to revise that figure.

J: What do you mean?

C: You'll see. Come on. Let's go.

SA1: Good morning, sir, madam. Are you looking for something special?

J: Yes, um, a diamond engagement ring, please.

SA1: I see – our diamond rings are over here, sir. If you'd like to browse and then ask me to show you anything you particularly like.

J: Thanks. Have you seen the prices?

C: I told you …

SA1: Is there something you'd like to see?

J: Um, they're lovely, but they're a little out of my price range.

SA1: Sorry we can't help you, sir. Goodbye.

J: Right, let's go somewhere less exclusive, shall we?

C: OK, but you're going to have to pay a bit more.

J: I'm not made of money!

C: No, I know, but this is a time when you have to push the boat out.

SA2: Can I help you with anything today?

J: Er, yes, I'm looking for a very simple engagement ring – perhaps one diamond?

SA2: And what are you looking to pay?

J: Well, around £500?

SA2: OK, this is £560.

J: It's small, isn't it?

C: You get what you pay for.

J: OK, I was hoping for something slightly more sparkly. How much is this one, for example?

SA2: That one's £1,400.

J: Right. I suppose, I was thinking of something a little less pricey.

SA2: What's your budget?

J: I suppose I could stretch to £1,000.

SA2: OK. This one costs £950.

J: What do you think?

C: I think it's lovely, and I think Julia would love it.

J: I should certainly hope so. This is definitely the last time I'm doing this.

Unit 4

🔘 1.35

It was day two of my first ever North Pole expedition back in 2001. I was twenty-three years old. There were two people on this expedition: me and a guy called Pen Hadow, who was very experienced, so he was really teaching me how to survive in the Arctic, and it was the morning of day two. We'd just taken down our tent and started skiing. Pen was in front, navigating, and I was following his tracks, dragging my sledge and I started getting a very strange feeling that something was wrong and I wasn't sure to start with. It felt like I'd forgotten something important. I couldn't quite figure out what wasn't right and I stopped and turned around and looked behind me. Looked back along our tracks and saw a polar bear, walking towards us.

Now, early in the spring, at the very start of the expedition, and this was very early March, 2001. Polar bears have been hibernating through the winter so they are hungry. They've just woken up, they are looking for breakfast and we are wearing black clothing. We probably look a bit like seals, which is what bears normally eat. Bears are also the largest land-based carnivore in the world, so they are quite big, scary predators.

And I turned around and shouted at Pen, who was in front. Luckily he heard me, and our bear drill swang into action. Now we'd practised what to do once in the car park of a café just before we left the UK, and the theory is that we had to stay where we were and try and convince the polar bear that we were bigger and scarier than, than it was.

As I have said, they are big creatures – the heavy, heaviest adult male ever recorded was, I think, just over a thousand kilos, so a tonne. They can move at nearly fifty kilometres per hour if they want to. Now our top speed, pulling sledges, was about three kilometres per hour, so we knew there was no way we could outrun the bear, so we had to stay where we were, try and look big, and scare it away.

Pen was in charge of the gun. We had a shotgun that we'd bought in Russia. That was his job. My job was to look big and to take off my skis, hold the skis in the air, make lots of noise, try and frighten away the bear. And Pen loaded the gun with two cartridges. There are two barrels in the gun; closed the barrels, pulled the triggers – there are two triggers, one for each barrel of the gun – click, click, and he said, 'The gun's jammed.' And I looked at him. He reloaded the gun – two more cartridges, pulled the triggers, click, click. He said, 'The gun's still jammed,' and everything went into slow motion.

🔘 1.36

The bear is walking towards us. Pen is reloading the gun again with a fifth and sixth cartridge. We had twelve cartridges to last eight weeks, so Pen is now half way through our supply of ammunition. He pulls the first trigger, click, and then he walks around his sledge towards the bear, and I remember thinking, 'Wow, Pen's gone mad, completely. He's going to get eaten. What do I do?'

And I couldn't – I felt quite calm and I couldn't quite think what to do. I thought maybe I could throw a ski at it or try and stab it with a ski pole or something, and then the bear stopped. Pen stopped. Bang. The gun, the gun goes off in the air. Big cloud of smoke, and I think it surprised Pen and me more than it surprised the bear. The bear looked up, looked down, turned around and walked off, and Pen turned round and said, 'Quick, get the camera and take a photograph,' and that was when suddenly I felt really scared and nervous. I couldn't even undo the zip on the sledge.

That was the morning of the second day of this expedition. We were out there for two months – fifty-nine days, but we never saw another bear that close.

One of the surprising things I've seen and one of the ways that the Arctic is changing – certainly in my experience – is that there is less and less evidence of polar bears being there at all. In 2001 we saw many, many sets, dozens of sets of polar bear footprints – of tracks in the snow in that expedition which lasted two months. Three years later I went back to exactly the same point – I followed the same route and I saw three or four sets, where three years before we had seen thirty or forty sets. So there is a lot less evidence of bears being around, which is tragic.

🔘 1.37

(P = Presenter; I = Interviewer; S = Steve)
P: A recent survey by the British Heart Foundation has revealed that only 38% of us would be motivated to do more exercise if our life depended on it. In other words, six out of ten of us would rather die than exercise!

We went out on the streets of London to find out how much exercise people are really doing, and if they're not doing it, what exactly is stopping them?

I: How much exercise do you do?
S: Oh dear, not as much as I should. I used to have an expensive gym membership, but I only went twice so I cancelled it. I'm not very sporty so I don't do any team sports like football or anything. I do love football, but strictly as a spectator, not as a participant. I have noticed that it's harder to keep the weight off than when I was younger though, so I've started cycling into work. That's about forty minutes of exercise every day. Better than nothing.
I: What stops you?
S: I'm just so tired after work – I get home, sit on the sofa and do nothing.

🔘 1.38

(I = Interviewer; M = Maria)
I: How much exercise do you do?
M: I'm revising for exams at the moment so I go running quite a lot, just to get some fresh air. There's nothing worse than being stuck inside all day. I think it helps if you have someone to go with – it's quite hard to motivate yourself, but if you arrange to go running with a friend, you feel you can't let them down, and that forces you to go.
I: What stops you?
M: The weather! If it's raining, or really cold, I can usually talk myself out of it.

🔘 1.39

(I = Interviewer; S = Sam)
I: How much exercise do you do?
S: I run up the stairs, and that's it. Well, at the weekends I do a few hours of housework – I should think that burns off a few calories. I hope so anyway, because when I've finished I sit down with a cup of tea and a packet of biscuits. I certainly don't go to the gym if that's what you mean. Can you imagine me in Lycra? Ha ha.
I: Is that what stops you going to the gym?
S: Er, not really. It's finding time to fit it in around everything else I have to do. I've got three kids under five, so there's no way I have time to go to the gym or anything like that. But I reckon I run a marathon every day just running around after the children!

🔘 1.40

(I = Interviewer; T = Tim)
I: How much exercise do you do?
T: I go swimming and I work out at the gym. I try to do some kind of aerobic exercise for about thirty minutes three times a week, and I do weights a couple of times a week. At the weekends I often go for a brisk walk in the country, and my girlfriend's trying to get me to go to salsa classes – she says it's a really good workout.
I: What stops you?
T: Nothing really – unless I've pulled a muscle or something, and it hurts. I love it. I sit at a desk all day long, and if I don't do some physical exercise at least three or four times a week, I feel really out of shape. But it isn't just about weight loss – exercise gives me a general feeling of wellbeing.

Unit 5

2.01

My dad is the most ritualistic person I know, and many of his rituals involve his car.

We've never kept domestic animals in our house, but my father's car is as close as you'll get to the family pet. In fact, to be honest, the car probably gets better treatment and more affection than a pet would.

Each night, the car is tucked up in its garage under a cosy blanket. Nobody – but nobody – is allowed in the garage in case they accidentally brush against 'the precious one', causing who knows what damage.

When we were children, on the rare occasions when my dad would get the car out of the garage (for births, deaths, marriages and national disasters – and then only if the buses weren't running), we would have to wear plastic bags on our feet in case we had a sudden urge to vandalise the seats with our school shoes.

We would never be allowed to shut the car doors ourselves … in case we slammed them too hard, I suppose. I mean, three, five and seven-year-old girls can do untold damage to a car by slamming the door shut.

Nowadays, we don't have to wear plastic bags on our feet, but the 'Starting the car and setting off' ritual has never changed.

He'll start the engine and then sit there for at least five minutes with the engine turning. As repulsive fumes pump out into the fresh country air, he'll take out his pipe, and start tapping out his last smoke. Then he'll take a pinch of Players Medium Navy Cut (no other tobacco will do), stuff it in the bowl and spend a minute or two patting it down. Next, he'll get out his box of matches and give it a shake. He always gives his matches a shake. The pipe won't light first go – he'll have several goes at it, and finally, when the tobacco takes, he'll puff and puff until the car is full of smoke. With visibility dangerously reduced and a car full of choking passengers, he'll take the hand-brake off and reverse out of the drive at breakneck speed.

It isn't pleasant being a passenger, but we've always let him get away with this strange behaviour because he's the boss. None of us would dare to complain.

My father used to be a pilot in the Royal Air Force, and I often wonder whether he would indulge in this kind of ritual before take-off and whether his crew would let him get away with it because he was the boss. Probably.

2.02

(I = Interviewer; J=Jorge)
I: Tell me about weddings in your country.
J: Well, in Spain, where I come from, there is this ritual that happens after the rings have been exchanged between the groom and the bride. It is called 'las arras', and it consists of thirteen gold coins which the groom puts in the bride's hands. It symbolises their intention of sharing everything: all the worldly goods they are going to receive together.

2.03

(I = Interviewer; S = Sandra)
I: Tell me about weddings in your country.
S: Well, in Taiwan we use a black umbrella to cover the bride's head, because we believe that it can protect the bride from the evil spirits. So normally there will be an elder person to hold the umbrella when she leaves her house to the groom's house.
I: And will this bring her good luck as well?
S: Yes, prevent bad luck.

2.04

(I = Interviewer; I2= Ilhan)
I: Tell me about wedding traditions in Turkey.
I2: Weddings in Turkey are quite different to how they are in the UK. There are a lot of people at the wedding. There are sometimes as many as four or five hundred guests, and one of the most interesting things, I think, about Turkish weddings is the fact that the guests at the wedding pin gold, money, banknotes, on the bride's and groom's costumes, on the bridegroom's suit and on the bride's dress. I think, from what I can understand, that this money and gold is used by the bride and groom to set themselves up for their new life together, living in their new house, their new home, to buy things like a fridge, and other things they might need for their future life together.

2.05

(I = Interviewer; L = Laila)
I: Tell me about wedding traditions in Morocco.
L: Oh, Moroccan weddings are elaborate affairs. Preparations take weeks, and the whole community is involved! The bride gets lots of attention in the days leading up to the wedding – a group of women, usually older than the bride, but connected to her in some way, give her a sort of milk bath which is supposed to purify her. Then she has her hands and feet decorated in henna. This ritual symbolises prosperity. It looks beautiful, and there's another custom which says that the bride isn't supposed to do any housework until the henna wears off.

2.07

a
'Well, I try to remember my wife's birthday every year, and on the way home yesterday I stopped to buy her some flowers – I think that's romantic, but she just thought I'd done something wrong.'

b
'I'm very romantic, but I think most women are. I remember meeting my boyfriend for the first time. It was in a club and I remember seeing him across the room and thinking, 'He's nice.' He was wearing a black T-shirt and really nice jeans. I even remember what he said to me – he said 'Do you want to dance?' When I asked him recently if he remembered meeting me for the first time, he had no idea.'

c
'I don't know. I don't think my partner would say I'm romantic because I always forget to buy him presents or say nice things to him. But deep down I think I am romantic. Since I met my partner, I've stopped looking at other men. Well, I haven't stopped looking, but I have stopped fancying them.'

d
'No, I don't think I'm romantic really. I don't like all that romantic nonsense. Women expect you to buy them presents and remember their birthdays. And they try to make you give up football and all those things I enjoy. I can't be bothered with all that. Maybe that's why I haven't managed to find a girlfriend!'

Unit 6

🔊 2.12

(I = Interviewer; JC: Jean Crowshaw)

I: How did you become a restaurant critic?

JC: Well I've been working for newspapers for more than twenty years. I started out as a journalist when I was twenty-three, and I've worked for several newspapers since then including this one. Then, when the last restaurant critic retired, I was asked to take his place. And I've been doing it for the last thirteen years.

I: How can you do this job and stay so slim?

JC: Yeah, that's a good question. I mean, I eat out two or three times a week. But as a matter of fact, to write about a restaurant and its cuisine, I need to taste the food, but I don't need to clean my plate. When I'm covering a restaurant, I always take three friends with me. Everyone has to order a different dish. So then I taste about two bites of everything on their plates, and then I eat the same amount of food on my plate. Then I stop eating. And that's not just so that I stay slim, it's so that I can remember all the different flavours.

I: Do you take notes?

JC: No, I don't write anything down because I don't want to draw attention to myself. So while I'm eating, I'm making mental notes about the restaurant. How does the room look? Is the lighting too dim, too bright? Is the service efficient or is it slow? How is the food presented? Are the waiters doing their job well? Do the customers look happy? Then, as soon as I get home, no matter how late it is or how tired I am, I write down my impressions – I write pages and pages of notes.

I: You must be pretty well-known on the restaurant circuit. Do you wear a disguise?

JC: What like a wig? Ha ha, no, I couldn't do that. Like I said, I've been working around the Manchester area for some thirteen years now, so inevitably, I do sometimes get recognised, but by that time it's too late for the management to call in another chef or change the serving staff.

I: Do people get upset if you give them a bad review?

JC: Oh yes, but the bad reviews are the most fun to write! Once, a restaurant owner called my editor and threatened to come in with a gun – I don't think he did in the end.

I: Who pays for your meals?

JC: The newspaper pays for the meals. No food is accepted for free.

I: Have you had any particularly good or bad experiences that stand out in your memory?

JC: There was the waitress who tripped and poured my son's dessert and a glass of wine in my lap. I wasn't too pleased at the time, but I managed to see the funny side of it later. But there's one thing I really hate and that's when the waiter keeps asking 'Is everything all right?' Good, experienced waiters never ask that – they don't need to because they can tell if everything's all right just by looking at the customers' faces.

I: Have you met any rude waiters or waitresses?

JC: I've experienced every kind of waiter and waitress – rude and moody, chatty and enthusiastic, flirtatious and over-familiar. The best waiters are those who are attentive but not intrusive. I can't stand those waiters who squat down beside you to take your order, and then proceed to tell you their favourite items on the menu, because they ate it on their holidays in Greece … this kind of invasion of your privacy is totally unacceptable.

I: What's the best meal you've ever eaten?

JC: It was in Italy, in Umbria. I was travelling with my husband, and we stopped in a very rural place where we had the meal I'll remember for the rest of my days. Olive oil pressed from the restaurant's own trees, lamb with so much flavour that it defines what the meat should taste like – wonderful bread, handmade pasta, local wines. It wasn't a formal restaurant, but I've never forgotten it and I've never enjoyed a meal more.

🔊 2.14

nought point two five
one million, two hundred and thirty-four thousand, five hundred and sixty-seven
seventy-fifth
oh two oh, double seven eight two, four double three five six
five sixths
the twenty-seventh of July, twenty twelve

🔊 2.15

a Manchester United won three nil.
b Rafael Nadal is winning two sets to love.
c My grandfather was born in 1908.
d It's really cold – ten degrees below zero.
e Nought point seven seconds – it's a new world record!

🔊 2.16

(W1 = Waiter; W2 = Waitress; M = Man; Wm = Woman)

W1: Busy tonight, isn't it?

W2: Yeah. Who's the man on table 4? He looks familiar.

W1: Oh, that's Burt Sinclair. He's a big cheese in the hotel industry, so if you butter him up, he'll give you a nice big tip.

W2: Oh right – I could do with a bit of extra cash.

M: Excuse me! Excuse me!

W2: Yes, sir. Can I help you?

M: Yes, you can. The service in here is very slow this evening. We've been sitting here for ten minutes and we haven't even seen the menu yet.

W2: Oh I'm terribly sorry, sir. We're very busy tonight. I'll get you the menus immediately.

W1: How are you getting on with the big cheese on table 4?

W2: Well, he obviously thinks he's the best thing since sliced bread, and so does the woman with him.

W1: That's his wife.

W2: His wife! Oh!

M: Excuse me!

W2: Yes, sir. Are you ready to order?

M: I'm afraid not. It's so dark in here that we can't read the menu.

W2: Oh, one moment, sir. I'll bring you a bigger candle. There, is that OK?

M: Yes, yes, that's fine.

W2: Would you like a few more minutes, sir?

M: No, no. I'll have the steak.

W2: Right, and how would you like it, sir?

M: Medium rare.

Wm: And I'll have seafood pasta and a green salad.

W2: That's one steak, medium rare and one seafood pasta. And to drink?

M: The Chablis.

W2: Who would like to taste the wine?

Wm: I will. Hm. It could do with being a bit colder. Can we have the wine chilled, please?

W2: That's no problem – I'll just fetch an ice bucket.

W1: Everything OK with table 4?

W2: They're tricky customers. I feel like I'm walking on eggshells.

W1: Just remember the tip.

M: Excuse me!

W2: Yes, sir.

M: I think the wine is corked. It certainly tastes very strange.

W2: Oh, I'm terribly sorry, sir. I'll bring you a new one immediately.

W1: Big cheese doesn't look too pleased. What's up?

W2: Oh dear, it's all going pear-shaped now. The service is slow, the restaurant's too dark, and now the wine's corked.

W1: Calm down. You have to take it all with a pinch of salt. If you start taking it personally, you've had it.

M: Excuse me!

W2: Yes, sir?

M: I'm afraid this steak is overcooked. I asked for medium rare.

W2: I'm sorry, sir.

M: And there's another problem.

Wm: It's my seafood pasta – I think the prawns are off.

W2: Oh dear. I'm very sorry. I'll talk to the chef.

W1: It's not looking very good for the tip, is it?

W2: That's not funny.

M: Excuse me!

W2: Grrr.

Unit 7

🔊 **2.21**

1
My favourite beach is in Cape Town. It's called Camps Beach, and I love it, because the location is spectacular. But if you want to swim there, I'd advise you to wear a wetsuit because the water is freezing.

2
My favourite beach is in the south of France, but nobody knows about it. It took a while to convince my girlfriend that it was worth climbing down a very dangerous cliff to get there, but she had to admit that it was worth it.

3
My favourite beach is in Sardinia. I've travelled to hundreds of beaches in different countries, and I can now confirm that the best beach in the world is Cala del Morto.

4
Holiday brochures claim that the best beaches are in faraway places like the Caribbean or the Indian Ocean, but I can assure you that there are wonderful beaches nearer home. For example, my favourite beach is in Cornwall, and I can drive there in a day.

5
My favourite beach is the man-made beach along the River Seine in Paris. In summer, they import a load of sand and encourage people to go there to sunbathe and relax. I think it's great for families who can't afford to go away on holiday.

🔊 **2.22**

Paul
We decided to do something really special for Christmas. We both love skiing so we managed to book ten days in a small ski resort in the French Alps. When we arrived there, though, we found out that the temperatures had been unseasonably warm. Basically, there was no snow. Well, there were a few centimetres of snow very high up on the black pistes, but we weren't allowed to go there, because it was too high and too dangerous. So we had to find other ways to entertain ourselves, and in the end, this was really good because we were forced to relax. We didn't have to get up early to go skiing, so we could go out until late at night and sleep in in the morning. We read books, had long lunches, went for walks and drank lots of hot chocolate. At the end of the holiday, we felt completely relaxed.

🔊 **2.23**

Amy
When I was 18, I was desperate to go to Guatemala to see the volcanoes but I wasn't allowed to go there alone – my parents thought I was too young. So my brother agreed to come with me, and we carefully planned a three-week tour. We set off from London, and our destination was the Guatemalan city of Antigua, but we had to stop over at Miami for a few hours. Anyway, we finally took off from Miami,

and during the flight, my brother asked a fellow passenger if he'd been to Antigua before. He replied that he had, and it was one of the most beautiful islands he'd ever come across. At that point, we realised we were on the wrong plane, going to the wrong holiday. Obviously we couldn't get off the plane there and then, so we had to carry on and then sort ourselves out when we landed. There were no direct flights from the Caribbean island of Antigua to the Guatemalan city of Antigua, so we had to go back to North America and start again. We lost a week of our holiday, but in the end it just made us appreciate Guatemala all the more.

🔊 **2.24**

Rachel
When I told my friends I was going on a cycling holiday in Andalucia, they thought I was joking. But I thought it would be fine. OK, I don't actually own a bicycle, but I do go to the gym twice a week. I even go on the exercise bike sometimes. In preparation, I went to a specialist bike shop to get some cycling gear. The helmet was compulsory, so I got one of those, but I didn't think I needed to bother with the padded cycling shorts. The man in the shop recommended them, but I thought they looked stupid, so I didn't get them. I should have listened to the man. As soon as I met the other people I knew I was in trouble. One man had recently cycled from London to Edinburgh – for fun! Our Spanish tour leader looked as if she was about to set off on the Tour de France. I made a big effort to keep up on the first day, but by the evening my bottom was in agony, and I couldn't sit down. Fortunately we didn't have to carry anything – there was a car that took all our baggage from one place to the next. But I have to admit that I got a lift in the baggage car a couple of times. I never realised that Andalucia was so hilly.

🔊 **2.26**

(F = Frank; A = Angela)
F: Have you ever had a holiday romance, Angela?
A: I have actually … many years ago!! When I was twenty I went travelling to Australia – I went to Sydney – and while I was there I met Brad.
F: Brad?!!!
A: Yes, I know. Come to think of it, he did look a bit like a film star, with his blond hair, and lovely white teeth. Anyway, we met through a mutual friend, and she arranged our first date. And that was it – the beginning of a lovely relationship!
F: Ahh!
A: We got on so well together. In fact, I really thought I'd met my soulmate. Do you know what I mean? I thought we may end up together.
F: Yeah – I know what you mean. So, what happened next?
A: Well, eventually my visa ran out and I returned to London. We then spent six months on the phone, swapping letters and parcels. But long-distance

relationships are really difficult, and neither of us wanted to give up our lives and move to the other side of the world. Basically, our relationship wasn't strong enough to survive the distance.
F: What happened?
A: Well, in the end, he met somebody else.
F: Ah.
A: And to be honest, I was relieved.
F: So have you ever heard from him again?
A: No, but the funny thing is that I heard through our mutual friend that he met a Dutch girl and ended up moving to Amsterdam!

🔊 **2.30**

(T = Tim; S = Sal.)
T: What are you doing for the long weekend?
S: I'm off to Paris.
T: Oh great – I love Paris.
S: Oh yes, you know it pretty well, don't you? Can you believe this is my first time there? Do you have any tips?
T: Well, there's so much to see. I'd definitely recommend the Eiffel Tower. Take the glass-sided lift – when it comes out into the daylight, the views are spectacular.
S: That sounds like a must. What about museums?
T: Well, of course the most famous museum is the Louvre, but it's probably best to avoid it because of the queues, but make sure you go to the Musée d'Orsay. It's one of the best museums in the world. You'll have to queue there too, but it's well worth the effort. Where are you staying?
S: In a little hotel in the 3rd arrondissement.
T: Oh, that's a really nice area. While you're there, make sure you walk around the backstreets because there are some lovely little shops – oh, and while you're there you should go to the Picasso museum. You won't be disappointed.
S: Oh, I love Picasso. And how should we get around? What are the taxis like?
T: Um, I think it's probably best to avoid taxis, because the traffic can be very slow. If I were you, I'd use the buses or the metro. They're very good.
S: Wow, that sounds great.
T: And whatever you do, don't leave Paris without tasting the oysters at Bofinger.
S: Bofinger?
T: Yes, it's a restaurant in Rue de la Bastille. It's the best place for seafood, and the décor is fantastic.
S: I think I need to write this down. How do you spell Bofinger?

Unit 8

🌐 **2.32**

(I = Interviewer; W = Woman; M = Man)

1

I: What do you think makes a face attractive?

W1: For a woman, smooth skin and good bone structure.

I: And for a man?

W1: Um, nice white teeth, sparkling eyes and a square jaw. That's what I like anyway.

2

I: What do you think makes a face attractive?

M1: Big eyes, full lips and a big smile.

I: Like Julia Roberts?

M1: Exactly.

3

I: What do you think makes a face attractive?

W2: It's probably easier to say what I don't like. On a man, I don't like a small nose – it doesn't have to be enormous, but a little turned-up nose on a man looks silly.

I: So you don't like Brad Pitt then?

W2: Well, I like everything about him except his nose!

4

I: What do you think makes a face attractive?

M2: High cheekbones, especially on a woman. Like Marlene Dietrich. She's my ideal woman. I love her arched eyebrows.

5

I: What do you think makes a face attractive?

W3: I love dimples.

I: Do you mean a dimple in the chin?

W3: Yeah, I quite like that, but I meant dimples in the cheeks when somebody smiles – it's so cute.

🌐 **2.33**

(JO = Jean Oldham; RT = Rita Taylor; MH = Michael Hirst)

JO: Personally, I'm dead against cosmetic surgery of any kind. I work on a women's magazine, so you can imagine how many beautiful models I've met. But I'm also in daily contact with women who are not physically perfect, and I have to say that the most beautiful women I know are not models – they are the intelligent, interesting women whose life experience shows on their faces. I believe that true beauty comes from within, and no amount of cosmetic surgery can give you that.

RT: Yes, I agree with you, Jean, but not everybody has the confidence to let their inner beauty shine out. Plastic surgery can actually give people that confidence. I really don't think there's anything wrong with trying to improve on what nature has given us.

MH: Ah well, that's where I disagree with you, Rita. I think we should be grateful for what God has given us. The point is, it's selfish and indulgent of people to spend vast amounts of money on superficial improvements when there is so much poverty and sickness in the world.

RT: Actually, it's not that expensive, you know, Michael. I mean you could have your nose done for the price of a holiday, and quite frankly, cosmetic surgery can do more for you than a holiday, because the benefits last longer.

MH: Are you saying I need a nose job?

RT: No, of course not. I suppose what I'm trying to say is that plastic surgery nowadays is almost as routine as going on holiday. Basically, it's here to stay, and I'm afraid you just have to accept it.

JO: Well, I don't go along with that at all. Growing old is a natural part of life and if you ask me, what we need to accept is that we can't look young forever.

RT: Well, I would disagree with that, but let's leave it there.

🌐 **2.36**

(P = Presenter; DrH = Dr Hudson)

P: Now, you may or may not have read the best-selling self-help book, *The Secret*, but almost two million people have, and the movie version on DVD has sold one and a half million copies to date. To tell us what all the fuss is about, we have with us in the studio today psychologist and expert in the 'law of attraction', Dr Rick Hudson. Welcome.

DrH: Thank you – I'm pleased to be here.

P: Dr Hudson, *The Secret* is based on the 'law of attraction', the idea that like attracts like. This isn't a new phenomenon, is it?

DrH: No, no, not at all. The theory behind the 'law of attraction' has been around for ages. But it is the recent success of *The Secret* that has brought it to the attention of so many people around the world.

P: What exactly is the 'law of attraction'?

DrH: Well, put simply, the 'law of attraction' is all about positive thinking. We attract things we want and we also attract things we don't want. So, if you were the sort of person who was always cheerful and optimistic, you would give off good vibrations, and these good vibes would in turn attract positive energy, and good things would happen to you. Similarly, a stressed-out sort of person would put out stressed vibes, and they would attract more stress into their lives. Whatever you are thinking and feeling at any given time is basically your request to the universe for more of the same.

P: Hmm. So how can you apply this theory, this positive thinking, to your everyday life?

DrH: You can use it to make some very positive changes in your life. It depends what you want.

P: Where do I start?

DrH: Ha ha. Well, let me give you a very simple example – OK, let's suppose you're on your way to the supermarket on a Saturday morning, so you're arriving pretty much at the same time as several hundred other shoppers! The one thing that would improve your life at that moment is a parking space. So you start focusing on that space. You visualise the ideal parking space, right near to the supermarket entrance, and you imagine yourself swinging into the space as you arrive.

P: OK, I like that image.

DrH: And to make the positive vibrations really work for you, you need to imagine how you would feel if you already had that space.

P: I see.

DrH: Imagine that you already had that space – how would you be feeling?

P: Um, amazed?

DrH: Right, so you're still in your car on the way to the supermarket, but you're saying to yourself, 'I'm so happy I found a space. I'm delighted and grateful that I found a parking space so close to the entrance.' It works. Try it.

P: I must say, it sounds a bit too good to be true. Supposing I really, really wanted a ten-million dollar house with a swimming pool – would I just think about it, and hey presto it would materialise?

DrH: Well, if you wanted to start living your life according to the 'law of attraction', you'd have to learn a few simple techniques, and these are explained in *The Secret*. But basically, if that's what you really want, then yes, you can make it happen.

P: But don't you think it encourages people to be more materialistic? I mean, I don't need a house with a swimming pool. Isn't that just being plain greedy?

DrH: Listen, I'll give you another example. Imagine that a genie appeared in front of you and offered to grant your wishes. Would you ask for something small? Say a new bicycle? No. You'd be asking for bigger things. A business, a soulmate, a million dollars. The 'law of attraction' is like a genie.

P: Hmm.

DrH: And here's why it's important to think big. There is so much that can be improved in the world. There is much more you can contribute. But you cannot do this by being mediocre. You owe it not just to yourself – but also to the world – to THINK BIG.

P: Well, thank you, Dr Hudson. For more information, read *The Secret* or watch the DVD. I'm going to start visualising a Gucci handbag.

Unit 9

🔊 **3.01**

(OB = Oliver Bridge; RJ = Richard Jones)

OB: It's a cold, grey morning. The sky is overcast and it's drizzling. For me, these are ideal conditions to visit the mysterious and ancient Stonehenge, my favourite place.

As a child, when I first visited the stone circle, it was the sense of mystery that fascinated me – what are the stones for? How did they get here and what sort of ceremonies and events went on here? As an adult, what I love about Stonehenge is that it's been standing there for 5,000 years – and it endures. I love the fact that after so many millennia, it remains such an enigmatic and enchanting place.

It's a bit difficult to picture exactly how it was all that time ago, with only sixty odd stones left and half of those fallen down, but when it was complete, there would have been over 160 stones carefully laid out as a circle with a horseshoe in the centre. Two types of stone were used – sarsen and bluestone. The huge upright stones are sarsens weighing up to forty tonnes each. Then the inner circle is made up of bluestones, and they weigh a mere four tonnes each. The bluestones are so-called because they turn blue when they get wet.

Stonehenge is, without a doubt, one of the greatest engineering achievements of pre-historic times. The stones were huge, and not a single one can be found locally. One can only marvel at the phenomenal effort involved in bringing the stones here.

I'm joined by Richard Jones, an expert in Stonehenge history, to tell us about the latest theories about how the stones got here, and why they bothered.

Richard, these huge upright stones, the sarsens – I suppose they were dragged across the land?

RJ: They would have been dragged, yes, from the Marlborough Downs, about twenty miles away to the north of here.

OB: And the bluestones, they were, they came from Wales, is that right?

RJ: From South West Wales, from the sunny mountains of South West Wales. Yes, a good 250 miles away from here.

OB: So there must have been some really powerful reason for them to situate it here?

RJ: Yes, there must have been a very good reason to bring them all the way here. It can't have been easy to get these stones in place – they didn't have the wheel at that time. In fact, it must have taken them years.

OB: But the reason why it's located here remains a mystery.

RJ: Absolutely. Something was such an important draw that they had to bring all these materials to here, to this place. Why they brought them here, no idea. And you know, if you put twelve archeologists in one room, you'll have twelve different theories – but we will never know for sure because Stonehenge was built before written history began. So we don't know any written evidence of a motive, a reason for why Stonehenge is here.

OB: All we can do is speculate. No one really knows what went on here, and I've got a feeling that Stonehenge will always keep some of its secrets.

🔊 **3.02**

a

The big stones look like a doorway. The shape is very similar to those found in Japan at the entrance of some of our temples. I think it must have been a kind of temple, a religious place.

b

Well, apparently, the stones are aligned with the sun and the moon at certain times of the year – the solstices and the equinoxes. So I think it might have been a sort of prehistoric calendar. But it can't only have been a calendar. It was more important than that. I think Stonehenge must have been a place where people worshipped the sun and the moon.

c

I think it might have been a place where important ceremonies took place. It probably had a roof on it originally – if you think about it, it makes sense. It was obviously an important place, and it rains a lot round here.

d

We don't know, do we? It could have been a landing site for spacecraft from other planets for all we know. Some people believe it was. Personally, I think it's just a bunch of stones in a field.

e

Well, it's a mystery, isn't it? Even the archaeologists can't agree. There's one lot who have dug up bones, and they reckon they can prove that it must have been a cemetery. Then there's another group of archaeologists who think that the bluestones may have had special properties, and that's why they brought them all the way from Wales. Personally, I think it may have been a kind of healing place.

🔊 **3.03**

The double portrait, *Frida and Diego Rivera*, was completed in 1931 and was probably based on a wedding photograph. When they were first married in 1929, Diego was forty-three years old, and Frida was twenty-two. He was a celebrated artist; she was an unknown art student.

The physical difference between the couple is striking in this portrait – he is tall with enormous legs rooted to the ground by heavy work boots. By contrast, she is tiny and wearing doll-like shoes. She almost looks as if she's floating next to her larger-than-life husband.

With his palette and paint-brushes in his right hand, Diego Rivera is portrayed as an artist. In fact, at the time Frida painted this portrait, Rivera was the most famous artist in the Americas. The couple are holding hands, but you can see in the way Frida is tilting her head towards her husband that she seems to be deferring to him and giving him a place of importance in the portrait.

Diego is wearing a blue work-shirt, thus defining him as a working-class craftsman. Frida is dressed in traditional Mexican clothes, wearing a long green dress and a red shawl. These are in fact the colours of the Mexican flag.

A bird holds a ribbon above their heads, and on the ribbon are written the words: 'Here you see us, me, Frida Kahlo with my adored husband, Diego Rivera'.

Let's move on to the second exhibit, *Self-portrait with Cropped Hair*.

The relationship between Frida and Diego was a stormy one. *Self-portrait with Cropped Hair* was painted shortly after they had separated, following Diego's affair with Frida's sister. In this portrait, she looks like a man with her heavy single eyebrow and cropped hair. She's wearing a man's shirt and a baggy suit, which looks as if it might have belonged to her former-husband. She's sitting on a wooden chair with strands of her hair lying all around her. Diego loved her long hair and traditional Mexican dresses, so Frida painted this portrait as a sort of revenge for her husband's affair.

Finally, we have *Roots*, a portrait painted later on in 1943. In *Roots*, Frida is wearing an orange dress and lying on a dry barren landscape with roots and leaves growing out of her body. With her elbow resting on a pillow, she looks quite comfortable. In fact, in this painting, Frida does not appear to be anguished as in many of her self-portraits. She often goes back to the theme of nature, and here she seems to be nourishing the Mexican earth. This painting was completed after Frida married Diego Rivera for the second time. The couple were unable to have children, and *Roots* expresses Kahlo's desire for fertility and to be a part of the life cycle.

🔊 **3.04**

(I = Interviewer; TB = Trevor Baylis)

I: Trevor, let me start by asking you what gave you the idea for the clockwork radio?

TB: Well I was sitting where I am now looking at that television over there, and I was um actually watching a programme about the spread of AIDS in Africa, and they said the only way they could stop this dreadful disease cutting its way through Africa was with the power of information and education. But there was a problem. Most of Africa doesn't have electricity. The only form of electricity available to them was in the form of batteries, which were horrendously expensive. And so I said to myself, hang on, hang on. Now, this is where dreams play an important part in everybody's life. Um, the beautiful thing about a dream is you can do anything you like in your dreams, right? Now why I am saying this to you is because I could see myself listening to some raunchy number by Dame Nellie Melba on my wind-up gramophone, mmm? And then I am thinking to myself, blimey, if you can get all that noise by dragging a rusty nail around a piece of old bakelite using a spring, surely there's enough power in that spring to drive a small dynamo which in turn will drive my radio, and so I was stirred enough to get off my backside and go to my, my shed and actually find enough parts to actually start doing those first primitive experiments …

I: And, um, how long did it take you to design a prototype from the idea?

TB: Well, from the actual, from the concept to, er, having the first in-a-box model out there it would have taken me two to three months, I guess, so yes, it took about two or three months.

I: So you got, you got the prototype, how easy was it from that point on? How easy was it to find a backer and set up production?

TB: Well first things first. I did know that there are these thieves about that will steal your idea. So I found a lady called Jackie Needle, a patent attorney, and I said to her 'Jackie, I want to write up a patent, can you help me?' So we did a search and couldn't find any clockwork radios of the kind that I had done, and she filed for a patent to me, for me, and therefore then I had a starting date, as it were. Now I knew that nobody pays you for a good idea, but they could pay you for that piece of paper, so then I went round every British company I could think of with a confidentiality agreement, and they all talked down to me. 'Oh yes, I think we're, I think that we are working on something like this, aren't we Johnny?' You know all that old sausage. Um, I mean it was so humiliating … and in the end, quite frankly after about three or four years of this, I thought, I have had enough of this. Why do I need this? I was fifty-six or something when this happened. So I was given a chance through the BBC World Service to meet up with the guys from the BBC *Tomorrow's World* programme, and they said, 'Come on, we'll do the story.'

I: So the whole thing got off the ground. How long was it then before the production of them started?

TB: Well, the important thing was funding. The *Tomorrow's World* programme was seen by a fellow in South Africa, a chap from a company called Liberty Life. He came to my house here, and we sat out there, and he said, 'Look, um, we can help you make this happen, provided we can share in its success.' I said of course, and so we formed a company called Baygen, Baylis Generators, and he wrote a cheque for three-quarters of a million pounds whilst I was in this room.

I: And how many radios are produced each month?

TB: Well, I'm sure they might tell me differently, but I'm sure they must be doing 200,000 a month.

I: And finally what advice would you give to someone who had a good idea?

TB: Don't go down the pub and tell everybody about it. That's the first thing, right? Get on to the Patent Office. Get their literature, and read all about it, right? Nobody pays you for a good idea, but they might pay you for a piece of paper which says you own that idea. But remember, somebody might already own that idea, so you must do a search first. There's no excuse afterwards.

🔊 **3.06**

(A =Alice; B = Brigit.)

A: Oh, I'm so pleased you can stay here while we're away and keep an eye on the place.

B: No problem. It'll be nice to have a change of scenery for a couple of weeks.

A: Now, there are a few things I need to tell you. Did you get the keys in the post?

B: Yes, I've got them here.

A: OK, to open the front door, you need the small key.

B: Right.

A: You need to turn it twice anti-clockwise.

B: OK. And I suppose the big key is for the back door?

A: Exactly. Now, if you need the heating on, you just need to turn up the thermostat.

B: OK, and where do I do that?

A: There's a dial in the hallway, between the sitting room and the kitchen. Just turn it until it clicks.

B: Right.

A: And then make sure you turn it down again before you go to bed.

B: Of course.

A: Right – the TV's in the sitting room, and you use the silver remote control to switch it on and off, and the smaller black one for changing channels. Are you likely to watch a DVD?

B: Er, no, it's OK.

A: Now, what else. The smoke alarms are always going off in our house. The best thing to do is to have the fan on when you're cooking – just press the red button above the cooker to turn it on. You can't miss it. And if the smoke alarm goes off, just stand under it and wave your arms.

B: OK. Is there anything else?

A: Oh yes, I know what I haven't told you. Do you like coffee?

B: Yes, I love it.

A: Well, there's a coffee machine next to the cooker. It's very easy to use. Basically, plug it in at the wall, and the on/off switch is at the back of the machine. Then you put a filter into the filter holder and put the coffee into the filter. Put water into the thing above it, and make sure the lid's on tight. Then put a cup under the place where the coffee comes out. The machine will warm the water up to the right temperature, so you just have to wait a few seconds. When the cup's full, take it off and your coffee's ready. Anyway, I'll leave you the proper instructions.

B: Oh good, thanks.

A: That's it then. Oh, and Molly needs a walk twice a day, and don't forget to let her out before you go to bed – we wouldn't like her to have an accident.

B: Molly? You didn't mention …

A: Oh didn't I? She's no trouble, are you? Yes … oh yes, you're lovely … down girl, down.

B: Urgh!

Unit 10

🔘 **3.09**

Joe Smedley

Children are much easier to reach with advertising than adults are – they like it and they pick up on it really fast. So, it's the advertiser's job to capitalise on this. We have a term 'pester-power', which means the marketing potential of children nagging their parents to spend money. And I'm not just talking about toys here – our aim is getting children to pester parents to buy something for the whole family, like a holiday or a car. What we try to do is to produce adverts that appeal to both children and adults.

Another key concept for advertisers is the 'playground pound'. Children want what their friends have – playground credibility is very important. In other words, brands give children a sense of identity and help them fit in with a peer group.

So you can see children are a very important market for us, and in return, we like to promote education. This is something that's already happening in America. Companies donate free computers and in exchange they can advertise their brands on book covers and posters. I think it's fantastic – the kids benefit and the companies get brand loyalty from a very early age.

I'd love to be a child today. They really know what they want and they have so many more choices. Advertisers respect children's opinions.

🔘 **3.10**

Sally McIlveen

Basically, children are being brainwashed by all the advertising that goes on around them. Quite honestly, if the children in my school remembered any of their schoolwork as well as they remember the advertising jingles they hear on television, my job would be a pleasure.

Usually the pupils at our school wear uniforms, but Friday is a non-uniform day, and that's when you really see the power of advertising. The kids are dressed from head to toe in labels, mainly sports stuff like Adidas, Nike, that sort of thing. And they all look the same!

There's a great deal of pressure on parents to buy children all these labels and gadgets, and I feel so sorry for the families who don't have much money because the pressure is just the same.

I really believe it's time the government put a stop to all this aggressive television advertising.

Mind you, it's worse in America apparently. Schools are actually being subsidised by companies like McDonalds and Pepsi. OK, the school gets free equipment from these big companies, but then the children have to add up burgers or multiply cans of Pepsi in their maths lessons. It's terrible to think that the schools end up promoting a product that's not even good for the children.

What I think is really sad is that children are being forced to be consumers from such

an early age. I don't think all this choice is liberating for children – it just means that they're encouraged to be materialistic instead of focusing on more important basic values, such as kindness and respect for others.

🔘 **3.11**

(P = Presenter; S = Shelley Russell; J = Jim Falmer)

P: Good evening and welcome to *Talkback*. Recently, the tabloid press have been under fire yet again, this time for their apparent disregard for truth and accuracy.

In the studio tonight we would like to welcome Shelley Russell, Oscar-winning actress, and Jim Falmer, editor of *The Daily Post*.

Shelley Russell, let's start with you. Do you think there should be greater restrictions placed on the press and the stories they print?

S: Yes, absolutely. I can't open a newspaper or magazine without reading stories full of false information about myself or people I know. It's getting …

J: Sorry, but I can't believe that you're actually complaining about free publicity. I mean, I remember, Shelley, before you were famous, you were begging us to write features about you … anything …

S: If you would just let me finish – of course the press have been important. I'm an actress and I understand the power of the press. But the thing is, I rarely seem to read anything true about myself these days. Take last week – your paper wrote this story about me and my co-star, who incidentally happens to be married to a very good friend of mine – taking a bath together in my hotel room.

J: Oh that. That was …

S: Hang on, I haven't finished. You went on to say that the bath was filled with $5000 worth of champagne. Now, …

J: Well, that was just a bit of fun. I don't think you should take that too seriously.

S: Oh really! You don't think that it's at all serious that my co-star's children woke up to the headline: SHELLEY GETS BUBBLY WITH SHAUN IN CHAMPAGNE BATH or that his wife is now filing for a divorce …

J: Look, I don't know whether …

S: Anyway, to get back to what I was saying … The point I'm trying to make here is that famous people have families with feelings. I am sick of the gutter press making up stories just so that they can splash sensational headlines across the front page and sell more newspapers – it's irresponsible and it messes up people's lives.

J: Look love, you're just angry about that particular article because the photos we printed of you weren't very flattering. Anyway, we made a public apology and said that there'd been some inaccuracies in the article.

S: Yes, but what you didn't say was what

the inaccuracies were, so …

P: If I could just come in here. I think we need to address the root of the problem. Jim Falmer, why do certain newspapers continue to print these stories when it's obvious that they are not true?

S: To increase circulation and make more money.

J: If you would let me answer the question – I think we have to look at the relationship between fame, the public and the press. The public are fascinated by fame and scandal, and they love to read about their favourite stars. The problem is, it's not always clear what's true and what isn't. I mean, if a newspaper prints something scandalous or embarrassing about a famous person, they're bound to deny it, but that doesn't mean it's not true.

S: Are you trying to say …?

J: No smoke without fire, if you ask me.

P: Well, I'm sorry to interrupt you, but we'll carry on after this short break for some travel news …

🔘 **3.13**

(I = Interviewer; G1 = Girl 1; B1 = Boy 1; B2 = Boy 2; G2 = Girl 2; G3 = Girl 3; B3 = Boy 3)

1
I: Excuse me. Do you mind if I ask you how do you feel about seeing this movie?

G1: A bit nervous actually. I don't know quite what to expect, but I think I'm going to be scared.

2
I: Excuse me – are you feeling nervous about seeing this movie?

B1: Yeah a little uneasy, I must admit … but I've brought my girlfriend, so I can hold her hand if I get scared.

3
I: How do you feel about seeing this movie?

B2: I'm looking forward to being frightened to death.

4
I: What are you expecting from this film?

G2: To be scared stiff – hopefully.

5
I: Do you think you're going to enjoy seeing this film?

G3: Er, no – I don't think enjoy is the right word. But I've heard so much about it that I can't wait to find out what it's all about. In fact, I feel quite apprehensive, but I love horror films, and this one sounds as if it's going to be really scary.

6
I: Any expectations?

B3: Well, I've been visiting the website for a while now and I'm really looking forward to finding out what happens. I expect it to be absolutely terrifying!

🔘 **3.14**

(I = Interviewer; G1 = Girl 1; B1 = Boy 1; B2 = Boy 2; G2 = Girl 2; G3 = Girl 3; B3 = Boy 3)

1
I: So, how was it for you?
G1: Extremely disappointing. I wasn't the least bit scared, and you know from the start that everybody dies, so there's no suspense. Anyway, the characters are so annoying that I felt like killing them myself. It does not live up to the hype.

2
I: What did you think of it then?
B1: Absolute rubbish. My girlfriend fell asleep, and I spent the last half of the movie with my eyes shut – not because it was scary – but because the camera angles made me feel sick. Don't see it if you suffer from motion sickness. In fact, just don't see it.

3
I: So were you frightened to death?
B2: No way. After all the hype, it was a massive letdown.

4
I: What did you think?
G2: Over-hyped nonsense. I spent most of the time waiting for something to happen. I feel completely disillusioned.

5
I: Did the film live up to your expectations?
G3: No, it didn't. I don't think I've ever been so bored in my entire life, and I still haven't got a clue what it's about. In fact, there's no story to speak of. This film is a perfect example of hype over substance.

6
I: Your verdict?
B3: A total waste of time. I was bored out of my mind. The website was much more entertaining than the film.

Unit 11

🔘 **3.16**

1 Acquired Immune Deficiency Syndrome
2 Bachelor of Science
3 Curriculum Vitae
4 Do-it-Yourself
5 Frequently Asked Questions
6 Master of Business Administration
7 North Atlantic Treaty Organisation
8 Organisation of Petroleum Exporting Countries
9 Doctor of Philosophy
10 Personal Identification Number
11 United Nations International Children's Emergency Fund
12 Value Added Tax

🔘 **3.17**

(I – Interviewer; Mrs B = Mrs Barrington; Mr B = Mr Barrington)
I: What is Saffron going to do when she leaves school?
Mrs B: Until a few months ago, she was going to go to university, but she's changed her mind. Now she reckons she's going to make it in the pop world.
I: And how do you feel about that?
Mr B: We think she's making an enormous mistake.
I: But surely she can go back to her studies if her music career fails?
Mr B: That's true, but once she gets a taste of freedom, she'll find it harder to go back to college. I just think it's such a waste – in three years' time, she'll have got her degree and she'll still be young enough to try out the music business. At least if it doesn't work out she'll have a qualification behind her.
I: Have you discussed this with her?
Mrs B: Of course, but she's made up her mind. We're just hoping that she'll get it out of her system and then come to her senses and go back to her studies. When I left school I didn't go on to university, and I've regretted it ever since. I just don't want her to make the same mistake I did.
I: Will you support her while she's trying to be a pop singer?
Mr B: You mean financially? No. She won't be living at home, and we can't afford to pay for her to live in London, so it's up to her to make it work.

🔘 **3.19**

Tom's second story
While I was travelling, I got an incredibly painful tropical ear infection after I fell into a stinking latrine. Feeling like death, I lay in bed with a raging fever for what felt like a lifetime. Wracked with pain, I couldn't face eating anything and I lost so much weight that I looked like a skeleton. Eventually, I managed to get hold of some antibiotics which brought me back from death's door.

🔘 **3.20**

(I = Interviewer; S = Sam)
I: Ah, come in. Sam, isn't it?
S: Yes.

I: Well Sam, tell us a little about yourself.
S: Um, well, I'm 24, and I was born in Swindon. I like football. In the winter I go skiing and in the summer, I like sailing and windsurfing. Oh, and I'm a black belt in karate. Well, I say I'm a black belt. In fact, I'm a brown belt but I'm taking my black belt in a few days, so … um, anyway, I graduated last year, and now I'm looking forward to getting a job.
I: OK. And why do you think you'd be right for a position in this company?
S: Oh, well, er, I'm interested in what your company does. Um, I haven't really thought about it.
I: In your opinion, what are your greatest strengths?
S: I'm outgoing and friendly, so I get on well with people.
I: What would you say your weaknesses are?
S: My weaknesses? I can't think of any. Ha ha. Oh, I know – I tend to be at my best in the afternoon. Mornings are tricky.
I: Right. And what are your long-term objectives?
S: To be the best I can be – and to make lots of money.
I: What would you like to be doing in five years' time?
S: Lying on a beach in the Caribbean! Ha ha.
I: Do you have any questions you'd like to ask us?
S: Er, no. I'm fine.
I: Right, well, we'll be in touch.

🔘 **3.21**

(I = Interviewer; L = Layla)
I: Ah, come in. Layla isn't it?
L: Yes, that's right.
I: Well Layla, tell us a little about yourself.
L: OK. I graduated from university last year, and since then I've been travelling in Asia and Australia. That was a great experience, but now I'm ready to embark on my career and I'm very keen to work for a company like yours.
I: OK. And why do you think you'd be right for a position in this company?
L: Well, I've always been interested in working in the media. I think I'm well-suited to this kind of work because I work well under pressure. I don't have much experience yet, but anything I don't know, I'm willing to learn.
I: In your opinion, what are your greatest strengths?
L: I'm highly motivated and conscientious. I'm a team player, but equally I can work on my own.
I: What would you say your weaknesses are?
L: I would say my greatest weakness has been my lack of proper planning in the past. However, since I've come to recognise that weakness, I've taken steps to correct it.
I: Right. And what are your long-term objectives?
L: I'd like to gain some experience in this field for a few years, and then decide which area I want to specialise in.

I: What would you like to be doing in five years' time?

L: Ideally, I'd like to be managing my own team.

I: Do you have any questions you'd like to ask us?

L: Yes, I'd like to know a bit about the training opportunities in this job.

I: Yes, that's a good question. We believe in on-going training here, and we provide regular opportunities for our staff to attend relevant courses.

L: Oh, that sounds great.

I: Right, well, thank you for coming in Layla. We'll be in touch.

Unit 12

🌐 **3.22**

Room 1

This is obviously a family room. The leather sofa and armchair are nice, big, comfortable seats which suggests that the priority here is comfort rather than style. I imagine a family with young children sitting on the sofa to watch a DVD or listen to a story.

There are far too many cushions and I'd say a woman was responsible for those. Cushions may look attractive, but nine times out of ten, they don't make seats more comfortable. But that's typical of the different ways men and women approach homes – men tend to be more practical, whilst women are more concerned with aesthetics.

So with that in mind, I imagine a woman will have chosen the candlesticks and house plants, and she will probably have been responsible for the family photos on the wall.

There are loads of different colours in this room with the green wallpaper, blue curtains and patterned carpet, but the big window and the mirror above the fireplace prevent the room from being too dark.

The room is rather untidy and I imagine both parents go out to work and so they don't have much time to tidy up.

I think the people who live here are laid back, sociable people who enjoy entertaining. I don't think they're the sort of people who would worry too much if someone spills a little wine on the carpet.

🌐 **3.23**

Room 2

This one's more difficult because there are very few clues here about the type of person who lives in it. I think it's a man because there are hardly any personal objects on display – for instance, there aren't any family photos around the place.

But there's plenty of evidence to suggest that this is a successful career person, someone who spends most of his time travelling. There isn't really enough furniture to make this look like a home. There are a couple of leather and chrome chairs which are probably Italian and worth a lot of money – he certainly has good taste and may work in advertising or the media.

I think this is somebody who doesn't actually spend much time at home, and when he does, he's obsessively tidy. You only have to look at how his CDs are organized on the shelves to see that he likes things to be in order. The lack of decoration suggests that he wants to be ready to pack his bags and leave at short notice.

He has little time to socialise, except in a working context, and probably never entertains at home. He's single, and may be the sort of person who has problems with commitment in personal relationships.

🌐 **3.24**

(I = Interviewer; L = Lizanne)

I: Lizanne, you're from America. What do you have for breakfast?

L: Er, eggs, bacon, pancakes, and a bit of toast on the side.

I: And what to drink?

L: Usually we start with orange juice and have lots and lots of coffee.

I: And your eggs – how do you like to have them done?

L: Sunny side up.

I: What does that mean?

L: That means that the yolk is facing upward – it's not been turned over.

I: Thank you.

🌐 **3.25**

(I = Interviewer; N = Nicola)

I: Nicola, you're from Germany. Tell me about breakfast. What do you have for breakfast?

N: Well, in Germany it's different. Some people like jam or cereals, but the typical breakfast is, of course, with cold meat like salami, bacon or ham, and cheese. And we always have hot bread rolls and coffee. But I don't like coffee very much. And, of course, boiled eggs – they are very important in Germany and very typical, with salt or pepper.

I: You don't drink coffee for breakfast. What do you like?

N: I like to drink tea.

🌐 **3.26**

(I = Interviewer; M = Michiko)

I: Michiko. What do you have for breakfast? What do you have to drink for breakfast?

M: We drink green tea for breakfast.

I: OK, and what about, what do you eat?

M: We eat rice, miso soup, pickled vegetables, er, grilled fish – like salmon, and Japanese omelette, and seaweed.

I: What, what do you have in the Japanese omelette? What does that …?

M: Japanese omelette is sweet taste, and it's different from the Western omelette.

I: And miso soup. What is in that?

M: Miso soup is a salty soup, which often has seaweed, vegetables and tofu.

Glossary

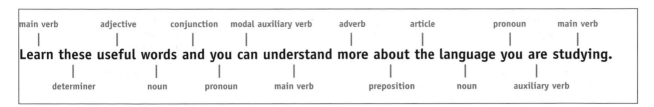

Learn these useful words and you can understand more about the language you are studying.

Agents are people or things that perform an action in a passive sentence.
*He was brought up by **his aunt and uncle**.*

Antonyms are words that mean the opposite of other words.
rich ≠ poor   dead ≠ alive   tall ≠ short

Back-shift is when a verb moves 'one tense back' in a conditional clause or reported statement.
*If you **were** a woman you'd understand.*
*'I can't come.' → He said he **couldn't** come.*

Clauses are groups of words containing a subject and a verb.
main clause   subordinate clause   main clause   time (subordinate) clause
I waited   but she didn't come.   I'll phone   when I get there.
Note: Subordinate clauses are introduced by conjunctions.

Collocation refers to words that frequently occur together.
common sense   get on well   Merry Christmas

Complements refer to adjective or noun phrases which give more information about the subject of a clause.
*She was **very happy**.   It's **my fault**.   I feel **a complete idiot**.*
Note: Complements usually follow verbs like *be, seem, feel.*

Conjunctions show a connection between one clause and another.
***Just as** we were leaving the hotel, I spotted a friend.*

Consonants are all the letters of the English alphabet except for the five vowels *a, e, i, o* and *u*.
b, c, d, f, g, h, j, k, l, m, n, p, q, r, s, t, v, w, x, y, z

Expressions are groups of words that belong together where the words and word order never or rarely change.
black and white   That reminds me.   How do you do?

Idioms are groups of words with a meaning which cannot be understood by taking the meaning of each individual word.
*My father **footed the bill**.   Let's **play it by ear**, shall we?*

Intransitive verbs do not take an object.
*He's **arrived**.   Is Marta still **sleeping**?   Stop **shouting**!*
Note: Many verbs can be either intransitive or transitive. It depends on the meaning or context.
*He **opened** the door. (Transitive)   The door **opened**. (Intransitive)*

Linkers show a connection between one sentence and another.
*Many motorists drive too fast. **As a result**, there are more and more accidents.*

Numbers can be cardinal (*1, 2, 3, …*) or ordinal (*1st, 2nd, 3rd, …*).

Objects usually come after the verb and show who or what is affected by the verb.
*She closed **the door**.   My dog hates **me**.   I've made **a cup of tea**.*
Note: Some verbs take both a direct object (DO) and an indirect object (IO).

*She gave **him** (IO) **a kiss** (DO).   He sent **her** (IO) **some flowers** (DO).*
*I teach **students** (IO) **English** (DO).*

Participles are the forms of verbs used in compound tenses and as adjectives.
*What are you **doing**?   I've **finished**.   It's **freezing**!   He's **injured**.*

Particles are the adverbs or prepositions that form part of a phrasal verb.
*turn it **on**   take **off**   get **on with** her*

Partitives are words or expressions that show that only part of something is being referred to rather than all of it.
***a piece of** cake   **a packet of** crisps   **a bunch of** flowers*

The **phonetic alphabet** is a set of special symbols which shows speech sounds in writing.
mother = /ˈmʌðə/   television = /ˈtelɪvɪʒən/

Phrasal verbs are combinations of a verb and one or two particles.
switch on   come up with

Pronouns are words used in place of nouns or noun phrases. There are many classes of pronoun.
Subject pronouns: *I, you, she,* etc.
　Object pronouns: *me, you, her,* etc.
Possessive pronouns: *mine, yours, hers,* etc.
　Demonstrative pronouns: *this, that, these, those*

Proper nouns are words that refer to a particular person, place or institution.
Janet, Madrid, the United Nations

Proverbs or **sayings** are short, well-known statements that give practical advice about life.
When the cat's away, the mice will play.

Register describes a level and style of a piece of language which is appropriate for the circumstances in which it is used.
I am very grateful for your help. (More formal)
　Cheers mate. (More informal)

Relative clauses are clauses that modify a noun or a noun phrase. They give additional information about the noun and are joined to a previous clause by words such as *who, that* or *which*.
*That's the man **who helped me**.   This the pen **(that) I lost**.*
　*Everyone is well, **which is really great**.*

Synonyms are words or expressions which mean the same as another word or expression.
mad = crazy   tolerate sb = put up with sb   I'm off now. = I'm going now.

Transitive verbs take an object.
*You're wasting **your money**.   He's cut **his finger**.*
　*I can't pronounce '**comfortable**'.*

Vowels are the letters *a, e, i, o* and *u*.

Phonetic symbols & Spelling

Single vowels

/ɪ/	ship	/ʃɪp/	(build, business, England, gym, lettuce, spinach, women)
/i:/	need	/ni:d/	(bean, he, key, niece, people, sardine)
/ʊ/	put	/pʊt/	(could, foot, woman)
/u:/	pool	/pu:l/	(flew, fruit, lose, rule, shoe, through, two)
/e/	egg	/eg/	(breakfast, friend, many, said)
/ə/	mother	/ˈmʌðə/	(arrive, colour, husband, lemon, nervous, police)
/ɜ:/	verb	/vɜ:b/	(learn, curly, skirt, word)
/ɔ:/	saw	/sɔ:/	(abroad, caught, four, horse, talk, thought, towards, water)
/æ/	back	/bæk/	—
/ʌ/	bus	/bʌs/	(blood, does, enough, onion)
/ɑ:/	arm	/ɑ:m/	(aunt, heart, laugh, past)
/ɒ/	top	/tɒp/	(cauliflower, what)

Diphthongs

/ɪə/	ear	/ɪə/	(beer, here, Italian, theatre)
/eɪ/	face	/feɪs/	(break, eight, fail, say, they)
/ʊə/	tour	/tʊə/	(plural, sure)
/ɔɪ/	boy	/bɔɪ/	(noise)
/əʊ/	nose	/nəʊz/	(aubergine, although, coat, know, shoulder)
/eə/	hair	/heə/	(careful, their, wear, where)
/aɪ/	white	/waɪt/	(buy, die, eye, height, high, my)
/aʊ/	mouth	/maʊθ/	(town)

Consonants

/p/	pen	/pen/	(happy)
/b/	bag	/bæg/	(rabbit)
/t/	tea	/ti:/	(ate, fatter, worked)
/d/	dog	/dɒg/	(address, played)
/tʃ/	chip	/tʃɪp/	(natural, watch)
/dʒ/	jazz	/dʒæz/	(age, bridge, generous)
/k/	cake	/keɪk/	(chemistry, kitchen, knock, toothache)
/g/	girl	/gɜ:l/	(foggy)
/f/	film	/fɪlm/	(different, laugh, photograph)
/v/	very	/ˈveri/	(of)
/θ/	thin	/θɪn/	—
/ð/	these	/ði:z/	—
/s/	snake	/sneɪk/	(city, message, race)
/z/	zoo	/zu:/	(has)
/ʃ/	shop	/ʃɒp/	(description, machine, sugar)
/ʒ/	television	/ˈtelɪvɪʒən/	(garage, usual)
/m/	map	/mæp/	(summer)
/n/	name	/neɪm/	(sunny, knife)
/ŋ/	ring	/rɪŋ/	(thanks, tongue)
/h/	house	/haʊs/	(who)
/l/	leg	/leg/	(hill, possible)
/r/	road	/rəʊd/	(carry, write)
/w/	wine	/waɪn/	(one, why)
/j/	yes	/jes/	(used)

Stress

Word stress is shown by underlining the stressed <u>syl</u>lable: <u>wa</u>ter, a<u>ma</u>zing, Japa<u>nese</u>.

Letters of the alphabet

/eɪ/	/i:/	/e/	/aɪ/	/əʊ/	/u:/	/ɑ:/
Aa	Bb	Ff	Ii	Oo	Qq	Rr
Hh	Cc	Ll	Yy		Uu	
Jj	Dd	Mm			Ww	
Kk	Ee	Nn				
	Gg	Ss				
	Pp	Xx				
	Tt	Zz				
	Vv					

Irregular verbs

Infinitive	Past simple	Past participle	Infinitive	Past simple	Past participle
be	was/were	been	let	let	let
beat	beat	beaten	lie	lay/lied	lied/lain
become	became	become	light	lit/lighted	lit/lighted
begin	began	begun	lose	lost	lost
bend	bent	bent	make	made	made
bet	bet	bet	mean	meant /ment/	meant /ment/
bite	bit	bitten	meet	met	met
blow	blew	blown	must	had to	(had to)
break	broke	broken	pay	paid	paid
bring	brought /brɔːt/	brought /brɔːt/	put	put	put
build /bɪld/	built /bɪlt/	built /bɪlt/	read	read /red/	read /red/
burn	burnt/burned	burnt/burned	ride	rode	ridden
burst	burst	burst	ring	rang	rung
buy /baɪ/	bought /bɔːt/	bought /bɔːt/	rise	rose	risen
can	could /kʊd/	(been able)	run	ran	run
catch	caught /kɔːt/	caught /kɔːt/	say	said /sed/	said /sed/
choose	chose	chosen	see	saw /sɔː/	seen
come	came	come	sell	sold	sold
cost	cost	cost	send	sent	sent
cut	cut	cut	set	set	set
deal /diːl/	dealt /delt/	dealt /delt/	shake	shook	shaken
dig	dug	dug	shine	shone	shone
do	did	done	shoot	shot	shot
draw	drew	drawn	show	showed	shown
dream	dreamt/dreamed	dreamt/dreamed	shrink	shrank	shrunk
drink	drank	drunk	shut	shut	shut
drive	drove	driven	sing	sang	sung
eat	ate	eaten	sink	sank	sunk
fall	fell	fallen	sit	sat	sat
feed	fed	fed	sleep	slept	slept
feel	felt	felt	slide	slid	slid
fight	fought /fɔːt/	fought /fɔːt/	smell	smelt/smelled	smelt/smelled
find	found	found	speak	spoke	spoken
fly	flew	flown	spell	spelt/spelled	spelt/spelled
forget	forgot	forgotten	spend	spent	spent
forgive	forgave	forgiven	spill	spilt/spilled	spilt/spilled
freeze	froze	frozen	split	split	split
get	got	got	spoil	spoilt/spoiled	spoilt/spoiled
give	gave	given	spread	spread	spread
go	went	gone/been	stand	stood	stood
grow	grew	grown	steal	stole	stolen
hang	hung/hanged	hung/hanged	stick	stuck	stuck
have	had	had	swear	swore	sworn
hear	heard /hɜːd/	heard /hɜːd/	swell	swelled	swollen/swelled
hide	hid	hidden	swim	swam	swum
hit	hit	hit	take	took /tʊk/	taken
hold	held	held	teach	taught /tɔːt/	taught /tɔːt/
hurt /hɜːt/	hurt /hɜːt/	hurt /hɜːt/	tear	tore	torn
keep	kept	kept	tell	told	told
kneel	knelt/kneeled	knelt/kneeled	think	thought /θɔːt/	thought /θɔːt/
know	knew /njuː/	known	throw	threw	thrown
lay	laid	laid	understand	understood	understood
lead	led	led	wake	woke	woken
learn	learnt	learnt	wear	wore /wɔː/	worn
leave	left	left	win	won /wʌn/	won /wʌn/
lend	lent	lent	write	wrote	written

Macmillan Education
Between Towns Road, Oxford OX4 3PP
A division of Macmillan Publishers Limited
Companies and representatives throughout the world

ISBN 978-0-2300-0919-6

Text © Sue Kay & Vaughan Jones 2009
Design and illustration © Macmillan Publishers Limited 2009

First published 2009

All rights reserved; no part of this publication may be reproduced, stored in a retrieval system, transmitted in any form, or by any means, electronic, mechanical, photocopying, recording, or otherwise, without the prior written permission of the publishers.

Review units by Peter Maggs and Catherine Smith
Project development by Desmond O'Sullivan, Quality Outcomes Limited
Designed by Keith Shaw, Threefold Design Limited
Photographic research by Sally Cole, Perseverance Works Limited and
Zoe Spilberg
Illustrated by Ed McLachlan pp12, 22, 32, 35(r), 44, 54, 59, 64, 67, 75, 76, 84, 86, 96, 108, 115, 116, 124; Adrian Valencia p35(l)
Cover design by Andrew Oliver

Authors' acknowledgements

We would like to thank all our students and colleagues at the Oxford English Centre in Oxford as well as all our teaching colleagues around the world who are using Inside Out – your feedback has helped us identify what we should keep and what we could improve. Particular thanks go to the following people: Paula Kler, Andrea Merckel, Marc Heffernan and students (Malvern House, London); Thorkild Gantner, Julia Strippentow, Andy Johnson (The London School of English); Meriel Steele, Will Gregson, Sam Gossen (Oxford English Centre, London); James Ford, Vanessa Shipley, Mark Fonhnsdoff (Bloomsbury International, London); Svetlana Petrovskaya (Pekhanov Economic Academy, Russia); Rita Collins (Masaryk University, Czech Republic); Suria Shukurova, (ITC – International Training Centre, Russia); Marian Davies and colleagues (Bournemouth Business School International); Gregory Rowen (British Council, Bangkok); Karina Fernandes (Cultura Inglesa Jundiaí, Brazil); Doris Urban (British Council, Milan); Sabina Politova Paunova (Orbis Pictus, Bratislava); Sarah Shaw (British Council, Thailand)
We are especially grateful to Peter Maggs and Catherine Smith for their Student's Book review units, to Mairi Macdonald and Julie Moore (authors) and Diane Nicholls (editor) for the CD-ROM, to Ceri Jones and Philip Kerr for the New Inside Out Workbook, and to Helena Gomm, Peter Maggs, Chris Dawson and Adrian Tennant for their important contributions to the New Inside Out Teacher's Book. We're also grateful to Scott Thornbury for allowing us to use extracts from his excellent book, An A–Z of ELT.
At Macmillan Education, we would like to thank Rafael Alarcon-Gaeta, Jemma Hillyer, Mo Dutton, Julie Brett, Katie Stephens, Penny Ashfield, Hazel Barrett, Claire Sparkes, Madeleine Williamson and Stephanie Parker for all their hard work on our behalf. Stephanie, in particular, deserves a special mention for the invaluable contribution she has made to this project. We would also like to thank Sally Cole and Zoe Spilberg (freelance photo researchers), Alyson Maskell, Celia Bingham and Xanthe Sturt Taylor (freelance editors), as well as James Richardson (freelance audio producer).
Keith Shaw has done a great job designing the book and we should also thank Andrew Oliver for his fabulous cover design.
Many thanks also go to the Macmillan production and marketing teams around the world whose enthusiasm and encouragement have been such a support.
Our biggest thank you goes to Des O'Sullivan (freelance project developer). Always thorough, always considerate and always there for us. We realise how lucky we are to be working with such a consummate professional.
Last but not least, we are so grateful to our families for their ongoing support and understanding.

The author and publishers are grateful for permission to reprint the following copyright material:
Adapted material from 'Bonfire of the Brands: How I Learned to Live without Labels' by Neil Boorman, copyright © Neil Boorman 2007, reprinted by permission of Canongate Books Limited, Edinburgh and Conville & Walsh;
Adapted material from 'Best of Times, Worst of Times' by Danny Danziger, copyright © Danny Danziger 1999, first appeared in The Sunday Times Magazine 26.09.99, reprinted by permission of the author and Capel & Land Agent;
Adapted material from 'How Cool Is That' by Caroline Rees, copyright © Caroline Rees 2008, first appeared in The Guardian 29.09.08, reprinted by permission of the publisher;
Adapted material from 'Where To Go To See A Masterpiece' by Robert McCrum, copyright © Robert McCrum 1997, first appeared in The Observer 12.10.97, reprinted by permission of the publisher;
Extract from 'For hip Amalia, used to clubbing until 4a.m, the prospect of dancing on the sticky carpets of a nightclub in Yeovil was not so exciting' by Viv Groskop copyright © The Guardian 2008, first published in The Guardian 26.06.08, reprinted by permission of the publisher;
Extract from 'Ben Saunders: explorer, adventurer, speck of red heat' by Andy Bull copyright © The Guardian 2008, first published in The Guardian 13.03.08, reprinted by permission of the publisher;
Extract from 'Are you ready to order?' by Jan Moir copyright © The Guardian Newspapers Limited 2008, first published in The Observer 22.06.08, reprinted by permission of the publisher;
Quotations from Collins Cobuild English Collocations 1995, reprinted by permission of Harper Collins Publishers;
Extract from 'The waiting game: Britain's most glamorous waiters and waitresses reveal all' by John Walsh copyright © The Independent 2008, first published in The Independent 14.06.08, reprinted by permission of the publisher;
Men's Health Magazine for adapted text from 'I smoke... and I work for Men's Health' by Greg Gutfeld, (December 1999);
Extract from 'Embarrassing parents' by Denna Allen copyright © The Mirror 1999, first published in The Sunday Mirror Magazine 16.05.99, reprinted by permission of the publisher;

Adapted material from 'Eight Minutes to Get Yourself a Date' by Jane Ridley, copyright © Jane Ridley 2000, first appeared in The Mirror 26.04.00, reprinted by permission of the publisher;
Extract from 'The King and I' by Hank Wangford copyright © Hank Wangford, first published in The Guardian 01.07.00, reprinted by permission of Sayle Literary Agency on behalf of the author;
Extract from 'You did WHAT?' by Michael Harvey © Solo Syndication 1997, first published in The Daily Mail 31.07.97, reprinted by permission of the publisher;
Extract from 'Sell a life: what price a life?' by Frances Booth copyright © Telegraph Group Limited 2008, first published in The Daily Telegraph 30.06.08, reprinted by permission of the publisher;
Adapted material from 'Why Students Love A Long-Haul to Hell' by Helen Chappell, copyright © Helen Chappell 1998 first appeared in The Daily Telegraph 29.03.98, reprinted by permission of the publisher.
Definitions from the Macmillan English Dictionary 2nd Edition © 2007, Macmillan Publishers Ltd www.macmillandictionaries.com
Word frequency graph and commentary from Frequency and the Dictionary LA13 by Dr Adam Kilgarriff, Macmillan English Dictionary 2nd Edition © 2007 Macmillan Publishers Ltd

These materials may contain links for third party websites. We have no control over, and are not responsible for, the contents of such third party websites. Please use care when accessing them.

The authors and publishers would like to thank the following for permission to reproduce their photographic material:
A&M Photography Ltd p101(tr); **Adidas**/p100(3); **Alamy**/Alibi Productions p15(t), Alamy/Andrew Bargery p61, Alamy/Blend Images p104(m), Alamy/blickwinkel p10(r), Alamy/David R. Frazier Photolibrary Inc p77(t), Alamy/Dennis Cox p77(Sydney), Alamy/Michael Gilday p31(b), Alamy/Mike Hill p117, Alamy/ImageState p72(m), Alamy/Art Kowalsky pp71(l), 88(bl), Alamy/Tom Mackie p120(l), Alamy/Francisco Martinez p110(t), Alamy/Ian Murray p15(b), Alamy/Nic van Oudtshoorn p114(b), Alamy/Redfix p102, Alamy/Ian Shaw p49(b), Alamy/Dorota Szpill p101(tl); **Banco de Mexico Diego Rivera & Frida Kahlo Museums Trust, Mexico D.F. 2009**/DACS p92; **Bananastock** pp80(5), 101(bl), 111(bl), 122(br & m); **BBH**, London p103; **Brand X** p72(tr); **Camera Press**/Paul Mowatt p94(bl); **Comstock** p53(ml); **Corbis**/Artiqu Photo p51(tmr), Corbis/Beateworks p121, Corbis/Fernando Bengoechea p120(r), Corbis/Johnny Buzzerio p111(m), Corbis/Fabio Cardoso p51(b), Corbis/ComStock p114(m), Corbis/Cultura p71(l inset), Corbis/Randy Faris p72(tl), Corbis/Patrik Giardino p85(b), Corbis/Girl Ra p56(r), Corbis/A. Green p26, Corbis/Jamie Grill p111(b), Corbis/Historical Premium p93, Corbis/Image100 p51(tr), 82(t), Corbis/Simon Jarratt p29, Corbis/Serge Kozak p10(mr), Corbis/LWA Dann Tardiff p80(t&m), Corbis/Simon Marcus p7, Corbis/Rob Matheson p110(b), Corbis/H. J. Martin p83(Kevin), Corbis/Minnesota Historical Society p25(r), Corbis/Markus Moellenberg p113, Corbis/Moodboard p71(m insert), Corbis/Warren Morgan p83(Tony), Corbis/Andrew O'Toole p71(r inset), Corbis/Michael Prince p53(mr), Corbis/Ben Radford p47(tm), Corbis/Frank Rothe p112(b), Corbis/Max Rossi p47(m), Corbis/James Strachan p91(b), Corbis/Luca Tettoni p58(bl), Corbis/Debi Treloar p94(toilet), Corbis/Bill Vaire p112(t), Corbis/Christophe Weidlich p19(b), Corbis/Elizabeth Whiting & Associates p21(b), Corbis/David Michael Zimmerman p94(zip); **Fotolibra**/Bernhard Howden p118; **Getty** p83(Mark), Getty/Aagmia p21(t), Getty/Allison Michael Orenstein p74(t), Getty/Dirk Anschutz p53(r), Getty/Tony Ashby p30(r), Getty/Juli Balla p58(tl), Getty/Gio Barto p83(Lara), Getty/Oliver Benn p77(Dublin), Getty/Francesco Bittichesu p51(tl), Getty/Cliver Brunskill p46, Getty/Joachim Chwaszcza p71(r), Getty/Robert Clare p28(t), Getty/Paul Conrath p41(mt), Getty/Marco Cristofori p90(b), Getty/James Darell p83(Sindy & Claire), Getty/Sam Diephuis p11(ml), Getty/Jody Dole p94(contact), Getty/Harald Eisenberger p41(b), Getty/Nicholas Eveleigh p42, Getty/Emmanuel Faura p39(l), Getty/Larry Dale Gordon p83(Karen & Erica), Getty/Steve Gorton p11(r), Getty/Fraser Hall p77(b), Getty/Patricia Heal p11(tl), Getty/Image Bank pp6(bl), Getty/Johner Images p49(t), Getty/Michael Kelly p70, Getty/Dan Kenyon p114(t), Getty/Kent Mathews p53(l), Getty/Frank Micelotta p8, Getty/Tara Moore p17(r), Getty/Derek P Redfearn p11(bl), Getty/Riser p6(tr), Getty/David Roth p83(Jim), Getty/Karin Smeds p48, Getty/StockFood Creative pp59, 60, Getty/Stone pp5(tl & bl), 33, Getty/Taxi Japan pp13, 100(bl), Getty/Caroline von Tuempling p55, Getty/David Trood p39(r), Getty/Garry Wade p10(ml), Getty/WireImage pp4(bl), 88(tl); **Martin Hartley** p37; **Head** p100(1); **Image Source** p74(b); **Cindy Jackson** p81; **Jupiter Images**/Deborah Jaffe p82(b); **Kappa** p100(6); **Kobal Collection** p106(m); **Macmillan Publishers Ltd**/Haddon Davies pp16(l,m,r), 18(t,b), 19(tr), 20(t,b), 28(b), 52, 94(razor,toothbrush); **Mary Evans Photo Library** p25(t); **Masterfile**/Raw File p5(br), Mastefile/Scott Tysick p10(l); **Museum of Rural Life** p123(b); **NASA Images** p4(tr); **Nike** p100(2); **PA Photos** pp30(tr),106, PA Photos/Russell McPhedran p 4(tl), PA Photos/Ma Zhancheng p4(br); **Penguin Press UK** p123(t); **Photolibrary** p77(Madrid), Photolibrary/Alaskastock p38, Photolibrary/Christophe Bluntzer p14(tr), Photolibrary/Corbis p97(tr), Photolibrary/Dex Images p41(mb), Photolibrary/Eyecandy Images p83(Craig), Photolibrary/Peter Fisher p56(l), Photolibrary/Flirt Collection p5(tr), Photolibrary/Raymond Forbes p51(t ml), Photolibrary/Fresh Food Images p122(tl), Photolibrary/Sylvain Grandadam p50(tl), Photolibrary/Tom Grill pp31(letters), 104(b), Photolibrary/LWA-Sharie Kennedy p73, Photolibrary/LWA-Dann Tardif p14(tl), Photolibrary/LWA-Stephen Welstead p41(t), Photolibrary/John Madere p17(l), Photolibrary/Lew Robertson p57, Photolibrary/Jochen Tack p94(teeth), Photolibrary/David Vinuales p111(tr); **Private Eye** p135, 137, 139, 143; **Rex Features** p62, Rex Features/Stewart Cood p47(bm), Rex Features/Everett Collection p99, Rex Features/Juergen Hasenkopf p47(t), Rex Features/Simon Hayter p50(br), Rex Features/Keystone USA p107(tl), Rex Features/Theo Kingma p79(b), Rex Features/KPA Zuma p105, Rex Features/MGM Everett p106(tl), Rex Features/Most Wanted p85(t), Rex Features/NBCU Photobank p47(b), 79(t), Rex Features/Sipa Press pp9(r), 97(b), Rex Features/Warner Bros p106(br), Rex Features/W. Disney Everett p63; **Robert Harding World Imagery**/Lee Frost p68-69, Robert Harding World Imagery/Bruno Morandi p71(m), Robert Harding World Imagery/Panoramic Images pp88-89; **Slazenger** p100(5); **Speedo** p100(4); **Superstock** p72(br), Superstock/De Agostini p90(t), Superstock/Newberry Library p24; **Peter Sylent** p27; **The Guardian**/Si Barber p119(t), The Guardian/Sophia Evans p14(bl), Guardian/Gareth Philips p119(b); **The Perception Laboratory**, University of St Andrews p78; **The Secret**/Edelman p84; **Stockbyte** p97(m); **Walk the Walk Worldwide** p40; **Andy Ward** p36.

Commissioned photography by:
Paul Bricknell p104(t).
Lisa Payne pp31(l,m,r).

Printed and bound in Spain by Edelvives

2013 2012 2011 2010 2009
10 9 8 7 6 5 4 3 2